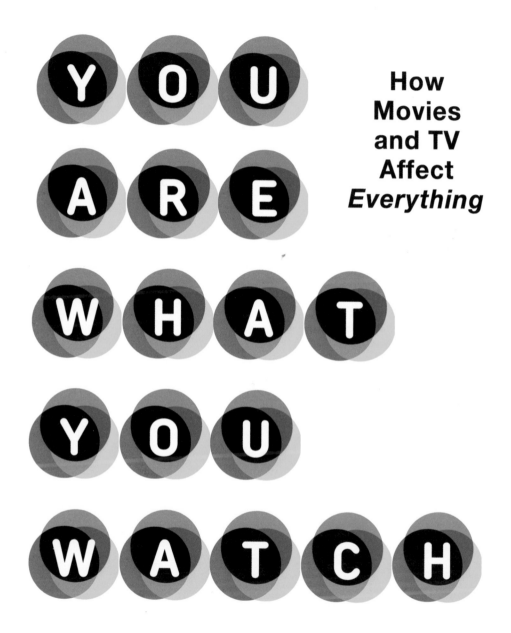

YOU ARE WHAT YOU WATCH

How Movies and TV Affect *Everything*

Walt Hickey

DATA VISUALS BY HEATHER JONES

WORKMAN PUBLISHING • NEW YORK

Copyright © 2023 by Walter Hickey
Data visuals copyright © by Heather Jones (art) and Walt Hickey (data)

Library of Congress Cataloging-in-Publication Data is available.

ISBN 978-1-5235-1589-9

Design by Janet Vicario

Jacket images by Mayli Stocks/Shutterstock

Workman books are available at special discounts when purchased in
bulk for premiums and sales promotions as well as for fundraising or
educational use. Special editions or book excerpts can also be created
to specification. For details, please contact special.markets@hbgusa.com.

Workman Publishing Co., Inc.,
a subsidiary of Hachette Book Group, Inc.
1290 Avenue of the Americas
New York, NY 10104
workman.com

WORKMAN is a registered trademark of Workman Publishing Co., Inc.,
a subsidiary of Hachette Book Group, Inc.

Printed in China on responsibly sourced paper.
First printing September 2023

10 9 8 7 6 5 4 3 2 1

For Michael

CONTENTS

INTRODUCTION

Every person is the result of something, the combination of nature and nurture and childhood and work and love and family. Every one of us has been molded into the people we are today by the environments from which we sprang.

I am a data journalist who covers pop culture. There are lots of environmental factors that caused me to become who I am—a solid upbringing, a decent head for numbers and a degree in math, the pathological need for attention that draws someone to journalism, and recent software advances that made big computation possible at a low price. But that's not *really* why I'm a data journalist.

I am a data journalist because I saw *Jurassic Park* when I was a kid. And I thought that mathematician Ian Malcolm was the coolest person I had ever seen. And I wanted to be like him.

If I hadn't seen *Jurassic Park*, I still would've been good at math. However, I wouldn't have thought it sufficiently cool enough to pursue in college. So, bam, not a data journalist. Note also that Ian Malcolm doesn't even do math in the movie. But it was his look, his affectation, his place in the world, his whole vibe—I saw it and I wanted it. There were other appealing factors that emerged along the way—the relative stability of quantitative professions didn't hurt—but really it began with Jeff Goldblum's performance. Because of him, I embarked on a series of expensive and difficult decisions that hewed me closer to what he was in *Jurassic Park*.

So, while pop culture might not quite make us into who we are, it does teach us how to yearn to be something that we just might become.

According to the 2021 American Time Use Survey, the average time an American is awake for is 15 hours, 7 minutes each day. That typical American then spends an aggregate of 2 hours, 51 minutes watching television and another 31 minutes doing things like reading, writing, going to the movies or theater for an average total of 3 hours, 22 minutes consuming media each day.

Movies and statistics? How could those mix?

Across a lifetime, that's 22 percent of our time on Earth!

Whether we admit it or not, consuming media is something to which we devote our lives. Nobody's forcing anyone to watch or read or listen, but we all do it. This of course makes the relative ignorance about the effects of media consumption confusing. There are lots of books talking about how things affect our well-being: food, exercise, work, travel, sleep. All are commonly accepted as having a substantial impact on our lives. But the thing we spend a fifth of our waking hours doing is dismissed as mere diversion, a distraction even, something we consume passively.

If anything, we tend to think that we're doing more *to* culture than it's doing to us when we discuss it, rate it, buy it, dismiss it, or argue about it—but that's wrong. When we do actually talk about how culture affects us, it often gets portrayed as a bogeyman, a brain melter, a violence inciter, a waste. This book argues that's not the case at all. Movies and television and books and music have incontrovertible effects on people, and those effects are complex, fascinating, and often rather good. Also, those effects influence us in ways that we could not imagine.

Everyone has a movie that changed their life. In writing *You Are What You Watch*, I sought to understand that; to figure out where the chills come from, the tears, the deep meaning in a favorite movie, and how all of that translates to our wider worlds.

In the pages that follow, we'll explore the physical—why horror movies are literally blood curdling, for example, or how the composition of air in a movie theater changes across the course of some films. We'll dissect the psychological magic of movies, the attentional tricks pulled off by incredible storytelling, how masterful movies play on how our minds work, why age matters, and how kids simply view things differently than adults.

This book is about how media and culture shapes us as individuals and collectively. It will prove that what we consume as "entertainment" changes our society in profound ways, including how we name our children, where we vacation, the pets we choose, and the careers we have. I have sought to clarify the too-often misportrayed relationship between pop culture and crime. I will show you how we really spend our time, how we learn, and how we mature. We'll also look at the deep reverberations of media among scientists, soldiers, and spies.

Then there's the economics of pop culture, how money fuels what art gets made and how that art fuels greater commerce—including theme parks—what movies get remade and how fandom evolves and is cultivated, and why nostalgia fuels an industry.

We'll go deeper and wider still, to consider the geopolitics of pop culture, how different countries have used their art and entertainment to accumulate global power. We'll track the rise of Hollywood and the US entertainment industrial complex, then consider how the United Kingdom, Japan, and South Korea have exported and parlayed their domestic cultural output into geopolitical might and influence.

Finally, we'll look at what lasts and why, how pop culture can transcend time and become canonical. And what making art does to those who make it, how where you create matters to what you create, and what undermines it, then we'll consider the health impacts of creating things.

Legendary critic Roger Ebert described films as "empathy machines," a technology that can place a viewer in the life and mindset of someone utterly different from them. Pop culture is that and so much more—including a vehicle to make us better. While other technologies are designed to optimize, to harvest attention for profit, to stoke conflict and turn it into revenue by forcing users to engage, books, films, television, and comics are downright generous.

As someone who works in a medium that he also loves, I am plagued by the fear that the more I understand what I love the less I might love it. I have seen data journalism take a thing apart and find it lacking, explore a system to find its broken parts, crack a game so decisively the allure of it evaporates under the heat of attention. I have seen great stories—about people who would be president, the greatest athletes of all time, unicorn companies—falter under the microscope of analysis.

I am pleased to report that, after dozens of analyses, the application of science to movies I love, and the digitization and quantification of sorts of films, that diminishing never happened. There are things that, under sufficient scrutiny, will collapse into their component parts, their tricks revealed, the hope they engendered gone. But culture is a deeper thing. Something fundamental about it resists reduction. And the very best of it leaves even the most seasoned critic with admiration.

In this book, I commit the tools of rationality, the advantages of statistics, and medical insight to consider the fundamental magic at the heart of the stories we love. My hope is that you'll emerge with an appreciation for what great pop culture can accomplish. Which is to say, this book will not make you a cynical viewer (or reader or listener), it won't erode your ability to love what you enjoy.

Rather, it might just teach you to value the things you watch, to appreciate them, to free yourself of guilt while learning what pop culture is doing to you along the way.

Because it turns out, you really are what you watch. And you might just like yourself more because of it.

CHAPTER 1

HOW CULTURE AFFECTS OUR BODIES

You're watching a movie in a theater when on-screen, out of nowhere, a serial killer attacks. Because you're scared, your body increases the amount of coagulant factors in your bloodstream, causing your blood to literally curdle.

By the end of the movie, the killer gets his comeuppance and your brain's reward center lights up like a firework. The part of your brain that links your actions to rewards is pumping on all cylinders. As you watch the villain get defeated, a process refined over millions of years of evolution triggers a dopamine gusher.

And you're not alone in this. You and everyone else in the theater has left a chemical mark behind as you exit. The air composition is noticeably different from when you entered: The level of CO_2 in the room is anywhere from 2.5 to 6 times higher than it was when you walked in, the level of airborne isoprene, which a person exhales when their muscles tense, having spiked each time the killer made the crowd flinch. There are also shifts in some 100 trace gasses in the theater that are different from what the crowd in the screening room next door is emitting as they watch a comedy.

We think a lot about the things we eat or drink or smoke and how they affect our bodies, but what we consume with our eyes and ears can have the same physiological effects as what we put in our mouths. We pretend we have control over our bodies, but the truth? When we absorb a piece of culture, a movie, a television series, a book, or even just a song, we cede control of our autonomy to another person, tossing them the keys to the whole operation.

Belfast, *directed by Kenneth Branagh, 2021.*

Heavy Breathing

The Williams Group at the Max Planck Institute for Chemistry, in Germany, researches the long-term viability of life on Earth. The planet's atmosphere is impossibly large and, as we've learned in recent decades, is based on an equilibrium thrown out of balance by the planet's "smartest" inhabitants. The largest source of volatile organic compounds on Earth is found in the Amazon rain forest—if we want to understand the composition and long-term viability of our atmosphere, we need to understand exactly what kind of compounds this rain forest pumps out.

From a 325-meter tower in the jungle, the Williams Group more or less samples the very breath of the world. Volatile organic compounds encompass any kind of chemical that living things emit into the atmosphere, the by-products of the various chemical reactions that living things are constantly orchestrating on a cellular basis. They're the molecular evidence of life, the by-products and chemical waste left behind by a plant, an animal, or an ecosystem. When you exhale, all sorts of these compounds will be found in your breath in minute quantities. So, when you're looking at a volume of life on the scale of a rain forest, the concentration of these chemicals can be meaningful on a climactic scale. Jonathan Williams, a doctor in air chemistry at the Max Planck Institute for Chemistry in Mainz, primarily studies these chemicals to figure out how they affect the ozone layer.

One day, on a trip to the rain forest, a student came up to Williams and said, "You know, I'm not sure that we're in the right place here in the Amazon jungle." Williams was taken aback. Working in the Amazon is a pretty glamorous assignment. Most students are keen to go there, which means they don't usually question the very foundation of the research they're doing.

"She had taken our *very* sensitive mass spectrometer that we use to measure these chemicals, and she just breathed into the mass spectrometer," explained Williams. "What she'd observed is, on her breath, there are high concentrations of many of the chemicals that we were measuring in rain forests."

Seven billion mouths, seven billion breaths. Were they missing a major source of atmospheric VOCs, or volatile organic compounds, literally right under their noses? We humans have managed to affect our environments in all kinds of ways, but are we doing so with breath alone? And what exactly are we exhaling anyway? The researchers would soon discover that the very composition of human breath—the direct evidence of the chemical reactions in our bodies—changes constantly, and one of the most reliable ways to affect that composition, and the body's internal chemistry, is through movies.

To determine the average chemical composition of human breath, their first thought was that they needed to get a whole lot of humans in one place. After returning from the Amazon to their normal base of operations in Germany's Max Planck Institute, their eyes turned to Coface Arena, home to the Bundesliga soccer team Mainz 05. In 2012, Williams and his group dragged out highly sensitive mass spectrometers capable of teasing out the smallest fluctuations in VOCs. Then they ran them during a match between Mainz and VfL Wolfsburg as a packed crowd of 31,069 cheered the teams on.

What they were looking for: significant spikes in certain chemicals that showed up when everyone got elated or when the home team suffered a blow.

"So we sit there, waiting and waiting and waiting," said Williams. "And then disaster for us: It ended in a nil-nil draw."

The question that would chew at Williams afterward: How does what we exhale change based on what we experience? And *why* would it? He needed to design an experiment where a mass of people congregated in a space for an hour or two, but in a way where there would be a guaranteed emotional response.

What Williams needed, he realized, was a movie theater.

"You subject them to an emotional experience—happy, sad, or fearful—and they react accordingly," he explained. "All we had to do was to put our instrument in the ventilation shaft of the cinema and we could monitor, in real time, the reactions of people to the movie."

* * *

The human mouth is an exhaust pipe. Chemical reactions going on inside your body produce waste chemicals, so you're constantly exhaling all sorts of by-products of chemical reactions. The most obvious is carbon dioxide. Humans inhale air, and the lungs extract some of the oxygen from that air, passing it into the bloodstream, where it's taken all over the body to fuel arguably the most important chemical reaction we do: respiration. The respiration reaction takes place in every cell, combining oxygen and sugar to produce the energy we need to live, with a by-product of carbon dioxide. That carbon dioxide is shuttled back to the lungs and then exhaled. The air you inhale is 21 percent oxygen and 0.04 percent carbon dioxide, and the air you exhale is 16.4 percent oxygen and 4.4 percent carbon dioxide. That's hardly the only such reaction: For instance, when your body burns fat, it produces acetone as a waste product, which is why some low-carb dieters experience "keto breath," or a hint of acetone on their breath. Tense your muscles and you'll start exhaling isoprene. If you smoke, your breath will have elevated levels of acetonitrile.

"On top of the CO_2, maybe about three orders of magnitude down in concentration, there's an absolute army of volatile organic compounds, hundreds of thousands, depending on your sensitivity," said Williams.

Those VOCs? They're from *you*. The body is a constant chemical reaction, and the waste from all the chemistry necessary to keep you alive has to go somewhere, quickly. You're exhaling not just CO_2 and water, but methanol, isoprene, ethanol, acetone, hydrocarbons, and thousands of other chemicals. And those chemicals might all indicate different things going on in your body, like increases in certain chemical reactions. That's what Williams and his team were looking for: direct evidence that the films they were showing to the audience—comedies, action films, thrillers—were somehow showing up in unique signatures on their breath, meaning that they had affected the body and the viewer on a level far deeper than mere sight and sound.

Over the course of 108 screenings of sixteen different films, they monitored air at multiple movies attended by 9,500 different people. After crunching the data, they noticed something remarkable.

"We knew that there was a connection between the scenes in the film and the chemicals that basically all human beings were broadcasting," he explained.

Some of what they found was obvious. When our hearts pump, the percentage of carbon dioxide we exhale increases. In *The Hunger Games: Catching Fire* is a fairly awesome moment when the dress worn by the hero, Katniss Everdeen, bursts into flames. Across ten screenings, at the moment Everdeen burst into flames, the percentage of carbon dioxide in the room would reliably pop. At the onset of the final battle, it consistently popped again.

These types of moments in various films were so visible and distinct in terms of CO_2 levels, the researchers found it was sometimes possible to identify a given film by its CO_2 signature alone.

But even more noticeable—and predictable—were the spikes in isoprene.

A film where isoprene levels jump around is a thrilling, exciting, perhaps frightening experience. During a film that's slow and steady, you're probably using all of your seat, not just the edge. Williams thinks this may have promise as a way to objectively evaluate the intensity of films, which could help produce a numerical rating to prepare parents and sensitive audiences for a feature.

In *Catching Fire*, the isoprene spikes that show up repeatedly are moments where your body wants to jump out of its own skin, the most reliable being a vicious surprise monkey

AUDIENCES IN A GROUP DRASTICALLY CHANGE THE AIR IN A ROOM

Carbon dioxide during multiple screenings of the *The Hunger Games: Catching Fire*

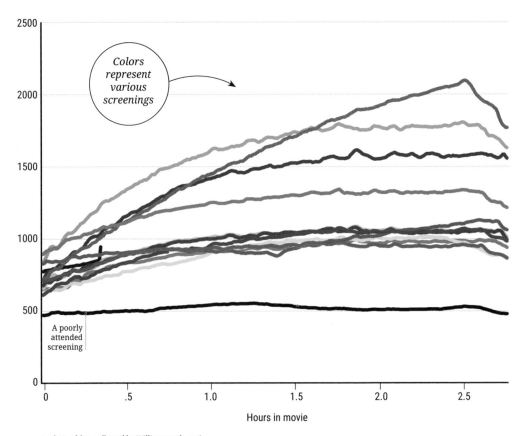

Analysis of data collected by Williams et al. 2016

attack that leads to the brutal death of a contestant toward the end of the film.

Most intriguing, though, was the amount of variation in VOCs: Although they were reliable between different screenings of the same film, Williams *had absolutely no idea* what caused them. Williams and his team might notice that a specific chemical would reliably spike in the air at about the same time in multiple different screenings, but they wouldn't know what the appearance of that chemical actually meant. The body remains a bit of a mystery.

Williams also recorded a range of gasses related to certain types of scenes but couldn't quite identify the molecules within them. The complexities of the human body, the sheer

MOVIES MAKE PEOPLE EXHALE THE SAME CHEMICALS AT THE SAME TIMES | Net levels of isoprene in each screening vs. expected levels

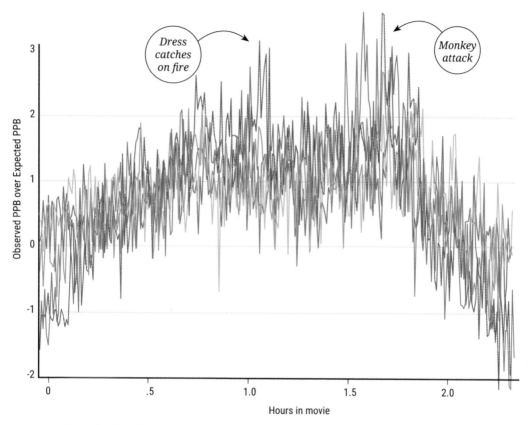

Analysis of data collected by Williams et al. 2016

depth of reactions that could be happening inside a given viewer, the understanding of the physiology simply isn't there yet, even if the technology to detect it might be.

Here's what we do know: Different movies create different reactions within our bodies, including repeatable chemical signatures for comedy, horror, or suspense. This means movies are far more than just sound and light—they're experiential works that resonate throughout our nervous, endocrine, and respiratory systems, affecting our entire bodies in ways we can measure but have barely begun to understand.

Onscreen Chemistry

For decades, Frits Rosendaal has been researching blood.

Rosendaal is a professor of clinical epidemiology at the Leiden University Medical Center in Leiden, Netherlands. An expert in how blood works, Rosendaal maintains a personal interest in the way that human blood winds through history. His PhD dissertation was about hemophilia, a disease of czars and kings and one of the oldest afflictions in human history.

The disease has been understood on a basic level for thousands of years: The Talmud says that if a boy dies of bleeding from circumcision and his brother or two cousins die, too, that family is exempt from required circumcisions, one of the most ancient recorded examples of epidemiology. The completion of Rosendaal's dissertation about hemophilia coincided with the height of the HIV epidemic, which often infected hemophiliac patients via blood transfusions. Eventually, Rosendaal moved from inopportune bleeding to the other side of the equation, inopportune *clotting*, specifically thrombosis, or when blood clots inappropriately, which can cause strokes.

There's a phrase for *bloodcurdling* not just in English but also in French, German, Dutch, and even Latin. Since medieval times, that frigid sensation felt in your blood when you're spooked has been compared to curdling. And that's precisely what Rosendaal and a group of his students decided to study on a lark.

"And then we thought, *Well, let's test it*," said Rosendaal. "Let's make people afraid and see if their blood curdles."

Rosendaal's daughter, a horror buff, was tasked with finding a film that made people afraid but wasn't bloody: They wanted to measure fear, not disgust, so it had to be spooky but not a slash-'em-up. The pick was *Insidious*, a 2010 James Wan film praised for its effective frights but containing virtually no violence and pretty much no blood, although filled top to bottom with intense and frightening jump scares. All flash, no splash.

For the control group, a staid, straightforward documentary was chosen: *A Year in Champagne*, which takes the viewer on a journey behind the scenes of six champagne-producing houses in France. It's delightful, and the closest thing to a demonic possession it contains is a 1957 Saint-Chamant brut for which you might sell your soul.

Next, they had to decide what to look for.

Blood clotting is one of the oldest systems in evolution. From the moment a body has blood vessels, those vessels can be punctured, so it's an evolutionary imperative to stop bleeding. And it's complex: Lots of factors are involved in the clotting system of a given person, including their blood type, genetic variants, and whether they have a blood disorder or are using certain kinds of birth control, for example.

What stroke researchers like Rosendaal measure is the relative equilibrium of these and other factors to determine if you're at a higher risk of stroke or are more likely to bleed. Long-term shifts in the balance of those clotting and anticlotting factors are what concern doctors, especially if certain behaviors put you at long-term risk of clotting or bleeding issues, though one's equilibrium can shift in the short term for all sorts of reasons.

Reasons like the body preparing itself to bleed.

Because our clotting system basically works as a cascade of things that happen in a chain reaction, it works best when it's fast, it's local, and it stops. When the body is under duress—when your adrenaline is up—one effect is that it escalates production of some blood coagulation factors. Adrenaline can't really be measured after the fact, so what Rosendaal did was take blood samples before and after the film to see if the balance of procoagulants and anticoagulants shifted.

He was trying to find out if those bodies watching the horror film were getting ready to bleed.

Twenty-four people volunteered to provide a blood sample for Rosendaal's study, then watch a scary horror movie, then give another blood sample. They all watched the two movies, two weeks apart.

During the control screening—the soothing Champagne documentary—86 percent of the participants saw a decrease in the level of coagulant Factor VIII, higher levels of which indicate the blood is more prepared for clotting. After the scary movie, 57 percent saw the Factor VIII level increase.

The results clearly illustrate just how much importance your body assigns to the things you watch. Even though your conscious mind understands that the images you're watching are invented, that you're not in real danger, your subconscious mind has a different reaction. Your sympathetic nervous system, the involuntary reactions your ancestors honed over thousands of years on a savanna, the instinct to take what you think you see as seriously as the things you actually see is what makes movies more than just a visual experience, but one that affects your whole body.

So even if you don't take movies seriously, your brain does.

Hooked on a Feeling

Our skin conducts electricity more or less efficiently, depending on our emotions. We know that when we're emotionally stimulated—stressed, elated, sad, any intense emotion, really—our bodies sweat a tiny bit, so little we might not even notice. And when those microbeads of sweat appear, our skin gets more electrically conductive. This change in sweat gland activity is called galvanic skin response, and it happens completely without your conscious mind having much say in the matter. If you feel emotionally intense, you're going to notice an increase in sweat gland activity. This is particularly useful from a scientific perspective, because it allows us to put an objective value on a subjective state of mind. We can actually measure your emotional state by tracking how your body subconsciously sweats, by running a bit of electricity through your skin. We can then turn the subjective, subconscious experience of emotional intensity into an objective number by figuring out how good your skin gets at transferring an electrical current.

Machines that measure galvanic skin response (GSR) measure the current that travels through a person's skin and can follow how a person's emotional state changes from one moment to the next. The higher the conductivity, the more intense you feel; the lower the conductivity, the more relaxed you feel. We can pinpoint the precise moments when things get intense according to your subconscious mind.

This is one reason that GSR—in addition to heart rate, respiration measurements, and other feedback—are components in a polygraph, the "lie detection" machine that in reality just spits out a bunch of graphs—*polygraphs*—that people interpret to identify acute moments of physical stress. These moments can be linked to "lying," but can also be linked to "talking to a police officer" or "taking a polygraph test" and "watching the last half hour of *Mad Max: Fury Road*."

Beyond its adoption by law enforcement, galvanic skin response remains a reliable and respected tool in psychological research—because it gets at the deeper level of physiological response underneath the ways that the conscious mind exerts control. You may not jump and scream at a jump-scare moment, but a GSR reader would show that your sympathetic nervous system took the moment *seriously* even as your conscious mind overrode the perception of a threat.

We know that it's possible to identify movies by biological signatures, that movies don't just exist as visual and audio entities but rather operate on a more physiological level, manifesting uniquely and repeatedly in signatures ranging from CO_2 composition of the atmosphere to the rewards center of the brain.

Here's what the output looked like when I strapped a GSR reader to myself and turned it on at the beginning of *Jaws* and turned it off at the end of the credits:

JAWS

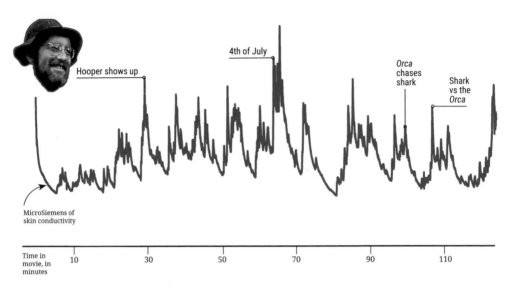

Author's analysis of personal GSR recording

The y-axis is in microsiemens, which are a measure of how conductive something is. (For the electrically curious, a siemens is the inverse of an ohm, a measure of electrical resistance.) The higher the value, the more incredibly tiny beads of sweat my nervous system decided to release to aid in fight-or-flight.

It's not really important to know the specific value at any given point—lots of things like baseline stress levels, humidity, weather, and temperature can affect the specific log of microsiemens, which is why it's not useful to line them up and see which had the "biggest scares." What we're interested in are those relative shifts seen in the chart, especially when the line goes up very quickly. Those are the moments when my brain saw something on-screen and my subconscious said, "Oh hell no!" and then released a preparatory flush of sweat from my palms. The reaction is logged by the electrical current in seconds,

and we can see the moments of intensity that define a classic horror-infused monster flick like *Jaws*.

Note how the shark attacks in the first hour of the film—serial-killer-style savaging on nameless bathers—give quite a shock time and again. When a character I personally like appears—Richard Dreyfuss's Matt Hooper—there's a jolt of intensity. What's telling about the success and accomplishment of *Jaws* is that Steven Spielberg, the director, manages your emotions perfectly in the first half of the film, giving you a scare but time to calm down, another scare then time to calm down, pacing the film methodically. But the Fourth of July scene is his manipulative masterpiece here. Despite evidence of a man-eater, the city fathers *insist* that the beaches remain open. So naturally, it's packed to the gills when we see the beach next. And worst of all, in addition to a legion of tourists, there are kids we've come

The Fourth of July, when Jaws *cashes in on the escalating tension of the first hour of the movie.*

to like and connect with playing on their boat in the canal just off the beach! It builds tension and then climaxes with a sequence of abject terror—*Where are the kids!?*—before ending with a long-sought confrontation between the mayor and police chief Martin Brody.

Our nervous system is most engaged when characters with whom we've bonded are in danger, not just when we're delivered the most convincing jump scare. Going into the movie, I assumed that the first shark attack would trigger the biggest reaction, the moment that jolts us into a reality where no one is safe. That, or it would be the most unexpected scare, perhaps when Ben Gardner's corpse makes a shocking appearance on his boat. But look at the chart again: Those big early jump scares cause spikes, but nothing like when the main characters are in danger.

The back half of the film pits three dudes we've come to root for on a boat versus one shark, the intensity popping higher and lasting

longer. The scares themselves aren't that different—it's the same shark in the same water hunting the same locals—but the emotional connection I developed for the characters had my nervous system jacked up. These guys losing a fight against an underwater menace is far more emotionally intense than the random bloody, violent deaths of act 1.

Raiders of the Lost Ark is an even more stark example, where we can really detect the rising action as the stakes of Indiana's adventure get more and more intense as the movie progresses. Though punctuated by a thrilling, iconic fight in the plaza, the action rises consistently through the first hour of the film as a college professor finds himself first in a treasure hunt, then in a heist, then in a *war*, and then in a brush with divinity itself. The stakes get dangerous after Indy's first experience with the Ark of the Covenant, when it winds up in the hands of the bad guys. Then the stakes get deadly, with Indy trapped in a sealed tomb

STEVEN SPIELBERG | Amazing stories

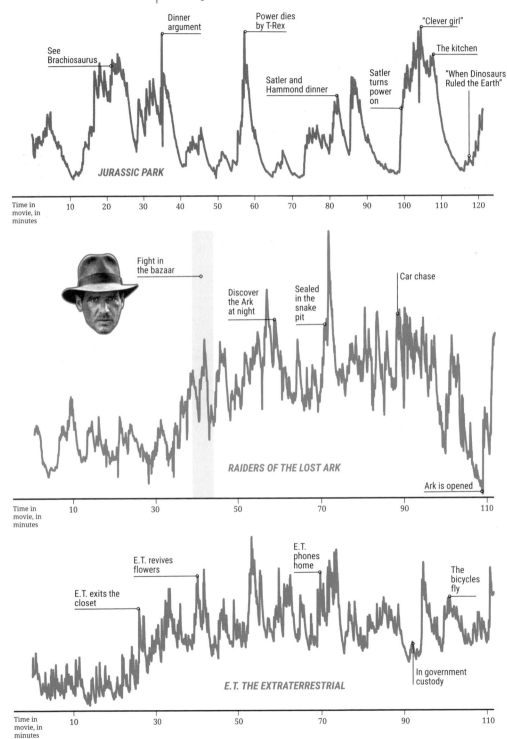

JURASSIC PARK

See Brachiosaurus

Dinner argument

Power dies by T-Rex

Satler and Hammond dinner

Satler turns power on

"Clever girl"

The kitchen

"When Dinosaurs Ruled the Earth"

Time in movie, in minutes
10 20 30 40 50 60 70 80 90 100 110 120

RAIDERS OF THE LOST ARK

Fight in the bazaar

Discover the Ark at night

Sealed in the snake pit

Car chase

Ark is opened

Time in movie, in minutes
10 30 50 70 90 110

E.T. THE EXTRATERRESTRIAL

E.T. exits the closet

E.T. revives flowers

E.T. phones home

The bicycles fly

In government custody

Time in movie, in minutes
10 30 50 70 90 110

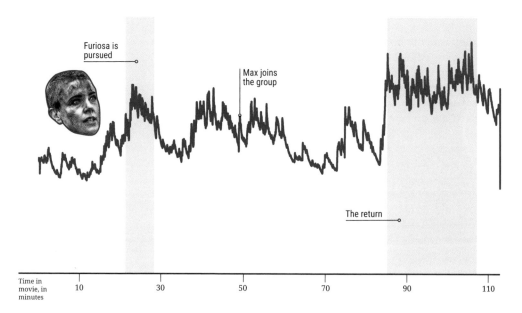

Furiosa is
pursued

Max joins
the group

The return

Time in
movie, in   10   30   50   70   90   110
minutes

surrounded by nothing but venomous snakes, eventually escaping only to have an explosive fight on a taxiing plane.

Even the high-speed chase that follows pales in comparison, but it's not until the end of the film, when (spoiler warning) Indiana and Marion survive a holy onslaught, that the viewer is at great risk of falling off the edge of their seat. You'd be hard pressed to find action and tension paced more capably than in *Raiders of the Lost Ark*.

Or take a movie like *Mad Max: Fury Road*.

First, this film should not exist. Developed over decades, it cost a fortune, was shot with real effects in a desert, and was universally believed to be an incredibly demanding experience for the actors. It was also directed by a master, George Miller, working at the top of his craft. *Fury Road* is probably the most insane thing anyone has contemplated making into a film. After Steven Soderbergh saw the film, he told the *Hollywood Reporter*, "I just watched *Mad Max: Fury Road* again last week, and I tell you I couldn't direct 30 seconds of that. I'd put a gun in my mouth. . . . I don't understand two things: I don't understand how they're not still

shooting that film and I don't understand how hundreds of people aren't dead."

This film is considered a miracle by many, and unquestionably one of the coolest movies ever made. And my GSR reading from the film reflected that.

The chart above reflects exactly how it feels to watch *Mad Max: Fury Road*. You start off enjoying the vibe, and then the most ridiculous chase scene you have ever seen—featuring a man held up by bungee cords playing an electric guitar that spits fire—ends with the protagonists flying into a dust storm. And somehow that feels *relaxing*. The chases continue, until finally Furiosa and Max have gone as far as they can to find that the green lands they were hoping to locate are gone. At that moment, the movie turns it all around, and they—along with the ragtag group they've assembled—make the audacious choice to turn their rig around and drive head-on into their pursuers in a bid to beat them back to home base. The final forty minutes of this movie are an adrenaline drip where your main thought is that Soderbergh is right: *How are all of these people not dead?*

The entirety of act 3 is a bare-knuckle ride to the death that demands to be watched without letting up for a single frame, a movie that continues shifting into higher gears despite starting off at full speed.

It was time to expand the experiment. Now a pool of seventeen people watched more than a dozen movies.

In these graphs, you can see the flow of the movies in real time. For action movies in particular, it's easy to notice the stakes and action increasing, whether it's Indiana Jones's adventure getting progressively intense or the tensions on the block in *Do the Right Thing* getting more fraught across the course of a hot day or the choices Rick Blaine has to make getting more acute and imminent as *Casablanca* progresses.

And this effect isn't limited to live action. Animated movies can make the most out of their quick run times. Whether it's *Wall-E* or *Princess Mononoke*, we can see how animated movies play around with time and intensity. Long, languid, slower periods punctuated by thrilling action set pieces allow the respective directors to control a viewer's attention and emotional valence over the course of the film.

We like to tell ourselves that the eye-catching moments, the enormous special effects, the huge battles and thrilling chases are what excites the brain. And that's true, to a point: I'm not bored at the end of *Fury Road*, that's for sure. But time and again, the moments that registered highest on my readings were when characters accomplished or endured something, not the moments of action.

In these graphs, you can see this effect over the course of not just one movie, but a whole franchise. Take, for instance, the three-film Lord of the Rings epic. Sure, the big moments—Gandalf on Khazad-dûm, the last march of the Ents, the charge on the Pelennor Fields—all get pops, to be sure. The action registers. But the truly engaging moments are when the characters come together, or when they have to leave.

This got much clearer the moment I saw the chart for *Fast Five*, a heist movie that evolved the Fast and Furious franchise from films about street racers to a series about a crew who carry out elaborate heists. A movie predicated on furious people driving fast would have its share of thrilling moments. And it does: when they break into the corrupt police department, or steal cars, or they're running amok in Rio carrying out the heist, and, still more, when they confront Hobbes, the cop played by Dwayne Johnson tasked with taking them all down.

Those moments—the flashy, expensive action set pieces—were not the ones that excited my nervous system the most.

That first colossal emotional peak forty minutes in isn't a car race, a fight scene, or an explosion but a montage of the crew being assembled. The moment where former friends and enemies comes together as a squad, and maybe something a little more.

The only conventional racing scene—the drag race about ninety minutes in—doesn't make as much of a dent.

You might think the huge surge in GSR at an hour and forty-five minutes is the big escape, the moment they get the safe and have successfully taken down the organized crime syndicate plaguing Rio.

But that big surge comes *afterward*.

The big emotional win, at about an hour and fifty-three, isn't just the absurd chase that leads the heroes through the streets of Rio dragging an enormous safe behind them, but the moment we realize *how* and *why* they got away with it, the twist that allows the crew to beat the bad guys and keep the dough. It's the moment when, recognizing their sacrifice, The Rock gives them a head start. It's when the music plays and the lights go on and they show us how they *really* stole the cash, followed by the elated moments where the victorious crew spends it celebrating.

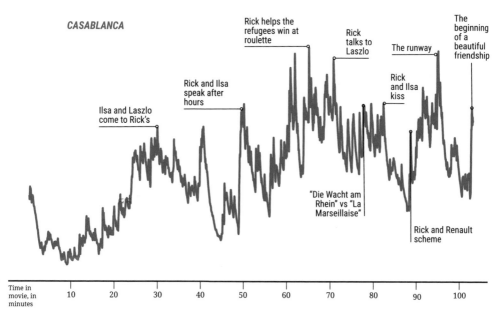

In Casablanca, *the stakes rise steadily as Rick's internal conflict, and the conflict swirling around the city, increasingly come to a head. The movie delivers best each time the true stakes and intentions of the characters are gradually revealed.*

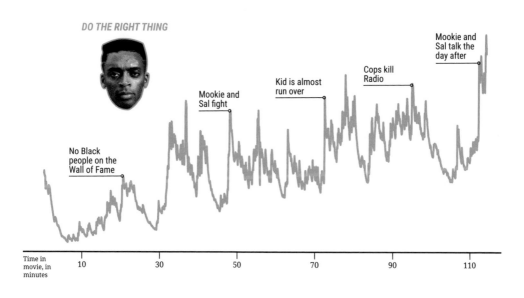

Spike Lee brilliantly escalates the palpable tension throughout Do The Right Thing, *with the film's hot summer day raising tensions on the block and culminating in the film's final, epic conflagration.*

Hayao Miyazaki's intricate and beautifully animated Princess Mononoke *tells a story of humanity's attempts to shape its natural environment and the tensions that causes. The conflict between the powers of the natural world and the powers of man clashing is an undercurrent of the film, but it occasionally gets extremely direct.*

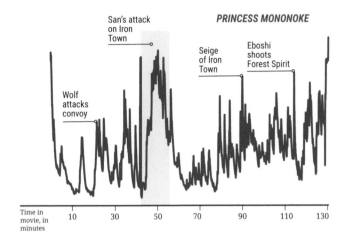

Pixar Animation's WALL-E *is a science fiction romance telling of how the last robot on a deserted Earth finds hope for the humans who abandoned it, and finds the companionship it never had.*

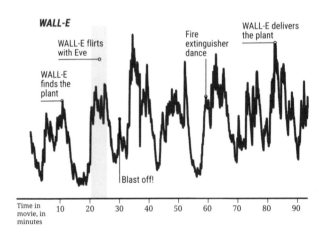

In Pixar's Up, *an old man with a bittersweet past confronts the difference between the life he wanted and the life he had. Though it appears to be a swashbuckling adventure, the moments that land are the ones where Carl's past meet his present.*

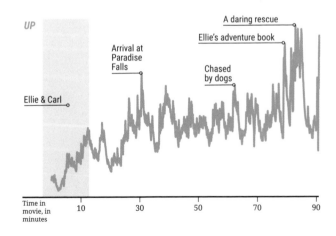

LORD OF THE RINGS | An emotional journey kicks into gear

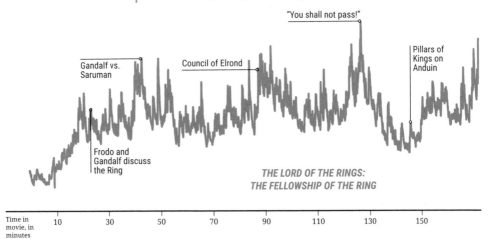

"You shall not pass!"

Gandalf vs. Saruman

Council of Elrond

Pillars of Kings on Anduin

Frodo and Gandalf discuss the Ring

THE LORD OF THE RINGS: THE FELLOWSHIP OF THE RING

Time in movie, in minutes
10   30   50   70   90   110   130   150

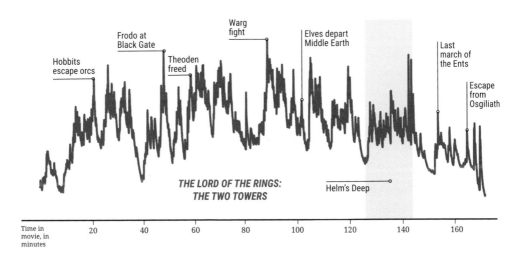

Warg fight

Frodo at Black Gate

Theoden freed

Elves depart Middle Earth

Last march of the Ents

Hobbits escape orcs

Escape from Osgiliath

THE LORD OF THE RINGS: THE TWO TOWERS

Helm's Deep

Time in movie, in minutes
20   40   60   80   100   120   140   160

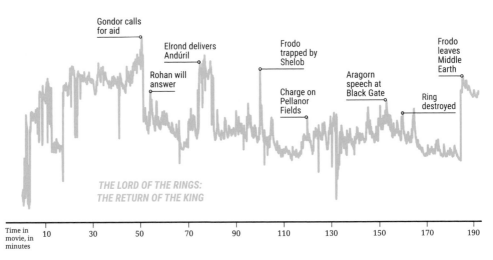

Gondor calls for aid

Elrond delivers Andúril

Frodo trapped by Shelob

Frodo leaves Middle Earth

Rohan will answer

Aragorn speech at Black Gate

Charge on Pellanor Fields

Ring destroyed

THE LORD OF THE RINGS: THE RETURN OF THE KING

Time in movie, in minutes
10   30   50   70   90   110   130   150   170   190

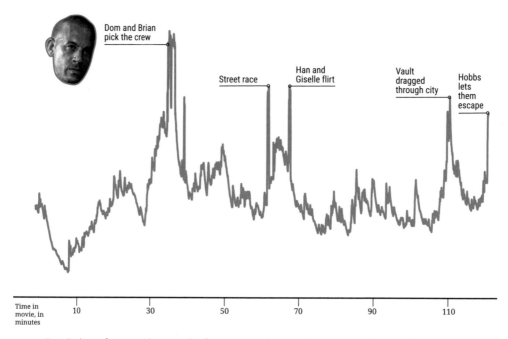

Despite its early reputation as a simple car racing story, Justin Lin's Fast Five *saw the crew become brilliant thieves executing one last heist. The best moments in the film aren't about the cars—they're about the drivers.*

It turns out that what makes good blockbusters stand the test of time is not how big the explosions are, but how much you *like* the ripped dude jumping away from the explosion. Even in the most audacious action flicks, the moments that resonate aren't the ones with danger or action for their own sakes, but the ones with the *characters* in danger, the people behind the action.

We know movies affect our bodies in real ways, that they can make our subconscious minds feel like they're in enough danger that they prepare themselves to bleed, that what we see on a movie screen can change what our bodies are doing chemically. And that our entire nervous system experiences films in a way that's discernible with electricity.

But for all those things to erupt, a movie has to grab us. We have to become invested in what's happening on-screen. And that comes before the physical part. For our bodies to go along for the ride, our brains must first buy a ticket.

PUNCTUATED BY ACTION

Action movies mete out moments of intensity over the course of a movie

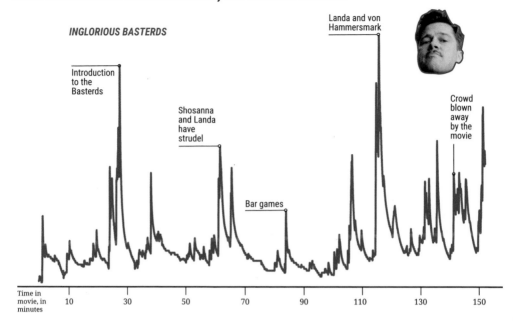

In a movie full of elaborate and violent action sequences, the scenes that resonate the most in Quentin Tarantino's 2009 war epic are the scenes where heroes and villains talk face-to-face.

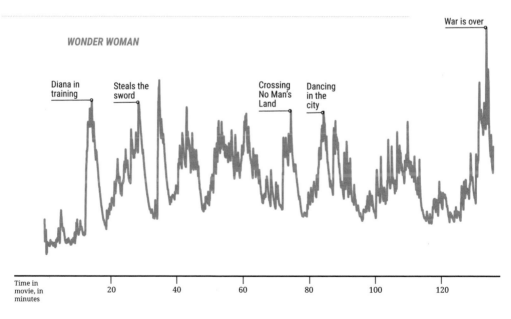

Diana's hero's journey sees the brain react most intensely not simply to the action sequences, but to moments where Diana achieves a personal milestone as a result of her efforts.

CHAPTER 2

HOW CULTURE CAPTURES US

The Prestige (2006)

If we want to understand how movies affect us, we need to understand how we watch movies. And so we first have to understand how we watch anything, how sight actually works.

Movies aren't just a way of making art—over time, they've been honed into direct manifestations of how we perceive the world. Directors don't merely direct the crew, the cast, the camera—what a director really does is manipulate the audience's eye. The best of them artfully bring together both technology *and* an understanding of attention to produce a film that works within the complexities of human vision, exploits the illusions of human sight, and captures the attention of every viewer in every seat.

If you want to understand human vision, you need to know that a central piece of it is the creation of illusions.

"An illusion is when the physical reality doesn't match the perception," said Dr. Stephen Macknik, who, along with Dr. Susana Martinez-Conde, is developing ways to restore permanent vision loss and communicate vision signals directly to the brain by understanding the fundamental nature of sight through illusions. "Therefore, if you're studying an illusion, it's actually a direct path to understanding what the brain is doing, because it must be from the brain doing that."

When you discover an illusion and can determine what's causing it, you're understanding something about how the brain works. It can be a visual illusion, like something by Victor Vasarely, or a cognitive one, like what a magician would do.

Your brain has more than two dozen cortical areas dedicated partly or completely to processing visual information. That's a colossal amount of real estate devoted to one thing, so it's clearly one of the most important things we do—according to our brains, anyway. The next closest sense, in terms of the number of brain cells or neurons devoted to its interpretation, is touch.

Compared with other senses, sight has by far the most illusions in both quantity and variety. There are plenty of auditory illusions, but when it comes to vision? We just keep finding more.

For years, illusions were thought to be bugs, errors, or mental goofs. After decades of research about the brain, that thinking is going out of style, and illusions are now believed to be not errors but essential infrastructure of thought.

"The point that our most complex sense has the most illusions associated to it," said Martinez-Conde, "that should tell you something—that illusions are not really something evolution is trying to get rid of. It's the opposite."

Given the brain's operational emphasis on vision, it leads to some interesting ideas about what, precisely, "vision" is. After all, we can "see" without using our eyes when we dream, and if I tell you to close your eyes and think of Superman, you will certainly conjure an image.

When we're seeing something in the physical world, light enters our eyes and hits our photoreceptors. Those convert the light into neural signals, which travel along the optic nerve through our brain's nucleus, then into the primary visual cortex, in the back of our heads. The latter is about the size of a credit card. Each square millimeter on that card corresponds to a different point in visual space, and each represents the smallest thing you can see.

The primary visual cortex is the first time information from our two eyes merges together, where we have the basis of binocular vision, the combined single image from two separate eyes. From there, elements of our vision go to different parts of our brains' visual system, where we comprehend action and motion, or object recognition.

If you want to know exactly how much one square millimeter of visual cortex can truly see, hunt around for the dimmest object you can see in the night sky. Given their distance, all stars are inherently smaller than the smallest photoreceptor in your eye. The "bigger" stars are actually not bigger, they're just brighter. The smallest thing we are physically able to see is therefore the dimmest star in the night sky.

But what you're really seeing is a slim fragment of reality at a given moment. Your brain is filling in blanks, stitching together a real-time approximation of what sight should be. We know this because our vision is far less precise than we might think.

The reality is that our eyes take far worse images than a phone camera, despite the enormous amount of real estate in our brains devoted to making sense of what we see. And that's why scientists like Macknik and Martinez-Conde are so interested in eye movements.

Right now, for example, you're looking at a book or an e-reader, or, if you're listening to this in audiobook form, you're likely looking at *something*. You have somewhere between 120 degrees and 180 degrees of visual field. So why move your eyes?

The reason is that the retina, which is the part of your eye that truly sees, is efficient, and only the very bull's-eye center of it—the fovea, itself the center of the macula—has truly great resolution. To see the world in high resolution, you need to dart your eyes all around, moving your fovea to take in an entire space.

Most of your retina is dedicated to peripheral vision, really seeing a resolution of only

Koskota (1976) by Victor Vasarely, the grandfather of Op Art, which integrates optical illusions into work.

about a tenth of a megapixel. A very small region at the center of your retina can see ten or more times that resolution. The macula and the fovea are at the center of the retina. They are the parts of your eye that are really, really good at seeing stuff. Our brains are able to move our eyes in clever ways to get a much broader and more complex level of detail than you would just staring at something dead-on. In fact, they're constantly constructing a composite image of what's in that fovea, without our ever noticing it.

If you had high resolution on your retina everywhere, like a digital camera has the same resolution across its entire field, you'd never need to move your eye. But notice, as you read this and the following sentences, how foggy things get in your peripheral vision. As you read this sentence, try to read what's going on just a line or two above. You can't, because your high-resolution vision—the part that might have 20/20 vision—is one one-thousandth of your visual field, or just 0.1 percent of what you can *actually* see.

Wanna know how big that is? Hold out your arm. Give a thumbs-up. Your thumbnail? That's it. That's your high-resolution vision. Everything else is peripheral.

And if you lose that thumbnail, you're blind.

Eyes Wide, Not Shut

So what does this mean for movies? You can go to the largest IMAX cinema in the world or watch a movie on an old cathode-ray television set, and either way your eye has the same range of visual acuity in what it can see.

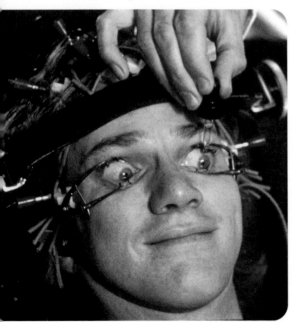

Stanley Kubrick knew a thing or two about what to do with viewers' attention.

Why then is the IMAX movie so much more immersive? Eye movements.

Eye movements are pointing your fovea to different places. Some species that don't rely much on their visual acuity don't have a fovea; their retina is basically the same photoreceptor density everywhere. Those species don't make a whole lot of eye movements, but we do.

We make about one to three per second. When you walk into an unfamiliar room, for example, and size it up over ten seconds, at best you're looking at thirty points of detail, or a little more than 1 percent of the average room. From that, your brain is nonetheless able to weave together a perception of space, one that you credibly believe is a true vision.

Since your eyes can see quite well only in one specific spot, your brain is able to do tricks—short, quick eye movements called saccades—that help it fill in the blanks by rounding out the visual scene with details that your peripheral vision doesn't capture. Perhaps, as you read this, there's a coffee cup on a table nearby that you can see out of the corner of your eye. Now, that coffee cup is not sprinting around a savanna. Since it's not dynamic, it's probably not a threat—your brain observes it, but declines to allocate more visual processing resources than necessary. If someone picks it up your eyes may, for a moment, pop over and steal a glance, but soon enough you'll once again focus on this page.

A different level of focus entirely is *smooth pursuit*, where you home in on one big thing only, locking onto it to see it in outstanding detail. Smooth pursuit is what happens when you see something *interesting*. It can be movement in the grass, a bird in the air, a car swerving up ahead, or something not random like a magician with white gloves moving a red ball in an arc over his head. Smooth pursuit happens when your brain is downright eager to closely follow interesting things in motion—because organisms that are bad at smooth pursuit also tend to succumb to predators, or don't hunt altogether.

The upside of smooth pursuit is that you're seeing in great detail—you can zone in on the gazelle in the grass, determine the type of bird with ease, or you can spot the unpredictable driver swerve and then estimate where he's going and take action to avoid him. The downside is that your brain cuts out all those saccades that keep you aware of what's going on in your peripheral vision. When in smooth pursuit, you likely don't notice what the magician's other, uninteresting hand is doing on the table to set up the next trick.

It is in the managing of these eye movements that film and TV directors succeed or fail. In fact, it is their entire job to effectively use the language of cinema and the visual field to steer our eyeballs around a screen so we see what they want us to see. Essentially, that's the basic cinematic difference between, say, an Oscar-winning movie and security camera footage. One has an active person deliberately attempting to steer your point of focus, and the other one doesn't.

You're also *not* seeing more than you realize. There are blood vessels in your eyes that are between your iris and the photoreceptors. Technically, they should be blocking your view like a tall man in a movie theater. But when raw vision information is processed, your brain just erases them for you as if you've never noticed them. When your eye moves to a new location, your brain makes you think you're not actually blind when you really are, a process called a saccadic suppression. Blinking does a version of this, too, called blink suppression. Your visual field goes completely dark for 100 milliseconds when you blink multiple times per minute, but you don't notice because your brain just carries the perception of sight along. You have visual blind spots because of your optic nerve, but your brain compensates, so you don't notice them in your day-to-day living.

Vision is also extremely demanding on our brains, which have evolved so the visual system runs efficiently and is therefore willing to accept shortcuts. When you look at a white wall, for example, you see only the edges of the wall—your brain simply fills in the middle. When you look at a blue sky, it's the same— you don't see the blue sky; you see the edges of clouds, and your brain fills in the blue.

This concept also applies to time. We will often see things for longer than they are actually there. In the real world, the speed of light is about 186,000 miles per hour. But in your primary visual cortex, your perception of light is considerably slower. When a given visual stimulus turns off, we know we see it continuing for thirty-five milliseconds longer because our brains are still moving and interpreting the signals. And then the signal in the brain might continue past the end of the real-world stimulus, because it's a little more efficient that way.

And although older generations of neurologists regarded that persistence of vision as a bug, it's the exact feature that makes film— which presents just twenty-four images per second—possible. Your brain is able to keep up with it because it's just quicker than the time it takes to turn a brain cell on and off.

Focus Group

Most people interpret attention as an enhancement of their focus. The idea is that if I'm paying attention to something, my vision of it is enhanced, and my understanding of it is somehow improved. But in practice that's not what's happening at all.

"Attention doesn't actually *enhance* anything," said Macknik. Not neurobiologically, anyway, because cranking up a signal to a neuron would also crank up the visual noise it must process. So your attention doesn't enhance vision. "When I look at you and I pay attention to your face," explained Macknik, "I'm not enhancing your face at all. What I'm doing is *suppressing* everything else."

When you're focused on something, everything that isn't *that* something is observed less.

"The rest of the visual field is actually dimmer," added Macknik. "It's actually *darker*."

Once you get how attention works, many of the ways we describe attention fall to ribbons. For example, multitasking? Not real. The concept of multitasking was invented in the early 1980s to sell computers, and then clever people attempted to convince normal people that they too would be able to multitask like their computers. And you certainly *can* do multiple tasks at one time. The only caveat is that you are not, in fact, doing several tasks at the same time. Rather, you're very quickly switching your attention between tasks, quickly enough that you can convince yourself that you are working on things simultaneously.

This is similar to what your eyes do, momentarily darting all over a visual field to keep up with the state of things. But instead of visual focus, it's attentional focus.

The brilliant color and action in the foreground consumes your focus, so you don't notice that upon closer inspection the backgrounds are just matte paintings.

Visual Shorthand

Dividing attention is a key tool of storytelling. If you pause an old Disney movie and take in the whole frame, you'll notice the old animation flat matte painting background. Dividing people's attention and subsequently taking control of their focus is the bread and butter of such staged magic. It's how directors cleverly feed your brain visual cues to ensure you're looking at the interesting part of the screen rather than allowing your eyes to wander and thus your interest to wane.

Every great movie twist and mystery is built on divided attention. Twists resonate only if the evidence for them builds in a slow boil, the clues becoming obvious to a viewer but also deftly placed in the attentional periphery of the viewer. Attention is therefore the very building block of suspense, which, when done well, is able to narrow our attentional focus. This is why having a *Law and Order: SVU* episode on in the background while we're working can—fairly seamlessly—turn into watching an episode of *SVU*.

A suspenseful Hitchcock short was shown to a number of participants who'd been asked to keep a tally of times they saw a gun in the movie. Some viewers were shown the film with the scenes cut up and placed out of order, as a way to disrupt the film's ability to seize and capitalize on their attention. Those viewers were excellent at mentally counting the number of appearances of the gun without much trouble.

The other group watched the unedited movie—a creation by a renowned master of suspense, no less—and then reported their mental tally. *These people performed terribly.* They were great at counting the appearances of guns early on, but once they were immersed in the movie, things changed. By act 3, they had clearly forgotten their one task in watching the film.

Moments of suspense decrease our peripheral vision and blind us to other things happening, on-screen or off. This management of attention is at the heart of detective stories, but also of how well a director pulls off a big twist ending.

Successful twists are hard-fought victories for directors. They really work only when a director manages to show audiences everything needed to discern the true state of things while also corralling their attention away from those clues so they fail to see what, in retrospect, is obvious. Twists fail for two reasons: Either the filmmaker puts too much evidence out there and the twist is obvious from the outset, or the filmmaker does not leave enough evidence before the big reveal, leaving the viewer confused.

When you consider the nature and process of vision and how it can be manipulated, the reason movies work begins to become clear. Your brain *wants* to assign credibility to the things it sees. Your brain craves action and interesting things and is more than happy to pay less attention to static things that bring a scene together. Think about *The Wizard of Oz*. The backgrounds are all matte paintings, the trees are plywood, the brick road contains absolutely no brick. But you don't have time to pick apart the paint job on the Emerald City—you're looking at the kinetic actors, you're taking in the colors, the flashy, visually arresting ruby slippers. Your brain is happy to buy into what it's seeing; it would rather accept the simplest visual solution over the most correct version.

Films work because your brain sees little reason for them not to. They work well with what our brains are willing to accept, because the very origins of movies—magic shows—were hotbeds of developing techniques to exploit our brains. Movies work so well on us because they are designed to appeal to our brains—always have been.

Events that happen in movies can have the same kind of effect on us that events in real life do because as far as our minds are concerned, the difference is immaterial. If most of what you see is made up by the brain anyway, and if you're focused on the screen, well, the screen is important and everything else can fade away for a time. And that's entertainment.

Center of Attention

A group of researchers at the University of Lubeck in Germany wanted to find a way to see just how often people looked at the same part of a movie screen under different conditions. To do this, they began by recording eighteen clips of different scenes that were each twenty seconds long. Each of the scenes showed just everyday moments from the area: eight of them showed people walking around in pedestrian areas or playing sports, another three showed cars, and yet another three were pretty uneventful, without much movement at all.

The researchers found that when watching the nondirected, natural video, people didn't really agree on where they should be looking. The 10 percent of the screen that was visually the most dense lured people to look at it only 30 percent of the time. It was otherwise rare for most people to look at the same place on the screen at the same time.

What happened when the researchers showed a shot that was composed on purpose?

Well, you could say that the researchers took it radically in the other direction, presenting trailers to *Star Wars: Episode III—Revenge of the Sith* and the Tom Cruise vehicle *War of the Worlds*. Here, the result was much more pronounced: The visually densest 10 percent of the screen drew 74 percent of eye fixations, meaning that the test volunteers were pretty much in visual lockstep when watching the trailers.

When they were watching the undirected scenes, people looked anywhere they wanted. When they watched the trailers—shorts deliberately designed to capture attention and guide the focus where the director wanted it—eyeballs were successfully herded.

Because, it turns out, our brains fall for the same dumb tricks in the same old ways.

Screens are big, so big we can't possibly focus on all of them at once. Good directors know how to make you aim your fovea at the part of the screen they want you to see. Great direction is just crafting a movie in such a way

that people intuitively agree on where to look. Bad direction is just the failure to coax an audience's eyeballs into a herd, where everyone's experience of watching something is theirs and theirs alone.

Liking What You See

Directors' degree of skill at massaging attention has a substantial impact on how well their creations are received. One study presented sixty-five commercials that aired during the 2014 Super Bowl to twenty-five participants wearing eye-tracking equipment. At the end of each, the participants were asked to rate the ad in terms of enjoyment on a scale of one to ten. The researchers also considered national polling on how each commercial was appraised.

The results were clear: About half the variation in the overall reviews of the ads was explained by how consistently people in the experiment were looking in the same vicinity as one another. The ads that rated highest all tended to also have the highest degree of consistency in where people were drawn to look at any given moment. When people all see something the same way, and that something is good, the visual manipulation is effective. To score unanimous evaluation as an output, you have to obtain—through direction alone—some degree of unanimity when it comes to input. It's the only way to guarantee that everyone's watching the same thing.

The ability to track viewer focus, enabled by cutting-edge technology used in laboratory settings and based on an understanding of the building blocks of attention, is powerful. It allows researchers to crack tough problems about how people process our visual world. It's considered serious business for research and development purposes, allowing companies and retailers to make decisions that can impact millions in sales. In the public sector, it can be used for bold, ambitious technological feats that facilitate safer roads and workplaces.

Eye tracking can also settle old arguments over classic films. Like *Star Wars*.

Upon release in 1977, *Star Wars* became a sensation, a movie that forever changed the culture that followed. This was perhaps not a surprise. It was the work of an obsessive director, George Lucas, who applied every iota of directorial knowledge he had to the film, borrowing the very best from movies that preceded it.

In particular, the attack run on the Death Star at the climax of *Star Wars* pulls heavily from a 1955 British war film called *The Dam Busters*, with the eponymous raid to bomb a dam serving as a direct inspiration for Red and Gold Squadrons' attack runs, which required the star fighters to score a tricky, direct shot. The director of cinematography on *Star Wars*, Gilbert Taylor, was responsible for the special-effects shots in *The Dam Busters*, and some of the dialogue in the film is lifted directly from the same. Lucas also deliberately made the run an homage to the film—and the impact is stunning.

The Empire Strikes Back followed *Star Wars*, but Lucas handed the director reins to Irvin Kershner. For *Return of the Jedi* in 1983, the honors went to Richard Marquand. Then, to some notoriety, after decades out of the directing chair, George Lucas returned to helm *The Phantom Menace*, the first of three prequel films that would feature the latest in special-effects technology to conjure the world

Lucas was never able to in the 1970s, when matte paintings and models were the tools of the special-effects trade.

The new world Lucas created for the prequels was extravagant, with details drenching every frame and dynamic digitally enhanced motion that was a feast for the eyes.

They were *hated*.

And not just hated. The Star Wars prequels became a touchstone of fan blowback. Many of the stories—particularly those that dwelled outside those of the core films, such as the television programming—became acclaimed in time. But the movies, well, they had problems.

Some critiqued the computer-generated imagery or special effects, and others knocked the performances or the writing. But the thing Lucas failed at in his second set of Star Wars films was grabbing hold of eyeballs, something he did incredibly well in the defining film of the series. Maybe that's because *Star Wars* pulled directly from the work of forebearers—films like *The Dam Busters* that were made by experienced cinematographers who knew how to manipulate attention the old-fashioned way—whereas the new films were quite literally inventing the field of digital photography in real time as they were created.

But in the end, the prequels forced the viewers to do way too much visual work. And I can prove it.

Half-Witted Scruffy-Looking Eye Herder

To wade deeply into the prequel muck, I decided to prove visually why they went so wrong. I persuaded a half dozen friends to don some gear—a Pupil Labs 3D-printed eye tracker constructed from two webcams and running the latest in open-source pupil-tracking software—and watch some of the most iconic scenes from each of the first six Star Wars films.

The clips I chose were the climactic fights of each film: the Death Star trench run of *Star*

Wars, the Battle of Hoth in *The Empire Strikes Back*, and the Battle of Endor in *Return of the Jedi*. For the prequels, we watched the duel between Darth Maul and Qui-Gon Jinn in *The Phantom Menace*, the battle in the arena on Geonosis for *Attack of the Clones*, and the duel on Mustafar in *Revenge of the Sith*. Finally, they watched the pod race in *The Phantom Menace*. Each clip was between ten and fifteen minutes.

FORCED PERSPECTIVE

"Always remember, your focus determines your reality."
—Qui-Gon Jin

Several participants donned eye-tracking goggles and were asked to watch key scenes from Star Wars movies. Some were better at holding their focus than others.

KEY:

1. Headband has two cameras, one looking out and one infrared looking at the eye.

Each screen below represents a different participant's view

EPISODE 1	EPISODE 2	EPISODE 3
The Phantom Menace	*Attack of the Clones*	*Revenge of the Sith*
The Duel of Fates	The Battle of Geonosis	The Battle of Mustafar

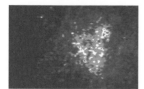

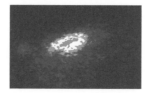

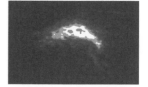

Viewers didn't have something to consistently focus on in the Phantom Menace climate.

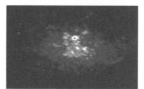

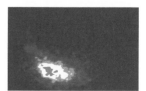

The Battle of Geonosis involved lots of chaos going on around the protagonists.

Distracting movements in the background can diffuse attention.

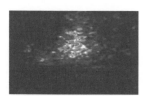

A climactic lightsaber duel is a good way to grab attention, even if the blades are moving all over.

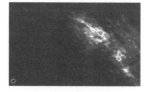

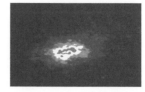

2. *Person watches films while the camera watches their eye movement.*

3. *After a calibration, the software knows where the eye is looking.*

4. *It follows the path and focus of the eye.*

5. *And makes these heatmaps based on the most visited location.*

EPISODE 4

Star Wars: A New Hope
Death Star Run

EPISODE 5

The Empire Strikes Back
The Battle of Hoth

EPISODE 6

The Return of the Jedi
The Battle of Endor

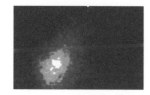

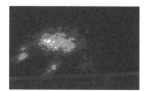

While the finale involves three separate battles—in space, on the moon, and in the Emporor's chamber—it's still pretty tightly focused.

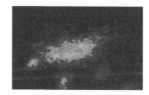

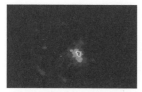
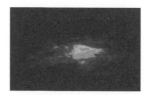

The Death Star assault keeps engrossed viewers staring dead-on in the center of the screen.

Author's analysis of six eye-tracking subjects

EYE TRACKING 101

An eye tracker works by pointing an infrared camera at your eye, then another camera at the room. You calibrate it, moving your eye around so the software can reconcile the angle of your eye with the calibration on the screen. For my Stars Wars experiment I was able to demarcate a television and then generate visual heat maps that plotted out where on the screen I was looking most during several short clips.

The Results

The first thing to notice is that the Death Star run of *Star Wars* is a functionally flawless piece of filmmaking, crafted so your eyes are glued to the dead center of the screen, fully rapt and focused. In the original films the center holds—there's a clear region of focus even if the eye meanders here and there.

In the prequels, not so much. There's no coherent focus in the climaxes of the first two films. Even *The Phantom Menace*, the only prequel shot on film, not digital, looks simple compared with the unfocused, all-over extravaganza of the Battle of Geonosis. Overall, the prequels lack the monomaniacal focus and intensity and stakes of the original trilogy, with the exception of *Revenge of the Sith*, which managed to grab some eyeballs with a twenty-minute light-saber fight. The speculation was not in short supply: Maybe Lucas was such a legend, no one told him he was off his game, or the lure of cramming delicious digital effects into every inch of frame was too great. Or maybe the advent of digital filmmaking meant that some of what used to work in manipulating attention wasn't as effective. In any case, the prequels are all over the map.

That said, there is one incredibly well-focused scene in the prequels, a sequence where George Lucas seizes your attention and never lets it lag, not for a second—the pod race in *The Phantom Menace*, a set piece from which your eyes positively can't meander.

NOW *THIS* IS POD RACING

One of the scenes that was best at holding the focus of viewers did as a matter of fact come from The Phantom Menace.

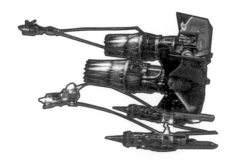

EPISODE 1
The Phantom Menace
The Pod Race

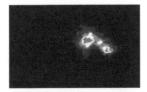

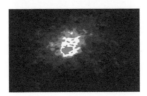

Author's analysis of six eye-tracking subjects

Kids are still learning where to put the eyes.

Appetite for Distraction: Kids and Viewing

Isabelle Mareschal studies visual perception. Early in her career, she studied simple ideas like how we gauge the speed of things moving toward us or determining the ideal amount of eye contact (three and a half seconds, by the way). Lately what has her interested is social perception, or why people look at things the way they do. She's particularly enamored with eye tracking because it can allow researchers like her to measure aspects of a child's development without having to ask them questions.

The work she's doing has the potential to gauge the developmental level of kids who might be nonverbal or who don't have strong language skills. Part of that work extends into how kids understand movies, and a key thing she found is that kids watch films *very* differently from how adults do.

The key difference: "Children might not be able to anticipate what's going to happen," she said, "whereas adults may anticipate and allocate their eyes to different parts of the screen."

Meaning: Understanding the visual language of film, the grammar of movies, is a *skill* that we gradually learn over time.

One study Mareschal worked on set out to find how different kids watched the same movie at different ages. She wanted to know if she could pick out differences in children's ages based on how they watch a short feature.

The study featured thirty-seven children aged six to fourteen who watched kid-friendly movies while being eye tracked. The results were all over the place: Infants tend to look at just faces, locking into one fixed spot where there is a human face. Younger kids, the ones in the younger group of that cohort, look all over the screen, taking everything in with less apparent logic. They fixate on more regions over a larger area compared with their older peers. The older kids are more likely to be herded along with their peers and look at intended focal points and follow the action as a director would want, particularly as they got older. By comparison, adults quickly put together a plot and identify the most interesting and relevant stuff, including the characters the directors want them to track closely.

"We were we were surprised at how much variability there was amongst the younger children," explained Mareschal. "We actually thought it would be a bit tighter, partly because one kind of difficulty when you use film is that directors, when they make a movie, always frame what is of interest."

What they found was that the variability among the children reflected the differences in their cognitive development. And lots of it comes down to context: Within this kind of research is an idea that the most *salient* thing on-screen—maybe the biggest or most colorful thing—attracts eyes first. But the semantics of the scene—what's actually happening in it—are what people grow into understanding.

For people producing visual content for children, there's a big emphasis on making the semantic elements pretty salient.

Ellen Doherty is the chief creative officer for Fred Rogers Productions, a nonprofit mainstay of the kids' television universe. They produce a slate of television shows—*Daniel Tiger's Neighborhood*, *Donkey Hodie*, and *Alma's Way* among them—that incorporate the best understanding of childhood development to reach kids.

As Doherty worked her way up the ladder of kids' television, she worked on shows where she interviewed dozens of kids every day. Along the way she developed an understanding of how kids think, how they express themselves, and how those two things are not always the same.

"I feel like as adults, sometimes we are biased in favor of people who can articulate things," she said. "And that's an unfair bias, because you can understand it and not know how to explain it. . . . And I think that that happens in different ways with young children."

The work being done by Doherty and others to make sure shows for children seize their attention commands an enormous amount of effort. For institutions like *Sesame Street*, Fred Rogers, or the Disney Channel, the hard-earned wisdom about how to help kids get the most out of screen time is their entire raison d'être—and it's changing faster than you might think.

"They've got it figured out, and it literally is a science," said Shannon Flynn, a director who works predominantly in the children's space.

Flynn cut her teeth as an acting coach on *Hannah Montana* for the Disney Channel. Since then, her filmography is a list of some of the most compelling kids' TV for a generation: *The Haunted Hathaways*, *The Thundermans*, *Bella and the Bulldogs*, *Sesame Street*, and *Helpsters*, which endeavors to teach the language and

LITTLE KIDS AND SCREEN TIME: THE GREAT DEBATE

Can we settle the never-ending debate of how much screen time is the right amount for kids?

Not yet. The Centers for Disease Control has general recommendations, but actual scientific evidence that screen time has a big impact on the health and futures of kids is simply not there. It's possible research will turn up that evidence at some point, but the kind of large studies that would advance that theory take years.

There is one study in progress with 11,000 kids under observation—and the early evidence is that, while higher time spent looking at screens is linked to some negative things (worse sleep, more anxiety, worse grades), the actual correlation is less than 2 percent. That means the link exists, but it's weak. It's vastly weaker than something like socioeconomic status, which accounted for about 5 percent of the variance. Indeed, it's not even clear if there is causation—because maybe kids who struggle with sleep fill that time with screen usage? Or perhaps kids who are anxious mollify those feelings with television. In general, it's extremely hard to disentangle all the factors that contribute to health and identify one bad thing, one root cause, such as screen time.

The "right" amount is still an unknown, and may stay that way for a while. The "wrong" amount is what parents should be looking out for. If screen time is undermining sleep, that's a big red flag; good sleep is well established as important for the health and development of kids. If it's getting in the way of schoolwork, then it's an issue. But if it's replacing time that would have been otherwise spent idle? There's not a lot of evidence that it's destructive. The worry shouldn't be about screens in particular, but time use in general. If they're sleeping enough and staying active, screen time shouldn't be too high on the list of parental anxiety.

---

logic of coding to preschoolers. She also had a hand in *The Not-Too-Late Show with Elmo*, which is widely regarded by late-night fans aged four to ten as the best thing to happen to bedtime since good-night songs.

Along the way, Flynn had a front-row seat to the shift from standard definition television to HD to the tablet-based kids' TV of today.

On shows from the Sesame studio, the key to holding attention is routine. Younger kids can't deal with the dynamism of the moving parts of your typical programming for adults, but older kids get bored by the lack of novelty and visually striking things. The solution is that the structure of every Sesame show is functionally identical, with the deviations from the formula being how you convey important information to kids. To keep the programming on the rails, Sesame falls back on strong, rigid plot structures that leave room for adaptation.

Helpsters, the program with the lofty goal of teaching kids about coding, is a colossal ask made even harder by the age range they're attempting to hit, from the youngest preschoolers through first graders. Here we're talking about kids who show up for the colorful puppets, the funny people, and the music, all the way up to first graders, who are old enough to get interested in the subject matter on its own.

"In our show," explains Flynn, "the person enters the doorway, they go sit at the desk, they say what their problem is, the leader of the group takes them to the board, they break down the component parts, and then they solve the component parts."

The show then comes together around how the problem was solved, and it always ends in a song. The songs are always the same style, with just a few things that relate to the problem itself changed.

Plot-wise it's not exactly *Dune*, but that's the point, according to Flynn: "The variations in that particular structure—kids notice those things. If there was any kind of variation on

WHY KIDS CAN WATCH THINGS OVER AND OVER

Parents often wonder what kids come away with when they watch TV. And of course the burning question posed by just about every parent of a TV-watching kid: Why is it that they can rewatch things a million times?

"The younger children were generally the more easily distracted," explained Mareschal. "Partly that reflects the fact that they're not necessarily following a plot [and] you can easily get distracted because you don't realize that there's a thread bringing all these things together."

Beyond the increased ability to focus more, older children retain a lot more about the shows and movies they just watched, whereas younger kids simply don't. And researchers like Mareschal aren't sure if it's because young kids have poorer memories than older kids. "They might have actually understood something," said Mareschal, "but they had already forgotten that the lion did this or something."

And that might explain why kids love rewatching TV episodes and movies endless numbers of time. They enjoy it in the moment, dipping in and out but still following it, but their still-developing memory betrays them in a good way, and they're able to enjoy it over and over with a fresh set of eyes.

That memory question is why lots of shows emphasize format. You can see this not just in kids' media—where the goal is to hold the attention of those who lack it—but in other formats intended for people who are half asleep or a little zonked, like late-night shows or morning shows like *Good Morning America*. They tend to rely on functionally unalterable formats—Elmo tells a joke, Elmo talks to Cookie Monster, a guest comes out, they play a game, and then he sings a song. This kind of rigid choreography allows for the programming to hold the attention of the youngest while offering room for customization that older kids and adults can enjoy.

that, they noticed. Because they know what the structure is, they'll pay more attention to the problem."

Direction is still all about managing attention, regardless of audience age. For adults that tends to mean *splitting* attention to achieve narrative goals. But directing for kids is all about

not splitting their attention, making the action incredibly easy to follow even after an attention lapse, and deviating from the expected only when you really, really want something to resonate. You ease children into a flow, and then you make them notice what's important by deviating ever so mildly from it.

This can mean producing things in ways that those who make things for adults might not even consider and deliberately designing things for little humans who lack context.

Beyond conceptual context, there's a visual grammar that adults grasp but two-to-fours watching *Daniel Tiger's Neighborhood* don't quite get. They don't know, for example, that a calendar flipping pages is meant to depict time passing, because they don't have a fully formed sense of time. They don't understand that a wipe transition means time has passed. They will learn that one day, but they haven't yet. And, according to Doherty, that's why every episode happens in real time, with songs as cut points.

That applies to concepts, too. "There comes a time in every children's show series life when you do the show about death," said Doherty. For *Daniel Tiger*, the writers were going to have Daniel's fish die, and then he would be bereft and inconsolable and have a funeral for the fish.

But Doherty explained that the show's child development advisers were strongly against it—because a four-year-old doesn't know that death is permanent. The theme of the episode was then changed toward asking questions, because that's what a four-year-old would do. They'd ask what the fish is doing, and then if the fish can't play today, whether it will be able to play tomorrow. In the end,

Daniel—and by proxy, the viewer—is able to get a working sense of the ineffable. Not that bad for twenty-two minutes and a song!

As we age, we basically increase our understanding of our own perception. Young kids haven't yet picked up on the intuitive rules of visual composition, or perhaps they *have* but decide to explore other elements of the space besides what's directly in front of them. But what we know for sure is that the kids are paying attention.

When Flynn made a show for a YouTube channel, she was privy to live comments from kids for the first time. Despite a career directing kids' television, what consistently surprised her was just how assiduous the viewers were. With repeated viewings and the ability to pause and rewind, they caught goofs and small continuity errors—an untied shoe in one scene, tied in the next shot—that would be overlooked by an adult following a plot but seem obvious to a kid just meandering about the screen for the thirtieth time.

And this might be why a seven-year-old can rewatch *Frozen* two hundred times and have it be almost like new every time. Whereas adults are more than ready to move on after viewing number sixty-four, a kid is not, because they've given up on understanding the essential nature of the work—in short, they're watching a different movie every time.

CHAPTER 3

HOW CULTURE REFLECTS US

One of the most famous books about stories is *The Hero with a Thousand Faces*, published in 1949 by Joseph Campbell, a professor of literature who codified the concept of the hero's journey and laid out the playbook on which human stories have been built from the very beginning.

The concept is simple: that there's a consistent character arc for heroes, from starting small to the acquisition of a mentor to leaving home and exploring the unknown and then returning from whence they came. Just to give you a glimpse into how much this blueprint has infiltrated pop culture, it has been the structure for Pixar movies, *The Lord of the Rings*, *The Matrix*, *Star Wars* (obviously!), and most superhero tales. If a movie has a budget of $50 million or higher, there's a good chance this is the play they have decided to run.

Understanding the basic shape of stories doesn't mean they're hacked or a rip-off—if we applied that logic to music, half the melodies in the Top 40 would be forbidden to use or adapt moments after they debuted. Some forms and expressions of art exist to be adapted and molded to reflect the times and tastes of their creators. Consider how Whitney Houston sang the national anthem at the Super Bowl versus

how Jimmy Hendrix played it at Woodstock or the Marine Corps band's rendition of it on Memorial Day. At some point the song is just the substrate; it's what a creator does with it that's interesting and revealing.

An agreed-upon format that is built on and adapted to the flavor of the tale is the crux of genre. If you want to learn about people and society, look at what's assumed in their art. We've been telling stories about vampires for hundreds of years, and though the beast stays the same, his motivations change with time. The United States has had workplace sitcoms for decades, but *30 Rock* didn't rip off *The Mary Tyler Moore Show*; it just played the same song in a new style. The script for Shakespeare's *Julius Caesar* hasn't changed by a word in more than four hundred years, but oddly enough the boss in the play sure tends to look like whoever's in the White House every time it graces New York's famed Central Park stage.

Genre, at its heart, is just a package of assumptions, tools in a tool kit.

But by taking a closer look at how and why different genres and story elements affect us, we can learn a lot about our society and ourselves, particularly our desires and fears.

There are many flavors of the hero's journey—where a protagonist is plucked from their ordinary life; faces danger, adversaries, and a serious ordeal; then returns home transformed—and we love them all.

We Can Be Heroes

Superheroes are older than dirt. Samson, Herakles—all the heroes of old possessed fantastic, above-average talents. One of the first stories people turned to after the creation myth was the heroic figure, the culture hero. Sometimes the hero was strong or crafty or a leader, sometimes he was endowed by gods, and sometimes, decisively, notoriously, he was not. Nevertheless, after heroes show up, people simply cannot shut up about them.

That lots of the most enduring and popular legends are just stories of heroic figures is a testament to their popularity. These stories—though they may lack the centrality and importance of other great myths that were more critical to the societies who told them—feature compelling figures who, most important to us, serve as personifications of the traits that a given society prizes.

In short, people tell on themselves when they describe their heroes.

The most straightforward demonstration of that ancient kind of heroism is the superhero trend. And although it can get tiresome for adult fans of the genre, it's important to not lose sight of the reality that admiration for an objectively heroic, empowered, positive figure has a measurably positive effect on kids.

Hero play, where kids pretend to be blessed with powers they do not possess, is critical for them because it's an opportunity to get prestige that they otherwise lack.

Why? First, the powers are great, superlative compared with those of any normal person. Kids spend most of their time surrounded by people who are bigger than them and able to make decisions they cannot. Second, superheroes inevitably *win*, which your standard-issue kid can't always count on doing. Batman doesn't have to settle for a compromise with his mom over dinnertime. For kids, life is a constant tug-of-war between their goals (getting the things they want or emulating things and people) and the obligations of an unjust society. But kids who pretend to be superheroes get control, coupled with an intuitive

sense of what's right. Most of all for kids, superheroes get accolades and recognition from other adults—and that prestige is something kids don't often get consistently.

Those with the strongest affinity for fictional heroes can also be those who most lack agency and prestige—nerds, children, nerdy children—so heroic stories are a way to borrow some of that cultural esteem. Bundling that heroic stature with religion (Samson), patriotism (Captain America), a moral code (Superman), or political goals (X-Men) is a great way to link those ideals to the prestige.

How to Build a Superhero

Superhero characters, at their core, are aspirational ideals.

So, where'd they come from? Tom Brevoort started reading comics when he was six, when his dad would pick up cartons of cigarettes and Tom would get entranced by the spinner rack near the checkout. He went to the University of Delaware to study illustration and eventually landed a gig at Marvel Comics in the summer of 1989, right as comics were getting red-hot. The market would implode shortly afterward, but Brevoort stuck around and climbed to the position of executive editor of Marvel Comics. During that time, he would bear witness to the creation of all sorts of heroes.

"The Marvel Universe is the world outside your window," claimed Brevoort. "In effect, the audience and the characters inhabit a world that is the same, and so the problems that they have to deal with are problems that are similar to the problems and the issues and the concerns that the audience may be dealing with."

It's rare that Marvel just creates a character out of thin air and launches a book about them. Even in the old days, that was rare: There's a reason why lots of the huge characters of today got their start in anthology series like Tales to Astonish or Amazing Fantasy. Even in the heady creative days of the early 1960s it was a lot to ask of an audience to spend their

THE SUPERPOWERS OF MARVEL COMICS

With various powers come various responsibilities

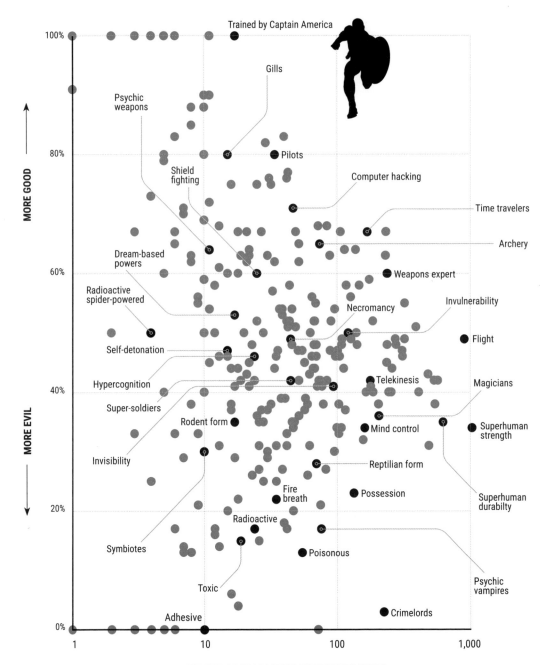

MORE GOOD

MORE EVIL

100%

80%

60%

40%

20%

0%

Trained by Captain America

Gills

Psychic weapons

Pilots

Shield fighting

Computer hacking

Time travelers

Archery

Dream-based powers

Weapons expert

Radioactive spider-powered

Necromancy

Invulnerability

Self-detonation

Flight

Hypercognition

Telekinesis

Magicians

Super-soldiers

Mind control

Superhuman strength

Rodent form

Invisibility

Reptilian form

Superhuman durabilty

Fire breath

Possession

Radioactive

Symbiotes

Psychic vampires

Poisonous

Toxic

Adhesive

Crimelords

1   10   100   1,000

NUMBER OF CHARACTERS THAT HAVE POWERS

BATMAN IS WORKING HARD!

Affinity for a heroic figure can have a profound effect on kids.

A 2017 study took 180 children and asked them to complete a boring, repetitive task for ten minutes. The kids were given the option to take breaks by playing a great iPad video game that had been conveniently placed nearby in the test area.

Some of the kids were told to ask themselves over the course of the task, "Am I working hard?" and an automated message of that question played occasionally.

A second group of kids was encouraged to ask themselves, "Is [their name] working hard?"

A third group of kids had the experimental test condition where they were given the option of dressing up as Batman, Rapunzel, Dora the Explorer, or Bob the Builder. They were prompted to ask themselves "Is Batman working hard?" (And yes, Batman *was* working hard.)

Across the experiment as a whole, the kids spent 37 percent of their time on the boring task and 63 percent of the time playing the video game.

But the kids who got to dress up as a hero? They spent 60 percent of their time focusing on the task at hand, living their best life as a defender of Gotham who would stop at nothing to complete the test. They worked harder, stayed more focused, were more immersed in the task, and were more dedicated when they were

A very, very hard worker.

pretending to be superheroes. Several children who were playing the game heard the prompt from the task and spontaneously responded, "Batman is working hard!" and dropped the iPad to return to work.

---

hard-earned paper route money on a new book sight unseen.

Introducing a new hero in the Marvel world is more complicated than you might imagine. Heroes need to be empathetic, but also empathetic in new and interesting ways. They are meant to represent an aspirational part of ourselves, the operative word being *part*. They succeed when they exemplify a virtue or a point in life, and when, even if you can't empathize with their totality, you can be drawn in by something that makes them

compelling. Perhaps you empathize with Daredevil because he's Catholic, or blind, or a martial artist, or lives in Hell's Kitchen. Or because he's an attorney, or he came from a single-parent home, or he dislikes corruption, or any number of those things—but you don't need to be a blind Catholic martial artist from a single-parent home in Hell's Kitchen who practices law and despises corruption. Because of all that, he's able to tell stories that other characters—for example, ahem, Episcopalian technologists from Forest Hills—can't.

Good vs. Evil

Where a superhero gets their powers can also have a strong bearing on what kind of hero they are.

Plenty of powers are just in the middle, without skewing one way or another. The power of flight, skill in martial arts, fencing, superhuman reflexes or agility, telekinesis, force field, and invulnerability—those powers are often just elements of the basic kit of anyone able to hang tough in the rough-and-tumble Marvel Universe, regardless of which team they're on.

Some powers seem to be possessed only by the good at heart. People with superhuman senses such as precognition (especially heightened awareness and night vision), empaths, multilinguists, time travelers, athletes, healers, archers, equestrians, and gymnasts all tend toward heroism rather than villainy. Hackers,

ANTI-HEROES OF MARVEL

How many comics a character was the antagonist and how many comics they were an ally

Character

Count of Villainous Acts	Character	Count of Heroic Acts
234	MAGNETO	261
218	SABRETOOTH	172
146	MYSTIQUE	150
144	VLAD DRACULA	138
138	JUGGERNAUT	96
116	VENOM	131
103	S.H.I.E.L.D.	85
74	DAKEN	83
63	ARES	68
60	BLOODY MARY	45
55	MAXIMUS THE MAD	68
50	RADIOACTIVE MAN	58

COUNT OF VILLAINOUS ACTS

COUNT OF HEROIC ACTS

clairvoyants, and pilots are also particularly inclined toward goodness. Interestingly, most of those powers tend to be very team-based or support types—the healing and the senses and the fast travel—or tend to be self-taught or involve discipline, such as the archers, horse riders, and gymnasts. Put together, the powers that break most heroic are the ones that are innately helpful to others or took a great deal of work to attain. It's odd to see hackers as good just as often as healers, but those are both roles that are most effective when they're part of a team. What this means is that the powers that contribute to the success of others—that is, people who help not only people in need but the super-people who help people in need— tend to be a special class of good. The powers that are more neutral and merely escalate one's own potential are a bit more of a dice roll.

Other powers are reliably linked with evil characters. Superhuman strength, durability, shape-shifting, armored suits, teleportation, pyrokinesis, using magic—all of those are popular powers that on balance tend to break bad. Immortals are bad about two-thirds of the time, and the ability to psychically possess other people tends to lead one down a dark path fairly often, as do claws, hypnosis, biological manipulation, and a reptilian form. Being poisonous or toxic is a reliable indication that

someone's not on the side of truth, justice, and the American way, nor is being sticky, or a demon, or radioactive, or a psychic vampire.

The more villainous power sets are interesting because they tend to involve either someone getting superior power from gifts rather than labor, or very offensive-oriented attacks like fire and claws, or deriving that strength and power from an external source like a power suit or magic. Also, several powers—hypnosis, possession—are inextricably linked to coercing people to do things they don't want to do. So, if the powers that skew toward team-based collaboration are the ones that most often skew positive, it's the antisocial powers—the ones based on intimidation or compulsion—that more often break bad. In Marvel's world, your ability isn't your destiny—there aren't too many powers that are exclusively good or exclusively bad—but when you get a gift you can't share, you're liable to succumb to the corruption that comes with power.

Heroism isn't only about *where* you got your powers, it's also about *how* you got them.

At Marvel, the origins of heroes were very much of the eras when those heroes were created. Jack Kirby, who was instrumental in developing early Marvel characters, was plugged into the science scene of the times. That's one reason so many of the heroes of that age got their

"*That's my secret. I'm always nuanced.*"

NATURE VS NURTURE

How you get your powers affects if you become a hero or a villain

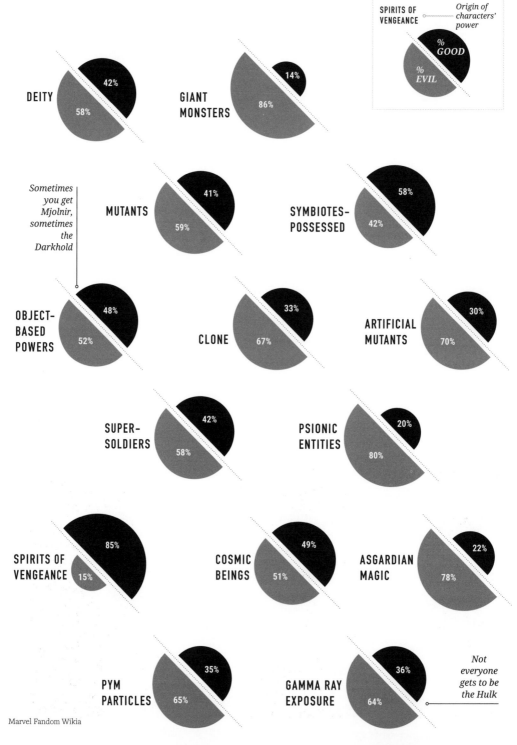

KEY:

SPIRITS OF VENGEANCE — *Origin of characters' power*

% **GOOD**

% *EVIL*

DEITY 42% 58%

GIANT MONSTERS 14% 86%

Sometimes you get Mjolnir, sometimes the Darkhold

MUTANTS 41% 59%

SYMBIOTES-POSSESSED 58% 42%

OBJECT-BASED POWERS 48% 52%

CLONE 33% 67%

ARTIFICIAL MUTANTS 30% 70%

SUPER-SOLDIERS 42% 58%

PSIONIC ENTITIES 20% 80%

SPIRITS OF VENGEANCE 85% 15%

COSMIC BEINGS 49% 51%

ASGARDIAN MAGIC 22% 78%

PYM PARTICLES 35% 65%

GAMMA RAY EXPOSURE 36% 64%

Not everyone gets to be the Hulk

BATMAN: ACTUALLY PRETTY GOOD AT STOPPING CRIME

How often do you have to fight Batman until you turn from a life of crime?

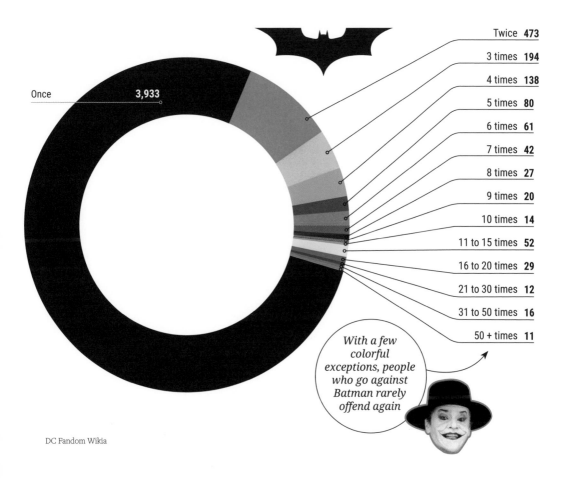

Once 3,933

Twice **473**

3 times **194**

4 times **138**

5 times **80**

6 times **61**

7 times **42**

8 times **27**

9 times **20**

10 times **14**

11 to 15 times **52**

16 to 20 times **29**

21 to 30 times **12**

31 to 50 times **16**

50 + times **11**

With a few colorful exceptions, people who go against Batman rarely offend again

DC Fandom Wikia

powers from the then-new science of the atom, which was pushing the United States to the forefront of global geopolitics. During the creative renaissance at Marvel through the 1960s, heroes came from space exploration (The Fantastic Four), from military nuclear weapons testing (The Hulk), and from the bleeding edge of the civilian science of radiation (Spider-Man and Daredevil).

The same radioactivity that in Japan created Godzilla created super-men in the United States. The early 1960s involved lots of space-flight tests. The H-bomb testing at Bikini Atoll brought verisimilitude to Bruce Banner's job. Iron Man's wealth and armor originally came

from the Vietnam War. The X-Men, with their mutant powers, emerged just ten years after the discovery of DNA's double helix structure by Watson, Franklin, Crick, and Wilkins and during a wildly productive time for genetic research.

But heroes aren't made in a lab. It's not a coincidence that very often the same thing that grants a hero their powers also empowers their enemies, be it mutation or scientific mishaps or radiation. It's from this point that we begin to understand one of the other most important things about developing a hero: the villains who oppose them.

"GOT YOU" PICTURES OF SPIDER-MAN

Spider-Man's best villains are all reflections of Spider-Man

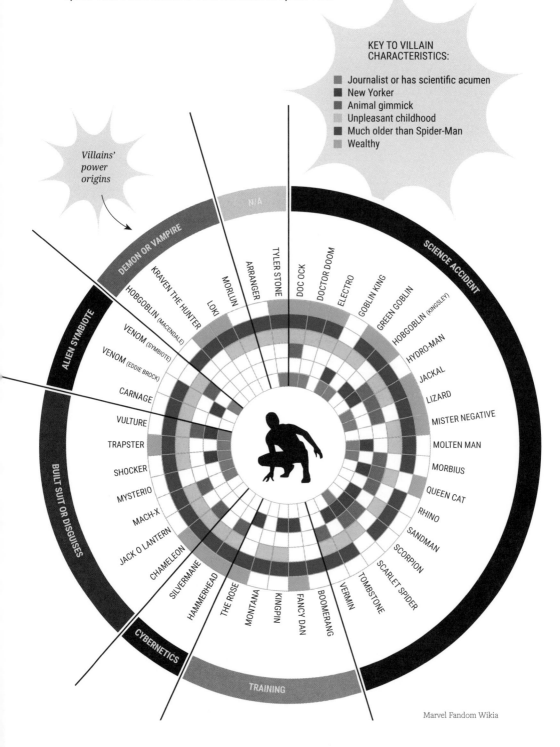

KEY TO VILLAIN CHARACTERISTICS:
- Journalist or has scientific acumen
- New Yorker
- Animal gimmick
- Unpleasant childhood
- Much older than Spider-Man
- Wealthy

Villains' power origins

Marvel Fandom Wikia

Villain in the Mirror

Many early superhero origins—Spider-Man, Ant-Man, The Incredible Hulk—are horror stories that later became optimistic. Horror, it turns out, is a great vehicle through which to understand the counterweight to the hero: the villain.

"On the basic level, Spider-Man has to fight somebody every month, and you're going to need to be inventing new people for him to fight with and to contend with," explained Brevoort. "And they all can't be the same, and they all can't be doing the same thing."

Spider-Man is a particularly useful case here because his rogues' gallery is chock-full of foils. Most Spider-Man villains have a great deal in common with Peter Parker or are in some way an inversion of him. A good chunk of them are the result of a science experiment gone wrong, just like Peter was—people like Lizard and Doc Ock and Electro. Lots of them riff on an animal for their branding, like Rhino, Chameleon, Scorpion, or Jackal. A bunch of them, just like Peter, built tech to aid in their work, like Vulture, Mysterio, and Shocker. Peter is poor, Norman Osborn is rich; Peter's from humble beginnings, Kraven the Hunter is an aristocrat; Peter's a hardworking journalist, Eddie Brock's a cruddy one. Spider-Man's enemies are old men, whereas Peter's just a kid.

The point is that by staking out these character traits—the specific manner in which some characters are the same as Spider-Man and the ways in which they're drastically different—we're actually learning more about who Peter actually is.

By being what Parker isn't, the villains can tease out more about who he is. By being what Parker is, they can reveal the elements of his character and the principles that actually differentiate them. He's a high school kid putting on a costume and taking on the responsibility of an adult while still a teenager, and his enemies reveal that.

The origin stories of superpowered heroes extends well before the comic book age, and if anything, the origin stories of villains date back even further. Superheroic fiction grew out of science fiction and horror stories of the late nineteenth century. Although science fiction would branch off from horror into something far more aspirational, it nonetheless originated in horror. And it wasn't the first time that horror birthed a genre (and it probably wasn't the last). But just as superheroes are a highly modern twist on an ancient story, horror is *the* ancient story.

Humans have been making up tales about things that go bump in the night as long as there have been stories, bumps, and nights. Ghosts and demons have been indelible fixtures of human stories going back ages, as have witches, and wolves, and that which is big and strong and mean and seeks to feast on the unprepared.

The only way to prepare, naturally, is to tell more stories.

Horror as a genre is also one of the most exciting because the concept is so adaptable. Everyone has a brain stem, and so everyone can feel fear and be scared. And yes, everyone dies. Comedy needs too much context and drama can be hard to pull off, but spooky plays anywhere.

As a result, horror is easily one of the most fashionable genres there is. Show me a story about a person who came back from the dead from any year in recorded history, and it's obvious what that society feared.

A Monster for All Seasons

A great example of how horror and villainy adapt with the times is to consider the vampire.

Vampires of earliest folklore tend to have two main unifying traits: They're revenants, which means they return from the dead, and they suck blood. In the earliest tales based in folklore, they would first visit their relatives and then other people. This originally explained why, after someone mysteriously died young, other people in their household and community might also begin mysteriously dying. Today we know the explanation is usually an infectious disease, but at the time

Vampire stories reflect the societal anxieties of their era.

rural peasants decided that vampirism—the deceased returned to drain the life of the living—was a reliable explanation. More importantly, it wasn't just an explanation, it was a solution: You can't kill what you don't understand, but you can disinter the offending ghoul and destroy the body. Vampires were a chance for people to take control of a situation they were otherwise unable to.

A letter sent in 1725 from an Austrian army official related a story about Serbian hajduks—peasant soldiers—who had exhumed a corpse, staked it in the heart, and burned it, out of belief that the dead man had killed some of their number. They called this creature the "vampyri."

At the time, the Counter-Reformation in central Europe meant that belief in magic was being suppressed. Vampyri didn't really fit anywhere in the existing cosmology of supernatural beings: Not angels, not devils, they riffed on the incorruptible bodies of saints, inverted the concept of the soul, and were really just phenomenally interesting constructs as a result. And so they spread like an urban legend.

Germany from the seventeenth to the eighteenth century had "the great vampire debate," where urbane Germans would investigate rural stories of vampirism. In the 1770s they became fruitful metaphors—an ancient thing sucking the blood out of peasants was shorthand for the aristocracy in certain lefty circles.

Politicians and tax collectors were unsurprisingly compared to vampires.

Modern vampire stories can be traced back to 1819, with "The Vampyre" by John Polidori. The story was begun the very same weekend as Mary Shelley's *Frankenstein*. Polidori was Lord Byron's personal physician, so perhaps it's no surprise that his story was where the creatures became distinctly bourgeois. Polidori's vampire, Lord Ruthven, is generally considered to be a mild pastiche of his employer: He is an aristocratic impostor, a lord because he's faking it and exploiting the system by taking unearned power. Critics panned it, but the public ate it up. Vampires were now firmly in the middle to upper class, agents of change in the social order.

In 1897, Bram Stoker wrote *Dracula*, and in doing so kick-started the modern age of vampirism. Stoker melded the fifteenth-century history of Vlad Tepes, largely made up of German propaganda about his bloodthirst and atrocities, and folded in some new lore about vampires. One of a dozen novels about vampires published in the 1890s, it hit big because Hollywood latched on to it and produced the incredibly popular Dracula films.

By the 1940s, Dracula had morphed into the subject of parody, chasing Abbott and Costello. It wouldn't be until 1958, when Christopher Lee donned the fangs in *Horror of Dracula*, that the creature would get a new life, specifically a sexy new life. Stoker's original story balances sensationalism with moralism, but Lee's interpretation was downright horned up for its era, and from there the "bloodgates" opened. The 1970s saw vampires become firmly erotic, and by the 1980s their transformation was compared to the changes that come with adolescence.

Vampires as villains have so much history that they work in all kinds of contexts. Do they represent the dangers of sexuality and promiscuity? Are they avatars of intergenerational power and wealth? The victims of a disease? *The* disease itself? Over the course of their history, vampires may lack a consistently specific identity, but that's because they have a larger general one: They're whatever threatens to take something essential from you.

The first question asked of a new medium after "So, it works?" is typically "All right, cool, so how do we use it to scare people?"

SYMPATHY FOR THE DEVIL?

We already know that our brains take the things we observe on screens seriously, particularly things like antagonists and threats. And that our brain's central visual bias is to focus most on things it finds interesting.

A study had subjects strapped into an fMRI machine to learn what was happening inside their brains when they saw people suffer pain on-screen. But not the pain of just anyone—only the bad guys. Subjects were shown a few films with sequences that included something that touched a person's palm: In some cases, it was a painful injection, and in others an innocuous object like a Q-tip. In some, the taped narration said things like, "Sarah is a musician in New York," and in others it was something like, "Matt's always believed in white supremacy." What the researchers found, first above all, was that the whole brain was way more engaged when the person subjected to the pain was objectively bad versus objectively good. Second, when the bad guy got the painful injection, the rewards center of viewers' brains—the striatum—were particularly engaged.

"We study psychopaths, we study narcissists, but we never study a psychopath with a backstory," said Glenn Fox, one of the authors of the study.

That villains are so attention grabbing is the very foundation of their appeal. But although we might root for the heroes, we *care* what happens to the bad guys. This at first appears to be a contradiction. But the brain's innate priority being survival, subconsciously we're drawn to assessing the fate of those who would seek to do us harm. As a result, just like a superhero gains character depth by whom she opposes, we the viewers derive moral meaning and appreciate the stakes of the conflict only through the villains. We'll root for a warrior, but we'll care about the fight only if the villain is sufficiently odious. If there's a villain you've never really been able to shake, that says a great deal about your own values and moral code.

Monster of the Week

An iconic, flashy, bombastic monster can achieve the kind of immortality typically reserved for the flashiest culture heroes. Medusa, after all, is more well-known than her killer, Perseus. The heroes might get the action figures, but the villains usually get the best songs.

Horror is among the first works to jump into any medium. England experienced its first major mass-market novel in 1719 with *Robinson Crusoe*. Decades later, a bunch of emo teenagers and young adults went on vacation in Switzerland, and the very smart one ended up writing *Frankenstein* while the middle-class friend penned "The Vampyre."

The earliest form of moving pictures were "trick films," which attempted to scare viewers. Horror movies also live on the bleeding edge of special effects, so tend to innovate with their low budgets to maximize impact with every inch of the frame. When television was just getting its sea legs and the comic book companies were grasping at straws before the modern superhero, they both set up horror anthologies to explore the medium. Scary storytelling—be it fictional (*Welcome to Night Vale*) or real (true crime, all of it)—were some of the earliest hits of the podcast boom.

Horror is a proof of concept for mediums, because if you can't make scares work, the medium is probably not all that good at communing with an audience. And just like an era's heroes will tell you what they hope for, the

same era's monsters will what show you what they fear.

When the Scooby-Doo gang breaks up a smuggling ring, or an insurance fraud, or an attempt to pilfer an inheritance, we learn not just about that individual bad guy at the center of it but the broken society in which they live.

Horror is so versatile and of-the-times because it's playing with a pretty loaded deck: Everyone from age one to 100 has a brain stem, and everyone can be scared. *Anything* can be scared. Fear is universal, transcending species

HAUNTED HOUSES

Whimsy plus time equals spooky.

Close your eyes and imagine a haunted house.

It's probably Victorian in design, ambitious, agglomerated architecture, fading paint, lots of spires and peaks, right? Have you ever wondered *why* that specific home design is indelibly linked to haunts?

Go back to a portrait of success in 1870: newly married, well off, a desire to purchase a house that's incredibly fashionable at the time or maybe even built new on some land outside the city. The colonial style is boring, so maybe it's Gothic Revival or a Queen Anne style? In any case, the fashion of the time is whimsical, exaggerated, *wonderful*.

Once the house is built or bought, very nearly all of that goes dreadfully out of style and never recovers, ever again.

Now imagine yourself as the homeowner. You've still got your whimsical house. It's still *fun*. You have kids who grow up wealthy, raised in the traditional

Victorian style—that is, you were strict and distant and ignored them. When your affluent, moody child grows up and becomes a novelist, the golden age he grew up in will later be rebranded as the Gilded Age. Eventually the stock market crashes a couple of times, you lose the house, and the key problem is this: When a boring colonial-style home deteriorates with age, it looks distinguished. When a fantabulous, whimsical home deteriorates with age, it starts to look spooky.

Not helping the matter is your ungrateful son, who sets his dumb Goth novels—the ones that became very popular, especially after the publication of *Dracula* in 1897—in unpleasant homes that happen to look exactly like the unpleasant home in which he was raised. The net effect is that these home styles are pretty much detested throughout the 1920s and eventually become a mockery. And the timing couldn't be worse, because it's exactly when the global movie machine is beginning its ascent. Soon enough, your house becomes visual shorthand for "dilapidated and spooky," despite the fact that no one has even built that style since 1880.

And this is how odd, whimsical, Victorianesque houses became standard in the horror genre. All because the people who founded the American science fiction and horror scene in the early 1900s had awful childhoods in oddly specific, briefly fashionable houses.

or upbringing. That's why horror plays so well, any time, any place. It's also one reason that, of the stories explicitly designed for children, so many have some kind of horror component. Horror defies the normal ways people like to split up into groups and can be interlaced with moral messages. Though less nuanced in this regard, fairy tales tend to pull pretty liberally from the horror tool kit: obvious good and evil, dire consequences for making the wrong choices, a palpable and simple lesson. Most kids' entertainment has horror DNA all over it, typically playing for the usual hits: simple morals, obvious monsters, clear heroes, compelling character design. Fairy tales, the grand-daddies of stories, are fairly monstrous.

And although some stories succeed or fail on the strength of their heroes or on the odiousness of their monsters, great stories blend the two. Most kids' movies don't strive to be overly clever; rather, their mastery replicated by few other genres is how unambiguous they are about the *stakes*. One study of children's films found that they tend to involve considerably more major character death than their adult counterparts. Disney, to some notoriety, has quite an impressive parental body count.

Villainy is the core innovation of children's literature, especially because kids crave a balance between stability, delivered by heroes, and variety, which comes from villains. More so than adult dramas, kids' shows excel at interrogating motivations and raising stakes as a way to advance stories. Adult dramas may have a single great villain over the course of their run, but it's rare that kids' shows contend with the same bad guy every week. If they do—if it's a Team Rocket or Gargamel situation—they never try the same thing twice; they're always innovating. This allows a given show to explore more about what's right and what's wrong without necessarily changing heroes week to week.

And variety is just plain good for business. Heroes tend to have one motivation: make the status quo better. But villains want all kinds of different stuff—money, power, fame, working out their anger. Villainous goals are nuanced in a way heroic goals have to be vague. Samurai Jack has one goal, to defeat Aku, but every week he's up against a unique spin on Aku's corruption with a specific mission Jack must foil. Superman fights for truth and justice, but his adversaries find a new scheme to mess with Metropolis weekly. The *Enterprise* crew just wants to find new worlds, but the universe throws a new problem in Kirk's lap each time.

Stories of adventure—with clear goals and a mode to obtain them—hearken back to the original Hero's Journey. Again, there's a reason that we keep coming back to those ideas, and it's because they're durable and worthwhile.

But standard hero-versus-villain tales only go so far. Once a viewer develops an understanding of the world, the cookie-cutter good guys and bad guys fail to cut it. Because the world we live in isn't filled with strictly good and bad guys. To get a true reflection of the world, you need kinetic stories about people who ride the line between doing the right thing, the lawful way, and the bad thing.

For that, you need *action*.

WHY ARE WE DRESSING UP AS GHOSTS AND SCARING TOURISTS?

Episode count of a given antagonist motivation in three seasons of *Scooby-Doo*

Distract from ongoing caper	14
Gain inheritance	5
Sabotage rival	5
Scare treasure hunters	7
Steal something	10

Seasons 1–3, *Scooby-Doo, Where Are You!*

48

KEY:

FILM TITLE
Main Character
Mother Father

Films listed in order of release

☠ Dead pre-film
✗ Killed beginning of film
⩘ Killed mid-film

? Never mentioned, unclear, or does not exist
♥ Alive
XX Abandoned or implied killed

SNOW WHITE AND THE SEVEN DWARFS
Snow White
☠ ☠

PINOCCHIO
Pinocchio
? ♥

DUMBO
Dumbo
♥ ?

BAMBI
Bambi
⩘ ♥

CINDERELLA
Cinderella
☠ ✗

ALICE IN WONDERLAND
Alice
? ?

PETER PAN
Wendy Darling
♥ ♥

LADY AND THE TRAMP
Lady
♥ ♥

SLEEPING BEAUTY
Aurora
♥ ♥

ONE HUNDRED AND ONE DALMATIANS
15 puppies
♥ ♥

THE SWORD IN THE STONE
Arthur
☠ ☠

THE JUNGLE BOOK
Mowgli
☠ ☠

THE ARISTOCATS
Three kittens
♥ ?

ROBIN HOOD
Robin Hood
? ?

THE RESCUERS
Penny
☠ ☠

THE FOX AND THE HOUND
Tod
☠ ☠

THE BLACK CAULDRON
Taran
☠ ☠

THE GREAT MOUSE DETECTIVE
Olivia Flaversham
☠ ♥

OLIVER & COMPANY
Oliver
XX XX

THE LITTLE MERMAID
Ariel
☠ ♥

THE RESCUERS DOWN UNDER
Cody
? ?

BEAUTY AND THE BEAST
Belle
☠ ♥

ALADDIN
Aladdin
☠ ♥

THE LION KING
Simba
♥ ⩘

POCAHONTAS
Pocahontas
☠ ♥

TOY STORY
Andy
♥ ?

THE HUNCHBACK OF NOTRE DAME
Quasimodo
✗ ?

HERCULES
Hercules
♥ ♥

MULAN
Mulan
♥ ♥

A BUG'S LIFE
Flik
♥ ?

TARZAN
Tarzan
XX XX

TOY STORY 2
Andy
♥ ?

DINOSAUR
Aladar
XX XX

THE EMPEROR'S NEW GROOVE
Kuzco
☠ ☠

ATLANTIS: THE LOST EMPIRE
Milo Thatch
? ?

DISNEY'S BODY COUNT

What happens to the parents in a Disney movie?

Movie	Character	Status
MONSTERS, INC.	Sulley	? ?
LILO & STITCH	Lilo	💀 💀
TREASURE PLANET	Jim Hawkins	♥ ✖✖
FINDING NEMO	Nemo	✖ ♥
BROTHER BEAR	Kenai	? ?
HOME ON THE RANGE	Cows	? ?
THE INCREDIBLES	Violet and Dash	♥ ♥
CHICKEN LITTLE	Ace Cluck	💀 ♥
CARS	Lightning McQueen	? ?
MEET THE ROBINSONS	Lewis	💀 💀
RATATOUILLE	Remy	? ♥
WALL-E	Wall-E	? ?
BOLT	Penny	♥ ?
UP	Russell	♥ ♥
THE PRINCESS AND THE FROG	Tiana	♥ ?
TOY STORY 3	Bonnie	♥ ♥
TANGLED	Rapunzel	♥ ♥
CARS 2	Lightning McQueen	? ?
BRAVE	Merida	♥ ♥
WRECK-IT RALPH	Ralph	? ?
MONSTERS UNIVERSITY	Mike or Sulley	? ?
FROZEN	Anna/Elsa	✖✖ ✖✖
BIG HERO 6	Hiro	💀 💀
INSIDE OUT	Riley	♥ ♥
THE GOOD DINOSAUR	Arlo	♥ ✖
ZOOTOPIA	Judy Hopps	♥ ♥
FINDING DORY	Dory	♥ ♥
MOANA	Moana	♥ ♥
CARS 3	Lightning McQueen	? ?
COCO	Miguel	♥ ♥
INCREDIBLES 2	Violet and Dash	♥ ♥
RALPH BREAKS THE INTERNET	Ralph	? ?
TOY STORY 4	Bonnie	♥ ♥
ONWARD	Ian & Barley Lightfoot	♥ 〜
SOUL	Joe Gardner	♥ 💀
RAYA AND THE LAST DRAGON	Raya	💀 ♥
LUCA	Luca	♥ ♥

Call to Action

As a genre, action works *only* if you have expectations about how a society operates. That way, you can be surprised and delighted when you see how a film manages to subvert and undermine those expectations. Tom Cruise as Ethan Hunt gripping the side of a plane is thrilling only if the viewer understands that *it is absolutely nuts*. Otherwise, the appeal is just watching a strange man with a nice smile ride a plane.

Magicians who perform for kids get this problem better than anyone: If you pull a rabbit from a hat in front of a young crowd, nobody's mind is blown, because they don't know enough about rabbits or hats to understand how genuinely impressive or unexpected the feat is. But if you pull a quarter from behind a kid's ear—an ear they have possessed their entire life and know for sure that quarters do not come from—well, their mind is blown.

Action is thrilling when one understands how things are meant to be, and the delight comes from the subversion of that: car chases, explosions, pitched battles. Great action sequences use cities in unexpected and interesting ways, whether it's a car chase on racetracks or an aerial dogfight between skyscrapers. But the action doesn't always have to be epic in scale: Remember the shock in *The Hunger Games: Catching Fire* when the dress bursts into flames? Because, you know, dresses don't spontaneously burst into flames.

Although lots of action movies involve fights, the fighting isn't the point—the physics

AVATAR BATTLE MAP

On Pandora

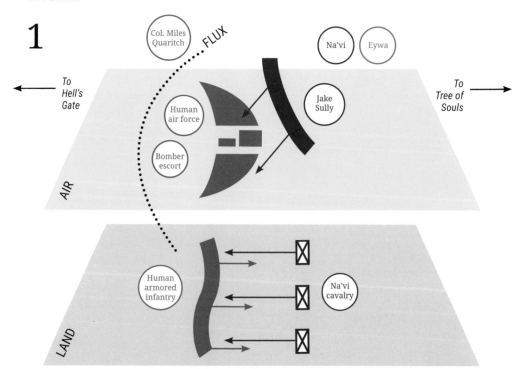

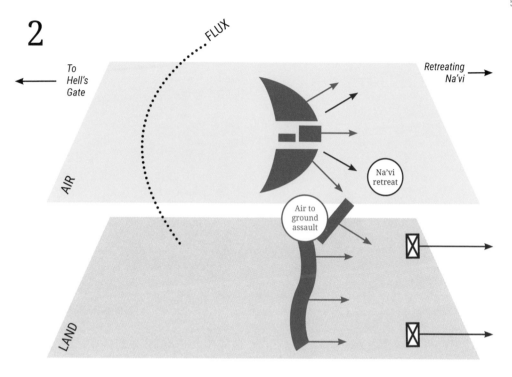

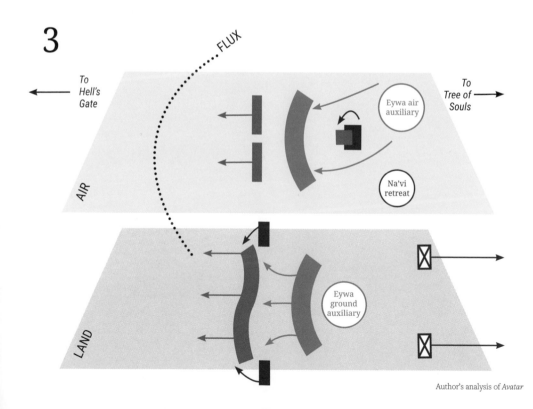

Author's analysis of *Avatar*

THE HOBBIT: BATTLE OF FIVE ARMIES MAP

At Erebor

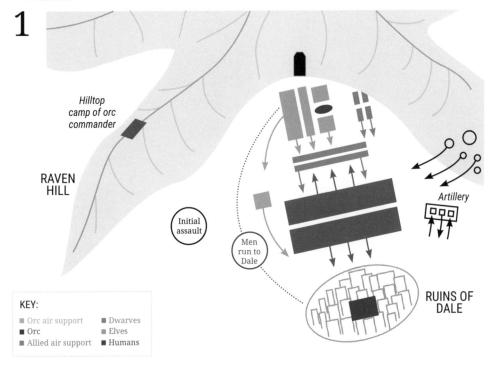

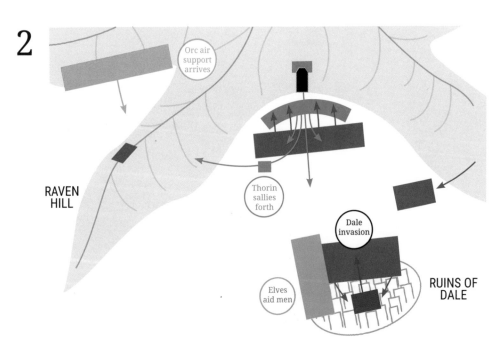

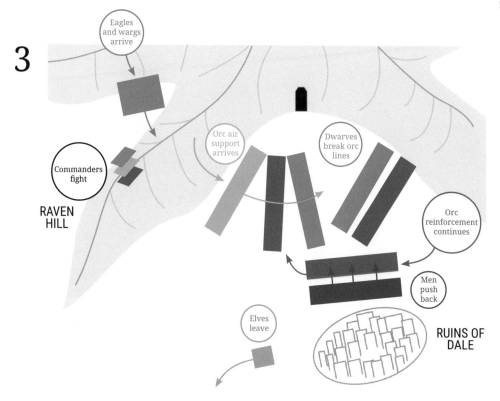

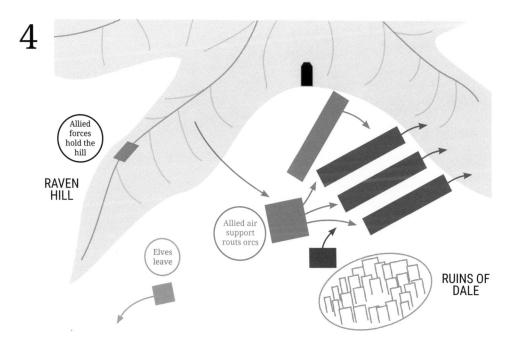

Author's analysis of *The Hobbit: The Battle of the Five Armies*

THE AVENGERS BATTLE MAP
The Battle of New York

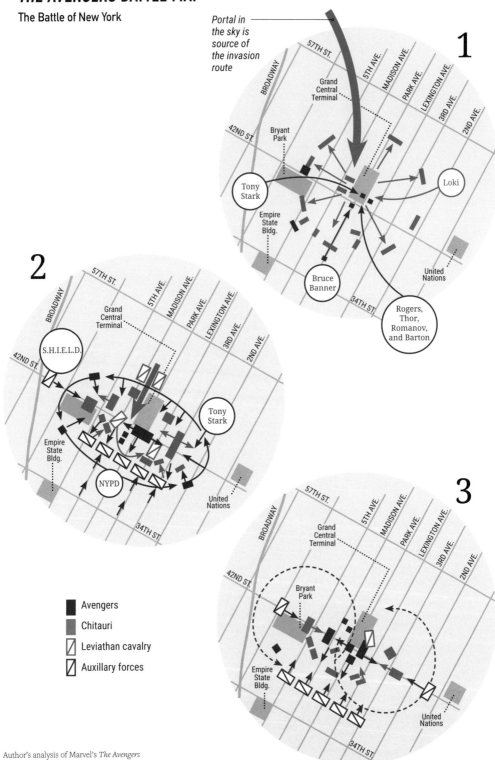

Author's analysis of Marvel's *The Avengers*

are. The part of you that might enjoy a boxing match is very different from the part of you that enjoys a movie sword fight. The former is appealing to that ancient brain stem, the fight-or-flight, but an action set piece is truly appealing to the developed part of your mind that understands how the world works, and it thrills you by confronting you with visual evidence to the contrary. In action movies, violence is choreography, not pain.

When someone's arm gets broken in a horror film, it's realistic and terrifying. This is because horror movies are mostly working with the base, lizard parts of the brain, the brain stem. When an arm is broken in an action film in a thrilling bit of fight choreography, a scene anchored in the visual cortex, we don't process it as pain but as a striking and innovative use of the space. It can be downright funny, if the destruction of the arm is played in such a way that subverts the expectations of what traditionally occurs with arms—that is, that they don't break. It's why Indiana Jones shooting a swordsman is funny, because the viewer knows enough of swashbuckling to expect a sword fight, only to be delighted by the inversion of that expectation.

That's one reason lots of the biggest action sequences deal violence and death on a massive scale but feel light and fun: They're handled less like brawls and more like dances.

Rules of Engagement

In film, there's a tough line to tread when it comes to battle, which by narrative necessity must often eject good sense and real-world strategy. A movie where a superior force of good guys attacks and routs a smaller army? Boring. Audiences need an underdog.

Sometimes the protagonists get placed in a desperate defensive position. In *The Hobbit: The Battle of Five Armies*, a loose coalition of allied forces emerges impromptu as a vast army of goblins and orcs assaults a disputed territory under the Lonely Mountain and the peaceful town of Dale, which is housing refugees. The aggressor is indisputable, the stakes

undeniable, and so the battle between peer armies is justifiable.

When the adversary is science fictional, the tactics can often remain classic. In *The Avengers*, the objective is simple: contain the invaders, encircle them, and drive them into a position of strength held by allied forces. Then, cut off the pinch point through which they're invading with Iron Man's daring charge into the enemy maw. Classic stuff updated for a modern age, albeit with significantly more glowing rocks and with transdimensional travel in lieu of over-water bridges.

In some cases, the heroic attackers must gain the advantage not by numbers but by guile, resorting to guerrilla warfare and ambushing an enemy with superior strength on favorable turf. This can be seen best in *Avatar*, in which simultaneous infantry and aerial battles are enjoined at the precise moment when the superior Earth forces encounter a communications problem. This of course gives the Pandoran forces a window to eliminate the bomber escort before it reaches its destination.

In each case, the heroes are at a disadvantage. Their loss in the fight would constitute a total loss of cities, people, and assets, while the adversaries bear no such existential risk.

All this destruction is naturally cathartic. Action makes flippant what's normally a source

King Kong wrecks New York, starting a trend.

THE BAD OLD DAYS

Movies where New York City is destroyed, by what destroyed it

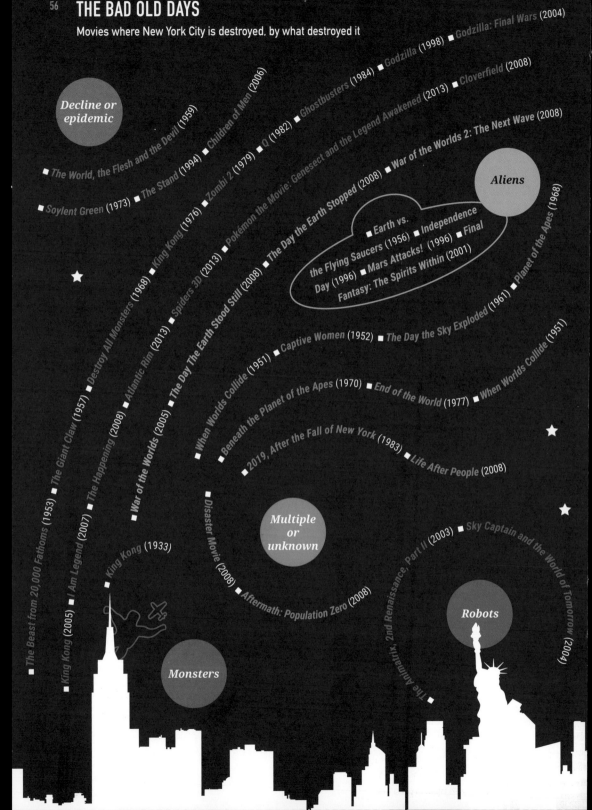

Decline or epidemic

Aliens

Multiple or unknown

Robots

Monsters

Godzilla: Final Wars (2004)
Godzilla (1998)
Cloverfield (2008)
Ghostbusters (1984)
Genesect and the Legend Awakened (2013)
Q (1982)
War of the Worlds 2: The Next Wave (2008)
Children of Men (2006)
The World, the Flesh and the Devil (1959)
The Stand (1994)
Zombi 2 (1979)
King Kong (1976)
Pokémon the Movie: Genesect and the Legend Awakened (2013)
The Day the Earth Stopped (2008)
Planet of the Apes (1968)
Soylent Green (1973)

Earth vs. the Flying Saucers (1956)
Independence Day (1996)
Final Fantasy: The Spirits Within (2001)
Mars Attacks! (1996)

Destroy All Monsters (1968)
Spiders 3D (2013)
The Day The Earth Stood Still (2008)

Captive Women (1952)
The Day the Sky Exploded (1961)

When Worlds Collide (1951)
Beneath the Planet of the Apes (1970)
End of the World (1977)
When Worlds Collide (1951)

The Giant Claw (1957)
The Happening (2008)
Atlantic Rim (2013)
War of the Worlds (2005)

2019, After the Fall of New York (1983)
Life After People (2008)

The Beast from 20,000 Fathoms (1953)
I Am Legend (2007)
King Kong (1933)

Disaster Movie (2008)

Aftermath: Population Zero (2008)

The Animatrix, 2nd Renaissance, Part II (2003)
Sky Captain and the World of Tomorrow (2004)

King Kong (2005)

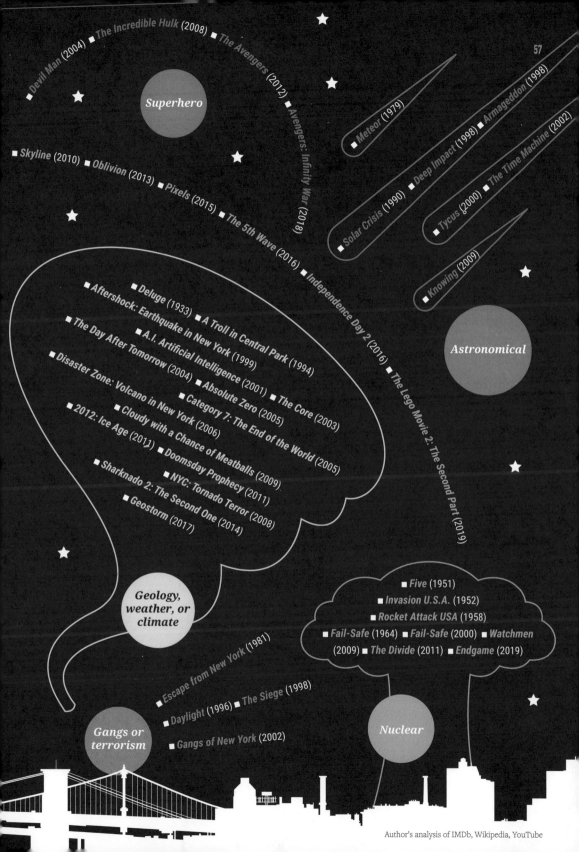

Superhero
- Devil Man (2004)
- The Incredible Hulk (2008)
- The Avengers (2012)
- Avengers: Infinity War (2018)
- Skyline (2010)
- Oblivion (2013)
- Pixels (2015)
- The 5th Wave (2016)
- Independence Day 2 (2016)
- The Lego Movie 2: The Second Part (2019)

Astronomical
- Meteor (1979)
- Deep Impact (1998)
- Armageddon (1998)
- Solar Crisis (1990)
- The Time Machine (2002)
- Tycus (2000)
- Knowing (2009)

Geology, weather, or climate
- Deluge (1933)
- A Troll in Central Park (1994)
- Aftershock: Earthquake in New York
- A.I. Artificial Intelligence (1999)
- The Day After Tomorrow (2004)
- Absolute Zero (2005)
- Disaster Zone: Volcano in New York (2004)
- Category 7: The End of the World (2005)
- 2012: Ice Age (2011)
- Cloudy with a Chance of Meatballs (2009)
- Sharknado 2: The Second One (2014)
- Doomsday Prophecy (2011)
- NYC: Tornado Terror (2008)
- Geostorm (2017)
- A.I. Artificial Intelligence (2001)
- The Core (2003)

Nuclear
- Five (1951)
- Invasion U.S.A. (1952)
- Rocket Attack USA (1958)
- Fail-Safe (1964)
- Fail-Safe (2000)
- Watchmen (2009)
- The Divide (2011)
- Endgame (2019)

Gangs or terrorism
- Escape from New York (1981)
- Daylight (1996)
- The Siege (1998)
- Gangs of New York (2002)

Author's analysis of IMDb, Wikipedia, YouTube

of great pain. Tokyo was leveled multiple times before in the real world, but postwar Japanese cinema had no scruples about leveling it again and again by whatever monster or threat came along. Disaster action is a way to take a shared experience and experiment with it, to build on it week after week. That way, an identity is forged not in the destruction, but in enduring it and rebuilding stronger than before. It's a reflection of the fears (annihilation) and the goals (survival from annihilation) shared by both filmmakers and audiences. New York has had destruction meted on it constantly. After 9/11, that didn't change in the slightest.

In fact, there are few things that have *not* destroyed New York City: It's been disintegrated, wiped out by an ice age at least three times,

leveled by a superstorm, attacked by aliens, hit with a tsunami, hit with a tsunami caused by aliens, damaged by asteroid or comet debris, and pummeled by giant bagels from the sky. A wide range of superheroes have also left dents in New York's urban hardware. The city has been volcanoed and earthquaked, nuked a bunch of times, blown to bits once, and attacked by vampires. The sheer number of King Kongs who've wreaked havoc on the place boggles the imagination; Godzilla as well. Mewtwo did a number on the place once, then of course the Sharknado, robots, the moon, an epidemic, and obviously, giant spiders. You'd think it would get old, but New York has been taken down endless times since the 1930s, and nobody appears bored by it.

WHO ARE WE FIGHTING IN ACTION MOVIES?

Percentage of top-grossing action films with this group as the enemy, by decade

As Hollywood made more money abroad, it stopped making those ticket buyers villains

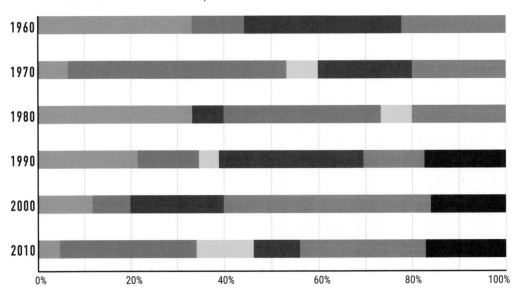

Real countries
US or UK
Fake countries
Criminals
Monsters, aliens, and robots
Corporations

The-Numbers.com

Worth Fighting For

Action reflects both the antagonists—the forces that a society believes want to destroy it, whether that's an external enemy, internal strife, or just the loss of control and increase in instability—and fears of society at the time. It does this by addressing those fears—and the antagonists—by reducing them to the point of farce. If you look at the action movies that made it into the top-ten grossing films their year of release, you'll see several patterns about who moviemakers consider an enemy. From the 1960s to 1990s, the bad guys were often from an actual country, like Russia or East Germany. But starting in the 2000s, that trend began to collapse. A decade later, the percentage of enemies linked to a specific state was at an all-time low.

The highest-grossing action films of the first two decades of the twenty-first century were far more likely to feature an adversary from a fake country—Sokovia, for instance—or be an alien, an artificial intelligence, or a big scary monster. If a specific country was made the enemy, it was often a historical film and the enemy was Nazi Germany or a similarly evil regime. Since the 1990s, a reliable percentage of enemies have also been corporations or wealthy antagonists using the levers of industrial power to achieve their aims.

That transition—from enemies that were often specifically another country to more ambiguous multinational corporations or neutral monsters and robots—came at a time when overseas revenue for movies was beginning to shift. That meant the market for what was considered a successful film could no longer be met exclusively with an American audience.

The items that action movie protagonists squabble over have also evolved, or at least gotten a little more specific. The "MacGuffin,"

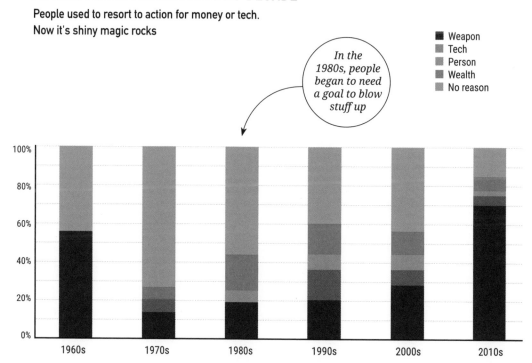

ACTION MOVIE MACGUFFINS BY DECADE
People used to resort to action for money or tech.
Now it's shiny magic rocks

In the 1980s, people began to need a goal to blow stuff up

- Weapon
- Tech
- Person
- Wealth
- No reason

Action adventure films that appeared in the top ten films of the year in that decade, The-Numbers.com

or object both the protagonists and the antagonists desire, has become more common as a result. Many of the 1960s and '70s action films were fought over honor or to stop a criminal or to prevent a terrorist attack; only the Bond films at the time featured an item like a nuke, a dirty bomb, a cryptography device, or diamonds as the object of pursuit.

By the '80s and '90s, some kind of target—be it technology, money, or a weapon—became the norm. The 1990s in particular featured a majority of films that had a *thing* at stake: bearer bonds, a bomb, or a piece of critical technology an antagonist wanted. And as the films of the 2010s saw a depersonalization of the adversary—not Russians or North Koreans but robots and aliens—the objects of pursuit were scaled back as well, in large part because of superhero films. The era of the important glowing rock came next, which

was the target in 33 percent of the forty action films of the decade, specifically because of the Infinity Stones of the Avengers movies, the kryptonite of the Superman flicks, and the various Allspark and derivative rocks of the Transformers franchise. Even when the target was not just a shiny rock, it was usually a shiny rock: the Arc Reactor, *Avatar*'s unobtanium, most vibranium, all shiny rocks. A whole decade spent chasing glow sticks.

In essence, the goal of action movies has become less varied and complex in the pursuit of the largest possible audience. It's difficult to quibble with the goal of "I need to collect this glowing orb, and if I do not, the world will end." The politics of that are rather clean. To be sure, action films have broadly tended to support a return to the status quo, preventing someone from gaining a new power or stopping an attack. It's uncommon to have action

BE CAREFUL WHO YOU VILLAINIZE

Box office revenue by origin

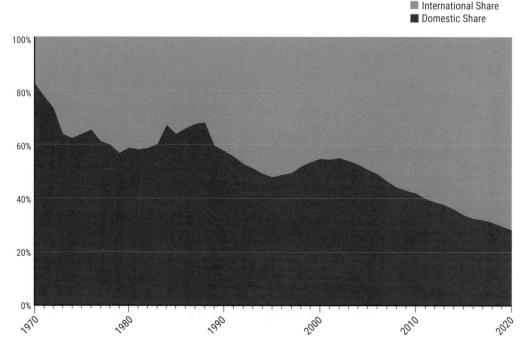

■ International Share
■ Domestic Share

films involve executing an attack or changing the status quo, at least outside of dystopian futures where the protagonists are functionally fighting for a return to the type of living we largely enjoy today. The trend does cause some problems, though, in that when the stakes are all-or-nothing, the suspense of the movie dries up rather quickly.

Which is why the best kind of action movie is a sports movie.

For Love of the Game

Not all action movies need to be about actually doing violence on an adversary or having the world at stake. Lots of movies are more functional action movies, like sports movies. Sports movies are just action movies with a specific set of rules to guide the action. The character arcs—honest people trying to beat well-funded bullies, old washed-up veterans coming back for one last job, ragtag teams learning how to come together—it's the same playbook regardless of whether it's a baseball team or a superfriends team.

Sports movies offer a little more excitement, if only because the teams usually end up winning in the end—but not always! It's a lot more palatable to end a sports movie on a message of "the team had a moral victory even if they did not personally win the World Series" than it is to end an alien invasion flick with the postscript that "The aliens did succeed in annihilating Earth, but we'll never forget that incredible season where we learned to play on the same team." No other genre, in fact, dangles such a pervasive possibility of failure as sports movies, which on some level actually makes them a bit more thrilling than a rom-com or superhero movie.

HOW CERTAIN IS THAT HAPPY ENDING?

Percent of films by genre in which the protagonist got what they wanted

Sports movies are the rare genre where the good guys often lose

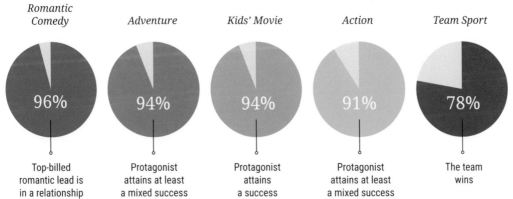

Romantic Comedy	Adventure	Kids' Movie	Action	Team Sport
96%	94%	94%	91%	78%
Top-billed romantic lead is in a relationship	Protagonist attains at least a mixed success	Protagonist attains a success	Protagonist attains at least a mixed success	The team wins

Author's analysis of IMDb

But there is one type of action movie that manages to invert the rule book, and in doing so reveals something fascinating about audiences who love it. If action movies show what people value on the outside, heist movies reveal what they think they're worth inside.

Honor Among Thieves

Heists reveal what we think about *work*. They are about what we do to get by, about labor, camaraderie, and who deserves what.

Heist movies tend to have an outsized impact on society compared with other genres. Nobody took out car insurance as they exited *Fast & Furious*, but movies showing bank robberies (accurate or not) reflect the expectations of what people want in terms of security from their banks. Media in general about people stealing stuff changed not only the way people steal stuff but also the way places guarding stuff try to prevent people from stealing it.

"There's always a fascination with crime of this sort, because it's happening to an institution that we live with every day," said Robert McCrie, a professor of security management at John Jay College of Criminal Justice in New York, where he has spent his career studying physical security.

Early bank robber films literally influenced the design of banks, which is absurd because they didn't represent how banks are actually robbed. Bank robbers don't get caught by valiant tellers or brave security guards—banks don't have money to fund private security forces anymore—and vaults are antiques.

HOW REAL HEISTS GO DOWN

Number of bank heists per year in the United States

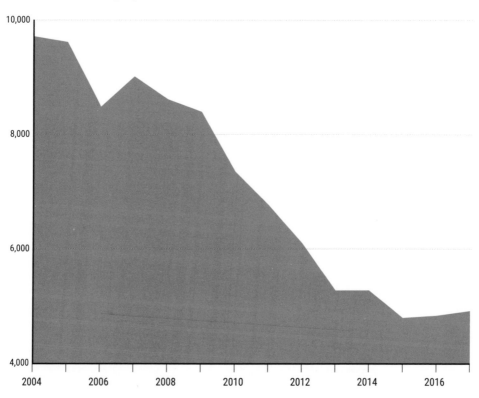

Federal Bureau of Investigation

Your typical banker has more money available at their fingertips than what was once found in the typical bank vault. But because of early heist films, banks actually began to take their security cues from cinema. Part of this was necessary to appease insurance companies, whose employees watch movies, too.

In reality, alarms and cameras don't stop robberies, nor does spiffy tracking equipment or much else on the mandatory list of things banks are required to do to defend against robbers. But the truth is, the reasons for half the bells and whistles in your standard bank is to appease the public's desire for ostentatious displays of security. Violent assaults on banks rarely happen in the United States—they make up just 3 percent of all bank robberies. And the money's insured anyway, so they'll just give it to you if you want, no fight no fuss. At the end of the day the only thing that actually matters regarding the success or failure of your typical bank robbery is the getaway. If a robber gets out of the bank before the cops show up, and if they get out of the vicinity undetected, the probability of success skyrockets regardless of the countermeasures installed.

So heist movies are fantasies—they aren't really about crimes. They take place in a bank the same way that *Jurassic Park* takes place in a zoo. Heist movies are instead about work and our relationships to our jobs.

Some of our earliest stories are heists— Prometheus and fire, the apple in Eden, Jason and the Argonauts—and they all come down to questions of who deserves what, and whether the small and weak deserve what the strong have.

Naturally, the importance of things has evolved since those tales were written. Theology and gilded garments no longer determine who has power and who lacks it. Modern capitalism means that heists are no longer spiritual in nature or about political riches and fortunes, but rather about capital.

The best example of this is *Ocean's Eleven*. The 1960 original—*Ocean's 11*—is markedly different, about a group of GIs bored with postwar life and the lack of remuneration for their World War II expertise. So they use those talents to rob five casinos in Las Vegas by bombing the power lines and punching bursars until they get the money.

The 2001 *Ocean's Eleven* updates that same occupational malaise for a postindustrial America. A coalition of has-beens with their potential wasted on trivialities come together to rob a casino owned by a vicious, vaguely European man who wields the weapon of capital to accrue a fortune. The gang before the movie is undoubtedly talented and possesses expertise, but they fail to use that know-how to become wealthy through honest work. When Danny promises them "eight figures, divided equally" he's making not just a plan, but a statement about his vision for what they deserve to earn from their efforts.

The backgrounds of the characters are particularly telling: Rusty is teaching amateurs how to play cards. Reuben is an older version of American capital who's been left behind by the global capital accrued by his corporate rival. Saul's age renders him useless to a society with a mandatory retirement age. The twins are twiddling away robotics knowledge working at a racetrack. Basher's a great thief stuck working with amateurs, Frank's been kicked out of honest casino work, Yen's a sideshow, Linus is picking pockets. Eleven men whose employment prospects have been rendered vestigial. It's the story the American working class wishes it could tell: Beat the house, score the entire stack, cue the fountains.

Heists are movies where people who have every justification for doing the wrong thing can still do it while remaining morally absolved— where the protagonists get the money by working hard and being competent at their job.

FICTIONAL HEISTS

Based on an analysis of 190 heist movies released from 1930 to 2018, inflation adjusted to 2018

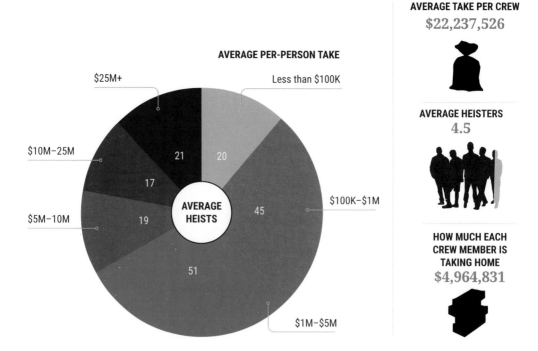

AVERAGE PER-PERSON TAKE

$25M+   Less than $100K

$10M–25M

$5M–10M

21   20

17

AVERAGE HEISTS

19   45 $100K–$1M

51

$1M–$5M

AVERAGE TAKE PER CREW
$22,237,526

AVERAGE HEISTERS
4.5

HOW MUCH EACH CREW MEMBER IS TAKING HOME
$4,964,831

Author's analysis of IMDb

The morality of heists

Heists emphasize craftsmanship and expertise over guile and brawn. And though a heist crew explicitly exists to undermine the established institutions of society, their defiance ends up reflecting it: A heist movie where you're completely unable to empathize with the crew in any way isn't a heist movie, it's a cop movie. And if you're successfully empathizing with the people about to rob someone, something about why they're doing that must make at least a little bit of sense to you. And if it makes sense to you, it's because they've successfully identified something unjust about the people who control the resources they seek to steal.

And if the people who control the resources in a society are unjust and the people who don't have those resources are right, then what does that say about the kind of society that would sustain that kind of systemic injustice?

The moral parameters of heists are interesting because stealing is one of the first things most people learn *not* to do. Whereas action movies have it comparatively easy, morally speaking—good guys versus bad guys—heist movies must persuade the viewer that the bad guys are the good guys. If action movies are about good and evil, heist movies are about right and wrong and how the natural order of

WHAT THEY TOOK

Film	Target	Crew	Haul	Per-Person Take
The Ladykillers (1955)	Bank	5	$1,529,791.30	$305,958.26
Ocean's 11 (1960)	Five casinos in one night	11	$90,994,375.70	$8,272,215.97
The Biggest Bundle of Them All (1968)	A B-17 bomber full of platinum	5	$35,186,602.87	$7,037,320.57
The Italian Job (1969)	Gold arriving in Italy from China	16	$26,693,284.94	$1,668,330.31
The Taking of Pelham One Two Three (1974)	Ransom for a train	4	$4,962,213.23	$1,240,553.31
A Fish Called Wanda (1988)	Diamond heist	4	$41,384,355.66	$10,346,088.91
Sneakers (1992)	Cryptographic system for the Russian government	6	$305,181.41	$50,863.57
Heat (1995)	Bearer bonds	5	$160,602,751.70	$32,120,550.34
Ocean's Eleven (2001)	Five casinos	11	$225,494,231.5	$20,499,475.59
National Treasure (2004)	Gold	2	$12,956,307,259.00	$6,478,153,629.32
Fast Five (2011)	Safe	12	$108,786,982.2	$9,065,581.85

Note: Gem heists, if otherwise unvalued on-screen, are valued at the median value of reported gems stolen per survey of *New York Times* archives

things is off, and how one crew of competent workers is going to subvert it for all of our sakes.

Today, most bank robberies are done by note-passers, where a person hands a teller a note indicating they have a weapon, the teller then gives the guy some money, and he leaves. It used to be a traumatic event for the general public, and now it's routine. The robber doesn't get much money and they usually don't succeed in ripping off banks for very long.

"The dramatic bank crimes of the past are fewer today for two reasons," said McCrie. "One is because banks themselves have changed, and the payoff has been less. . . . The crime of the moment is electronic crime, not the dramatic pulling into the bank shooting bullets into the ceiling to let everybody know *this means business.*"

Today, McCrie's students are mainly studying cybercrime. John Jay's got some two hundred people taking a minor in cybercrime, and it's beginning to crowd out things like physical security in lectures. The price of a bitcoin is so volatile it's ludicrous to attempt to print in a book. However, the value of a couple of stolen bitcoin is probably somewhat higher than the $9,295 average loot scored in a successful bank robbery in 2013.

Laugh Tracking

Heists are hardly the only format that serves as a barometer of the state of work. If heists are how people reconcile their relationships to their jobs and their lots in life when times are dysfunctional, sitcoms are how we reconcile our relationships to work and life when things are functional. Domestic and workplace situational comedies are basically as versatile a genre as one can get, and, as far as premises go, leave the widest room for interpretation.

The most persistent format for comedy in the United States is the televised sitcom. Whereas filmed comedies have ebbed and flowed at the box office, sitcoms remain persistently in demand. And their reliability of format is what makes them so interesting. Family sitcoms give us a glimpse into America's conception of what a family looks like. Based on their setting, we can get a sense of what people have valued over time. Workplace comedies have been around since the 1960s, for example, and through them we can see change in the workplace.

Movies take years to develop and shoot, but sitcoms are conveniently filmed just a few weeks before their release. In this sense, comedy is not just useful for society to work stuff out but to do it almost in real time.

In fact, formulaic art is one of the best ways to understand how a society ticks. Sitcoms, telenovelas, soap operas—they are how a culture reveals its least-common denominators, its assumptions, the sense of what a typical family wants in a given country. They show how people live, work, and talk. The latter is why they're often ideal for people learning English as a second language: They offer a chance to hear how people *actually* have conversations, versus the more clever or contrived feature films. They define a baseline, what's deviant but gradually becoming accepted, what previously abnormal or taboo lifestyles are punching a ticket into the mainstream.

In the 1960s, as the format was just finding its legs, in addition to the kind of domestic sitcoms still being made today, there were fantasy

WHERE ARE THE SITCOMS?

Locations of sitcoms that appeared in the top 30 shows of a year in a given decade

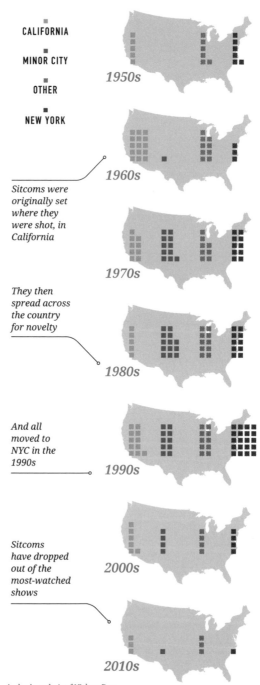

CALIFORNIA

MINOR CITY

OTHER

NEW YORK

1950s

Sitcoms were originally set where they were shot, in California

1960s

1970s

They then spread across the country for novelty

1980s

And all moved to NYC in the 1990s

1990s

Sitcoms have dropped out of the most-watched shows

2000s

2010s

Author's analysis of Nielsen Data

and surreal sitcoms like *Gilligan's Island* and *I Dream of Jeannie*. But there were also large numbers of sitcoms set in rural environs, a reflection of how much of the country was still on the cusp of urbanization. Military sitcoms were also popular, as the United States was going on three decades of war (World War II, Korea, Vietnam), with plenty of Americans with televisions who served, voluntarily or otherwise.

Just plotting out where the top-rated sitcoms of each decade were set reveals major changes in American society. In the 1960s, the vast majority of sitcoms were set either in the Los Angeles area where they were shot or somewhere outside a major city. That would begin to change in the 1970s, with about equal numbers of sitcoms set in California, New York, or other cities, as well as in other suburban or rural areas. This balance largely held through the 1980s, but then shifted dramatically in the 1990s, when New York City reigned supreme. Of the fifty-one sitcoms that made it into the top thirty programs for at least a year in the 1990s, twenty were set in New York City. This was the era of *Seinfeld* and *Friends*. But it didn't last: Perhaps seeing that the Manhattanites had overreached, the post-2000s has experienced a geographic rebalancing for the most popular sitcoms.

If there is one style of sitcom worth looking at above the others, one that has reflected societal change more accurately than the rest, it is probably the workplace comedy.

Workplace comedies grew from a niche of the 1960s and '70s—with *The Mary Tyler Moore Show* leading the way—to a rising force in the 1980s and '90s, with shows like *Night Court* and *Cheers*, which were hybrid workplace comedies, as were *Seinfeld* and *Frasier*. Families and groups of friends still served as the central gathering point for most shows on through the 2000s, but by the late 2000s, several pure workplace comedies emerged—*30 Rock*, *The Office*, *Boston Legal*, *Parks and Recreation*, *Scrubs*, *The Drew Carey Show*, *It's Always Sunny in Philadelphia*—that demonstrated the extent of the demand for shows set exclusively at work.

By the 2010s, it was hard to find shows that didn't reflect on the characters' work lives at all. Strict workplace comedies like *Brooklyn Nine-Nine*, *Bob's Burgers*, *2 Broke Girls*, *Superstore*, *Workaholics*, *Veep*, and *Silicon Valley* were all popular, not to mention shows that weren't technically workplace comedies like *The Big Bang Theory* that nevertheless were about friends who also work together. It's fair to say that work became more central for many Americans during this time, and television reflected that. It remains to be seen if the currently changing dynamic about work and a possible deprioritization of office culture in general will change that, but if it does, we'll probably see it first in sitcoms.

The Mary Tyler Moore Show *and* 30 Rock— *not so different from each other.*

To delve more deeply into what these other styles of stories do to us, we need to go beyond the boundaries of identity formation and repeated forms. Culture isn't a one-way street; it's a conversation. A show that's mostly about spaceships where an interracial kiss is normal isn't just making a statement. It can have the power to change the society that watches it.

Seen in Scene

If pop culture well done manages to reflect what people aspire to or fear or value or want, it stands to reason that it should also try to reflect the people themselves. Though it too often does not.

For more than a decade, the Annenberg Inclusion Initiative at the University of Southern California has analyzed how well films and television actually reflect the world at large. And they have found Hollywood wanting time and time again.

"Individually, we know that people like to watch and are drawn to characters that look or act like them in some component," said Katherine Pieper, the postdoc program director who runs the lab with Dr. Stacy Smith. "People are drawn to different characters in movies and identify with different characters."

And that's where Smith sees issues for many minority groups, from Asian Americans to Pacific Islanders to Muslims, Hispanics, Latinos, and others.

"Muslims account for a very small fraction of all speaking characters," said Smith. "And when they are shown, it's in such a negative light that it's going to perpetuate a whole series of harmful effects, whether it's identity based for in-group individuals that identify as Muslim or out-group members that maybe don't have a Muslim in their community."

And the science about media consumption shows that if every single person who looks like you in a movie is poor, or violent, or dangerous, it has a profound effect. There's lots of evidence for this around the LGBTQ+ community, particularly how media exposure and positive representations of gays and lesbians in relationships have had positive impacts on the perception of LGBTQ+ people on people for whom that was the only exposure.

Although not all impacts are necessarily positive or negative, the positive impacts are remarkable. Studies from the early 2000s showed that the attitudes of fans of *Will and Grace*, which featured a number of gay characters, softened toward gays and lesbians in the aggregate, even when respondents didn't have anyone in their social network who was gay. But that representation hasn't necessarily persisted across the whole LGBTQ+ community: Smith noted that transgender representation is nearly zero in film, with just four speaking trans characters across hundreds of movies.

"Showing characters in a negative light can have very deleterious effects on individuals, their own self-worth, their own value, how they might see themselves, negative attributes around their group, and then how other groups might view a particular identity," said Smith.

Even if it's just one movie, or one character, it's never just one movie or just one character. Those representations add up.

WHO REALLY GETS TO BE A PROTAGONIST?

Analysis of main character in top-grossing films

MUSLIM

In 200 popular films, 2017-2019:

6
■ ■ ■ ■ ■ ■

Had Muslim leads

51%

of Muslim characters were from films set in the past

1.6% of 8,965 speaking characters were Muslim

24% of the global population is Muslim

48.9% were in present day settings

11% were in the recent past

40.2% were in the historical or fantastical past

of 41 primary and secondary Muslim characters **58.50%** were immigrants, migrants, or refugees

AAPI

of the 44 films with AAPI leads or co-leads, 14 times it was Dwayne Johnson

67%

of AAPI primary and secondary characters fell into stereotyped tropes

58%

of AAPI men had no romantic relationships

41.8%

of AAPI characters experienced disparagement of some sort, six of which were racist/sexist slurs

37.5%

of AAPI women had no romantic relationships

HISPANIC

Of 94 Hispanic/Latino characters:

Spoke no English — **37.2%**

Spoke English, with an accent — **30.5%**

Were immigrants — **8.5%**

Of the 2019 Top-billed Latinos:

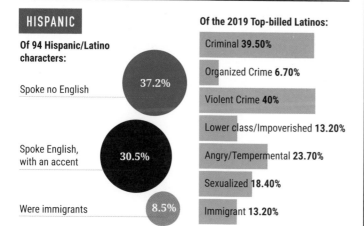

Criminal **39.50%**

Organized Crime **6.70%**

Violent Crime **40%**

Lower class/Impoverished **13.20%**

Angry/Tempermental **23.70%**

Sexualized **18.40%**

Immigrant **13.20%**

Annenberg Inclusion Initiative, 2021

CHAPTER 4

HOW CULTURE CHANGES US

Some people saw Twister *and thought, "Sign me up!"*

KFOR meteorologist Emily Sutton is flying down North Tenth Street south of El Reno, Oklahoma, headed toward US Route 81. To her right is Kevin Josefy, who's trained his camera on the entity slightly farther to Sutton's right: a tornado that just fourteen minutes earlier touched down a few miles south of Interstate 40, the artery connecting Barstow, California, to Wilmington, North Carolina, by way of Oklahoma City, where Sutton is a meteorologist for KFOR.

The tornado itself is a massive one. In real time, KFOR reports it's a mile wide, with winds of over 100 miles per hour. When the tornado crosses I-81 just two minutes later, things get much worse. It gets much, much larger, swelling from a mile-wide path to a 2.6-mile-wide path in a matter of seconds. And more importantly, true to form, it *twists*, and its eastern course swings north. Directly to where Sutton and Josefy are heading.

"Emily Sutton is *in the tornado*," Chief Meteorologist Mike Morgan says back at the station to the people of Oklahoma City, who are watching Josefy's camera feed as the audio breaks up.

Leaves are flying over the vehicle, being sucked forward toward the vortex that just cut in front of the vehicle. Soon it's branches flying over the truck, and Sutton feels a splash on the back of her neck. More branches fly over the truck, then a whole tree. The audio is still garbled because her cell phone signal is being shredded by the storm ahead. Oklahoma City sees Sutton's truck back up through an intersection—and then the camera smashes to black.

Sutton was born and raised outside Chicago, far from the Tornado Alley of the central Midwest. But in 1995, when Sutton was in elementary school at the height of her obsession with tornadoes, a little movie called *Twister* was released. The film, about a group of swashbuckling storm chasers trying to crack the true nature of destructive tornadoes, was a revelation.

"I think that was the first time I realized what storm chasing was, that a female could do that," said Sutton. "That was the first and only example I had."

Fast-forward a decade or so, and Sutton is an undergrad at the University of Missouri, which has a storm chase team. She saw her first tornado on her very first storm chase on April 22, 2004. On her second chase, she saw five tornadoes, one of which was an F3 in Kansas. After graduating with a degree in meteorology, Sutton quickly worked her way up the news meteorologist ladder to KFOR in Oklahoma City, Oklahoma.

If San Diego is where forecasters go for the easy life, then Oklahoma City—well, there's a reason why their NBA team is called the Thunder. Meteorologists (and everyone, really) is on call from Mother Nature at all times. There are ice storms, blizzards, wind events, and tornadoes. For starters.

"It's a meteorologist's dream," said Sutton.

The tornado she was chasing when her camera feed blacked out claimed eight lives, including those of two storm chasers, and injured another twenty-six people. Without advance warning, it would have been far worse. The National Weather Service determined it was one of the most powerful tornadoes ever sampled by mobile radar, and the single widest tornado on record, at one point with a forward ground motion of 180 miles per hour and up to 296-mile-per-hour winds.

"I realized that our back window blew out," said Sutton, explaining what happened during the live broadcast. "And so I just remained calm and kept driving backwards until we hit a guardrail. Then the camera fell down, so it made it look like we both died—that was pretty crazy."

Now that she has lived the equivalent of what happens in *Twister*, is she ready to put the movie aside?

"Oh my gosh, I watch it all the time," she said. "I love it so much that friends text me when it's on TV, all the time. No, I have a *deep* obsession with *Twister*."

Inception

Movies can have deep reverberations. These go beyond simply what people do and can alter trends and fashions for years to come.

Archery—along with rowing and running—is one of few sports that can claim to be ancient. People have been shooting bows and arrows for millennia. Through the early 2000s, archery remained a fairly niche activity, one with a cost-of-entry and equipment level that likely turned some people away from the sport. Niche was fine, but niche was also niche. USA Archery, the governing body that oversees the sport in the United States, pulled in around $1.5 million in membership dues and grants in 2009 and 2010. Their merchandise sales were about $158,000 per year in the same period.

In 2010, novelist Suzanne Collins happened to complete the final book in a trilogy set in a post-apocalyptic world where children and young adults are made to fight one another. That final book sold 450,000 copies in one week, eventually moving 1.2 million copies. In March 2011, Lionsgate announced that actress Jennifer Lawrence had been cast as the lead in a film that would come out in 2012.

When *The Hunger Games* movie debuted in 2012, USA Archery's membership dues swelled to $2.1 million per year, and merch sales had nearly quintupled, to $744,000. Those numbers would rise to $2.7 million in dues in 2015 when the final film was released, nearly double the level from 2009. Merch sales would hit just shy of $900,000, more than six times what they earned in 2009. People were buying lots of bows and lots of arrows and were also signing up to shoot them in sanctioned competition.

The Geena Davis Institute on Gender in Media commissioned a study on what prompted the surge. In 2012, the overall membership dues increased by about 16 percent, but that surge wasn't led by males. Girls' participation in national archery competitions *doubled* that year.

"For young girls it was more Princess Merida," said study author Caroline Heldman,

referring to the bow-wielding protagonist of Disney's *Brave*. "For older girls, in their teens, it was Katniss. Both had an effect—most of the girls who have taken up archery had seen both of them."

According to a survey of USA Archery members who were girls under age eighteen, 48.5 percent of them specifically cited Katniss Everdeen from *The Hunger Games* as having "some" or "a lot" of influence on their decision to take up the sport, with 36 percent citing the character Merida from Pixar's *Brave* as a motivation. Boys similarly didn't lack for archer role models—in the same survey, boys under eighteen cited *The Lord of the Rings*' Legolas and Robin Hood, but to a far lesser extent (22 percent and 21 percent) compared with the girls who pointed to Katniss as their motivation.

But movies and books can move the needle on much more than just hobbies.

ARCHERY ROLE MODELS

Competitive archers are taking inspiration from movies

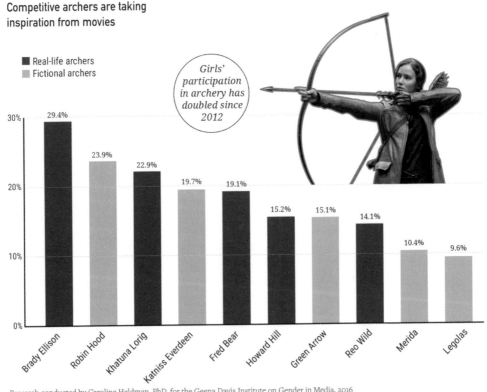

■ Real-life archers
■ Fictional archers

Girls' participation in archery has doubled since 2012

- Brady Ellison — 29.4%
- Robin Hood — 23.9%
- Khatuna Lorig — 22.9%
- Katniss Everdeen — 19.7%
- Fred Bear — 19.1%
- Howard Hill — 15.2%
- Green Arrow — 15.1%
- Reo Wild — 14.1%
- Merida — 10.4%
- Legolas — 9.6%

Research conducted by Caroline Heldman, PhD, for the Geena Davis Institute on Gender in Media, 2016

DOUBLE SECRET PROBATION

Between 1965 and 1975, the number of college students in the United States more than doubled from about 4 million to almost 9 million. A legion of kids in the 1970s became the first people in their family to go to college. In 1971, 38.5 percent of freshmen at American colleges and universities were from families in which the parents did not go to college. Those millions might have lacked direct insight about what exactly one does at college, but fear not: Pop culture was there to fill the gap.

Riding the tide, the 1978 film *Animal House* offered one hedonistic angle on how to handle a college experience. According to Google's Ngram Viewer, which tabulates mentions of words and phrases in the English language over time, the phrase *toga party* goes from virtually nonexistent until the early 1960s—the period covered in the film—where it briefly spiked, only to fade once again into obscurity by the '70s. But *Animal House* changed that, making college toga parties an institution.

The movie also preceded a significant rise in the formation of fraternity chapters that was not matched by sororities. Although both organizations saw increases in chapter formations during the 1920s, the postwar years, and the late 1960s, through most of the 1970s the rate of fraternity formation was in decline. But following the release of the film in 1978, there was a spike in the spread of fraternities, reversing the decline until the early 1990s.

TOGA! TOGA! TOGA!

Mentions of "toga party" in English language writing

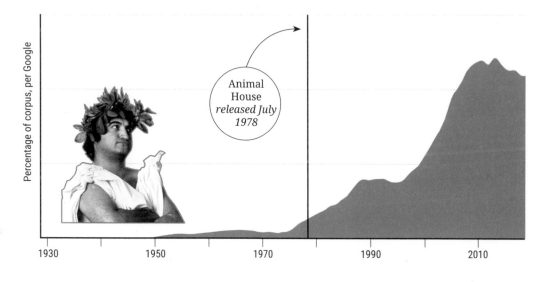

Percentage of corpus, per Google

Animal House *released July 1978*

1930   1950   1970   1990   2010

PEOPLE LIKE WHAT THEY SEE

American Kennel Club breed data

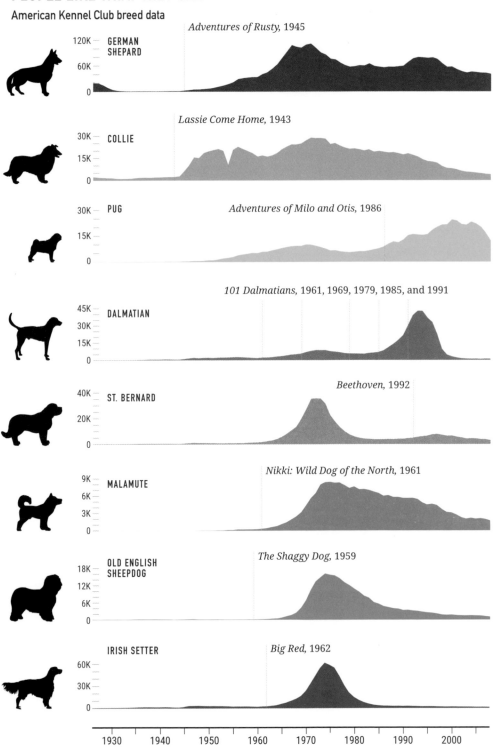

Adventures of Rusty, 1945

GERMAN SHEPARD

Lassie Come Home, 1943

COLLIE

PUG

Adventures of Milo and Otis, 1986

101 Dalmatians, 1961, 1969, 1979, 1985, and 1991

DALMATIAN

Beethoven, 1992

ST. BERNARD

Nikki: Wild Dog of the North, 1961

MALAMUTE

OLD ENGLISH SHEEPDOG

The Shaggy Dog, 1959

IRISH SETTER

Big Red, 1962

1930   1940   1950   1960   1970   1980   1990   2000

American Kennel Club Digital Library & Collections

The popularity of dog breeds are in constant flux, subject to fashion, social trends, availability, and more. One thing that can drastically alter the life of thousands of dogs is a star turn in a movie.

One Hundred and One Dalmatians is a particularly clear example of this. The film was originally released in 1961, when it was a commercial success, leading to a modest increase in Dalmatian registrations, according to American Kennel Club records. In the five-year period after the release of the film, from 1961 to 1965, there was a 22 percent increase in registrations for the breed. But the 1985 and 1991 rereleases were smash hits, the latter finishing as the twentieth-highest grossing film of the year. After the 1991 film, an average 38,261 Dalmatians were adopted in each of the following five years compared with 6,314 before the first rerelease in 1985. Ultimately, the breed peaked at number nine on the overall breed rankings in 1993 and 1994, compared with a low ranking before the rereleases.

Here are some highlights of the chart on the opposite page:

• After the release of *The Shaggy Dog*, there was a hundredfold increase in registrations of Old English sheepdogs.

• Registrations of Labrador retrievers had been increasing at a rate of 452 per year up until 1963, when *The Incredible Journey* was released, at which point it popped to 2,223 dogs per year.

• *Lassie Come Home*'s release in 1943 took the collie from a breed that averaged 1,674 registrations a year in the proceeding decade to an annual average of 13,215 dogs per year in the decade that followed. Within five years, the collie was the third-most-popular breed in America.

Heck, even movies where the entire lesson is "my god, this animal is impractical" can pump up popularity in a given breed. In the ten years preceding the release of *Beethoven* in 1992, which featured a rambunctious St.

Bernard, an average of 4,057 of the hulking creatures were registered with the AKC annually. In the ensuing decade, that rose to 6,434 per year, a 58 percent jump, potentially further bolstered by the successful 1993 sequel.

Although fraternities, pets, and hobbies are influenced by film on a large scale, their reach goes deeper still. The stratospheric and lasting popularity of Star Wars probably isn't news to you if you were one of the 1,119 Leias born between 1978 and 1987, when the first Stars Wars trilogy was released, or the 921 Anakins born from 1999 to 2008, during the second trilogy, or the 1,544 boys named Kylo born from 2016 to 2020 during the most recent spate of Star Wars series releases.

There were eighty boys named Xander born from 1987 to 1996, according to the Social Security Administration, but you get one moderately dreamy side character on *Buffy the Vampire Slayer* in 1997 and that's how all of a sudden there were 7,413 Xanders born from 1998 to 2007.

And although Roman names have always had their appeal, the thirty-four kids named Maximus born from 1990 to 1999 likely had some issues finding license plate key chains with their name at gift shops. That was probably less of a problem for the 9,916 kids named Maximus from 2001 to 2010, after the 2000 release of *Gladiator*, which tells the story of Maximus Decimus Meridius (commander of the Armies of the North, general of the Felix Legions, and loyal servant to the true emperor, Marcus Aurelius).

In the decade before the premiere of *Friends* in 1994, an average of 318 new Chandlers were born each year. In the decade that followed, the average was 1,792 new Chandlers per year. (Could it *be* any clearer?) Plus, haircuts weren't the only thing *Friends* character Rachel Green made popular. Her daughter's name, Emma, was fairly popular in the ten years before her birth on the show in 2002, with an average of 7,907 Emmas born annually. Following her birth in the season finale of *Friends*' eighth season—an episode that drew in 34.9 million viewers, the highest-rated episode of the highest-rated

BABY NAMES AND POP CULTURE | Based on US Social Security Administration data

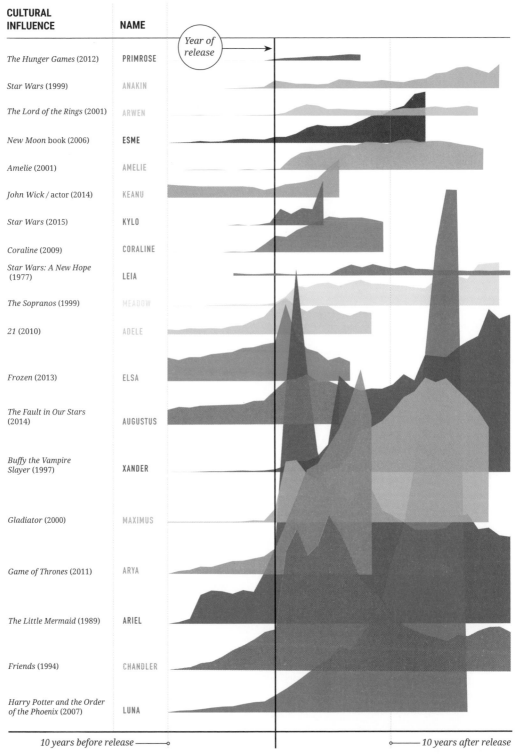

CULTURAL INFLUENCE   **NAME**

Year of release →

Cultural Influence	Name
The Hunger Games (2012)	PRIMROSE
Star Wars (1999)	ANAKIN
The Lord of the Rings (2001)	ARWEN
New Moon book (2006)	ESME
Amelie (2001)	AMELIE
John Wick / actor (2014)	KEANU
Star Wars (2015)	KYLO
Coraline (2009)	CORALINE
Star Wars: A New Hope (1977)	LEIA
The Sopranos (1999)	MEADOW
21 (2010)	ADELE
Frozen (2013)	ELSA
The Fault in Our Stars (2014)	AUGUSTUS
Buffy the Vampire Slayer (1997)	XANDER
Gladiator (2000)	MAXIMUS
Game of Thrones (2011)	ARYA
The Little Mermaid (1989)	ARIEL
Friends (1994)	CHANDLER
Harry Potter and the Order of the Phoenix (2007)	LUNA

10 years before release ——→   *10 years after release* ——

Social Security Administration

show on television that season, and the third-best viewership of any *Friends* episode—the name Emma skyrocketed in popularity, more than doubling to an average of 19,600 Emmas born annually during the following decade.

Names, although important to those who give and receive them, still may seem like a relatively small cultural impact. But what about the power to impact the very understanding of what a family should be?

One 2012 study that examined the effect of telenovelas in Brazil found that once television and the telenovelas that air on them were introduced into areas where they hadn't been available before, the structure and size of families changed in a given region. Researchers found that the portrayals of women on-screen were reportedly having an impact on family planning. The women on network Rede Globo's programs—where families were wealthy, happy, and, most significantly *small*—were being watched in communities where historically families were large, rural, and poor. The network reached about 183 million Brazilians at the time of the study, with the telenovelas routinely drawing 60 to 80 million viewers. Researchers estimated that the

introduction of Rede Globo's telenovelas, which depicted empowered women with control over their sexual agency, was responsible for about a 7 percent decline in the probability of giving birth from 1980 to 1991.

More often than not, when people see something on-screen, they want the thing on-screen. When the car called the DeLorean was released, it flopped. The doors opened up like wings and not out, so it was an impractical vehicle at an impractical price point. Then Robert Zemeckis featured the DeLorean in the Back to the Future movies as the quirky car of the quirkiest character in the film, and now they've held their value for decades.

If movies can accelerate trends, they can stymie them just as fast. When the comedy-drama *Sideways*, about a pair of friends traveling to California wine country, came out in 2005, it made $109.7 million at the box office, scored Oscar nominations for Best Picture, Best Director, and two supporting acting nominations, and won for Best Adapted Screenplay. But its impacts in California extended well beyond Los Angeles and all the way up to the Napa region, where it was set.

Doc and Marty in Back to the Future, *where the pair goes back in time to significantly enhance the resale value of DeLoreans, among other things.*

One of the film's tropes involves extolling California pinot noir while constantly ripping on merlot. Twelve years after the film's release, pinot noir production in California increased 170 percent, vastly outpacing the 7 to 8 percent overall increase in wine grape production. Merlot—the go-to grape of the '90s and also the subject of disdain of the movie's main character, Paul Giamatti—would take a different turn. A 2009 economic analysis out of Sonoma State University found a 2 percent decline in merlot sales over a three-year period after the film's release, a time period that saw a commensurate 16 percent increase in pinot noir sales.

Courting Viewers

The year was 2002. Eddie Prentiss was the owner of an indoor sports and entertainment space in Minneapolis, a huge warehouse. Prentiss was mulling over ideas for a new rec league to spice up the place. He remembered reading about some wooden bat leagues that were cheap to start up, something that might keep people coming through the doors.

His mind was drifting when he had a thought, something from the recesses of gym class: Why not dodgeball?

He told his wife, which he recalls well: "She's like, *Okay, good luck with that*."

Two decades later, Prentiss is the American ambassador on the governing council of the World Dodgeball Association, the architect of the professional game in the United States, and the organizer of twelve different National Dodgeball League World Championships. He is also a pro player himself for the Dallas Dobermen.

In June 2004, a Ben Stiller and Vince Vaughn comedy called *Dodgeball: A True Underdog Story* was released by 20th Century Fox. It would spark an enormous amount of popularity for the sport, but would also serve as a permanent albatross hanging over the institution. It accelerated the popularity of Prentiss's league, for sure, but it also threatened to throw a wrench into its credibility.

As we saw with archery, a moment in the spotlight can have a significant impact on a niche activity when it's presented as a hobby or favorite activity of a character in a movie.

But *The Hunger Games* wasn't an archery movie; it was more about a dystopian future class war. Archery was just the protagonist's hobby, something she looked cool doing that helped her advance the plot. But the effect a movie can have on an activity is actually larger when we're talking about movies *specifically* about sports.

In the early 1990s, hockey was having a moment. It was one reason why Disney opted to do a *Bad News Bears* but for hockey, a film that would eventually be released as *The Mighty Ducks*. The film made some $50 million at the box office, and that gave the executives at Disney an interesting idea. At the time, the NHL was looking to expand into nontraditional hockey cities, like Anaheim, for example, where Disney had a certain world-famous amusement park. The fee for a new franchise, coincidentally, was $50 million.

And so the Mighty Ducks of Anaheim were born. The Disney costume department was tasked with designing a logo, which they pulled from *The Mighty Ducks* film. The team debuted its official logo and colors in June 1993, right about when Buena Vista reported 370,000 preorders for *The Mighty Ducks* VHS rentals, an all-time record for Disney. The videocassette would remain in the top ten steadily, with the film and the NHL franchise boosting awareness of each other. *The Mighty Ducks* the film was the twenty-third most popular video rental of 1993, netting $54 million in revenue for Disney. By the end of the 1994 season, 80 percent of all NHL merchandise sold was Mighty Ducks merch.

The final film would come out in 1996.

HIT VOLLEYBALL MANGA *HAIKYUU!!* GOT READERS ON THE COURT

Enrollment in boy's high school volleyball in Japan

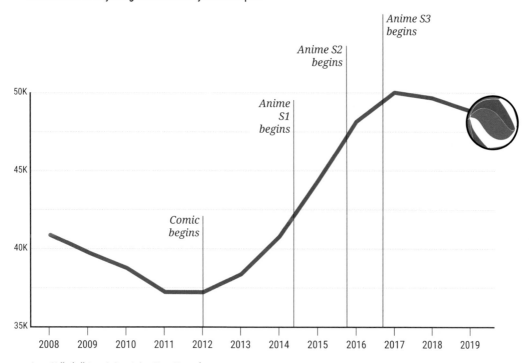

Japan Volleyball Association, Anime News Network

* * *

For many sports, it's hard to gauge the impact a movie has on the game. This is because sports movies tend to tap into existing fans of popular sports and generally are not made about unpopular sports, making it hard to measure shifts in popularity driven by a specific movie.

But sometimes it's incredibly clear.

In the late 2000s, high school volleyball was in decline in Japan, with the boys' side of the sport shedding about a thousand players a year. In 2008, there were just shy of 41,000 high school boys playing volleyball. By 2012, that was down to 37,000.

That year, the fate of the sport would change because Haruichi Furudate would adapt a one-shot comic published in 2011 into *Haikyu!!*, a serialized manga series about an underdog high school boys' volleyball team. The following year, it would become the twenty-second-

best-selling manga series in Japan, moving some 2,056,211 copies. An anime adaptation was then green-lit, the first season of which would debut in 2014. That year, the manga became an even bigger hit, selling more than 8.2 million copies and ranking as the third-highest-selling book of the year. In the years that followed, over its 2012 to 2020 run, *Haikyu!!* would reliably sell north of 5 million copies a year and never slip below the eighth-highest-selling series in any given year, with the anime going on to produce three additional seasons.

Haikyu!! was credited with completely turning around youth volleyball in Japan. The 37,000 boys who played volleyball in 2012 grew to 48,687 by 2019, an increase of over ten thousand players over seven years. For a country with only 3 million high schoolers, the rise was unprecedented. That wouldn't have happened had it not been for the 50 million copies of *Haikyu!!* in circulation.

And when Japan hosted the 2020 Olympics, *Haikyu!!* had its very own moment. Canadian Olympian Sarah Pavan, an avid fan of anime, used the show as a way to introduce people to the sport on her YouTube channel. American Erik Shoji, a libero on Team USA, became a fan after a team trip to Japan, and said in one interview, "I think *Haikyu!!* does a really great job of teaching the sport, and also showing some good technique in volleyball."

Japan's own Yuji Nishida went viral in a video, at one point spiking the ball similarly to *Haikyu!!* star Hinata in a match against Venezuela. During the following game break, the arena blasted the first season of the show's opening song. Japan would go on to win the match. It was the first time Japan's men had won in straight sets since 1992.

* * *

When Prentiss's dodgeball league began, it was mostly a midwestern affair, but all that changed with the league's first tournament in Las Vegas in 2004. The internet of 2004 was not the internet of today, but its characteristic desire to manifest ridiculous things in the real world was a thing back then—and the internet was absolutely down with dodgeball.

Since forming the league, Prentiss estimates that thousands of people have at one point or another hopped onto a court and played an officially sanctioned game of dodgeball, many of them compensated for it as professionals. Although the original film was a boost, it has caused hiccups.

"It's a double-edged sword," said Prentiss. "For about five or six years, it became almost a joke. The players that were really talented, that were really athletic, were getting ticked off. It's not a joke. These guys will play three or four times a week. Some of them are crazy ripped. We had five of our athletes that were on a Hanes commercial."

The National Dodgeball League has had struggles. Most leagues fail. It's the exception to persist, and through its national and then global expansion it survived.

"That film is almost twenty years old now, believe it or not," Prentiss said. "When it first came out, it was huge. We got so much with it." Through the decades, the ribbing from new fans, the prime-time appearances on dating shows, even a national broadcast on ESPN from *The Ocho* itself, the simple fact remains: Although dodgeball's rise as an actual professional sport was in no small part sparked by the deluge of interest in competing in a real-life high-stakes dodgeball tournament in Las Vegas with an enormous cash prize just like the movie, it endured mostly because it's an incredibly fun thing to watch and play.

Change of Scenery

It's not just what the characters do or drink or play that can have real-world implications. Setting aside the action, even the characters, the setting of a film or television show can encourage audiences to book vacations to places they never would have previously considered.

In 2000, one of the longest flights in the world was from London's Heathrow Airport to Auckland in New Zealand. The journey from the very center of the former British Empire to its one-time far-flung colony is arduous even by way of a Boeing 777: a twenty-three-hour trans-hemispheric shot in a pressurized metal tube, a flight so long it requires a stop along the way so it won't run out of fuel over the Indian Ocean. It is an uncomfortable, exhausting adventure that was then taken by about 200,000 travelers annually.

By 2002, however, that number had doubled. In the interim, New Zealand had not unearthed a new natural resource, no new industry had kicked off that demanded another

THE LORD OF THE RINGS EFFECT

Number of annual passengers to New Zealand

■ USA
■ UK
■ Germany
■ Canada

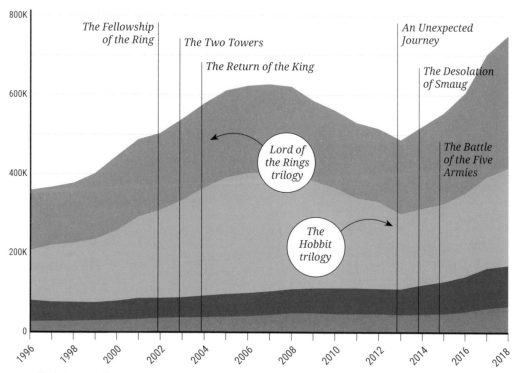

The Fellowship of the Ring

The Two Towers

The Return of the King

An Unexpected Journey

The Desolation of Smaug

The Battle of the Five Armies

Lord of the Rings trilogy

The Hobbit trilogy

Auckland Airport monthly traffic update (MTU) reports

200,000 people commute annually, there was no economic shift that encouraged Londoners to holiday 11,000 miles away. Nevertheless, another 20,000 people every month decided to embark on the worst plane ride on the planet, all because of a movie about a couple of hobbits.

The Lord of the Rings drove hundreds of thousands, if not millions, of people to visit New Zealand. And then when those numbers began to dip, The Hobbit trilogy did the same thing all over again. New Zealand's remoteness and the magnitude of The Lord of the Rings–induced bump make this a clear case, but the instinct to visit the pretty place you saw in a movie is an incredibly common urge. People visit remote islands in Scotland when the BBC broadcasts a cozy murder mystery set there.

They went to Rwanda after *Gorillas in the Mist* highlighted the jungles there. They're drawn to visiting Iowa because of *Field of Dreams*, which really drove home the "If you build it, they will come" avocation of the film.

Heck, it wasn't even the first time the region saw a boost in tourism because of a cultural export. The release of *Crocodile Dundee* and Americans' ensuing Australian obsession prompted a 20.5 percent increase in tourism from the United States to Down Under between 1981 and 1988.

This appeal is not lost on film studios either, several of which have gone through the arduous work of setting up theme parks to explicitly attract fans of their movies. Beyond their inherent appeal, films can revitalize aging

US

Dances with Wolves
+25% increase in tourism to Fort Hayes, KS

The Fugitive
+11% increase to Dillsboro, NC

Last of the Mohicans
+25% increase to Chimney Rock Park, NC

+65%

+25%

Close Encounters of the Third Kind
+75% increase to Devil's Tower, WY, in 1975; +20% now

Field of Dreams
35,000 visits to IA in 1991; Steady increase every year

Little Women
+65% increase to Orchard House, Concord, MA

Cheers
$7m in unpaid promotional advertising to Boston each year

Thelma and Louise
+19.1% to Arches National Monument in Moab, UT

Bull Durham
+25% increase to Durham, NC

Deliverance
20,000 annual tourists to Rayburn County, GA; Gross revenues $2M to $3M

500K

Steel Magnolias
+48% increase to LA

Dallas
500,000 visitors to Southfork Ranch, Dallas, per year

Bloodline
$65 million to the Florida Keys in local spending, 1,000 jobs

Miami Vice
+150% increase in German visitors to Miami 1985 to 1988

Forrest Gump
+7% increase to Savannah, GA

Narcos
Estimated 1 in 10 visits to Colombia is influenced by Netflix show

Captain Corelli's Mandolin
50% increase to Cephalonia, Greece, over 3 years

Saving Private Ryan
40% increase in American tourists to Normandy, France

Gorillas in the Mist
20% increase to Rwanda in 1998

Troy
73% increase to Canakkale, Turkey, in tourism

MOVIES, TV, AND TRAVEL

How movies get people to pack their bags

UK

+50%

Harry Potter
All locations
saw an increase
of 50% or more

Braveheart
300% increase in
visitors to Wallace
Monument the year
after release

Shetland (BBC)
53% increase to the
Shetland Islands per
2019 survey, in 6th
season

*All Creatures
Great and Small*
Generated £5m for
Yorkshire Dales

Heartbeat
Three times
the number
of normal
visitors to
Goathland
in 1991

Pride and Prejudice
150% increase in
visitors to Lyme Park

Middlemarch
27% increase to
Stamford in 1994

To the Manor Born
37% increase to Cricket
St Thomas between
1978 and 1980

39%

*Sense and
Sensibility* 39%
increase to
Saltram House

Mrs. Brown 25%
increase to Osborne
House visitors

*Four Weddings
and a Funeral*
The Crown Hotel was
fully booked for at
least 3 years

Notting Hill
10% increase to
Kenwood House
in 1 month

GLOBAL

10%

The Beach
22% increase to
Thailand in the youth
market in 2000

The Lord of the Rings
10% increase to New
Zealand every year from
the UK, 1998 to 2003

Crocodile Dundee
20.5% increase in US
visitors to Australia
1981 to 1988

Mission: Impossible 2
200% increase to
National Parks in
Sydney in 2000

Middle Earth is now just a thirteen-hour flight away.

Mr. Darcy's residence of Pemberly, accesible just off the M1.

attractions the same way they can put a shine on Madison County and its many bridges. Although the data's available only for the last film in the franchise, in the three months after the release of *Pirates of the Caribbean: Dead Men Tell No Tales* in May 2017, wait times at the Pirates of the Caribbean attraction at Walt Disney World averaged 31.4 minutes, 42 percent longer than the average 22-minute wait at the attraction in May through July 2016 and the 21.5-minute average of the same months of 2015.

Charts and Minds

Music has a symbiotic relationship with visual works. That movies and television can be enhanced and improved by music is obvious. Whether it's a Scorsese needle-drop, a jukebox musical, the song at the end of a prestigious television drama, or any musical cue that becomes permanently associated with an action sequence, movies and music have been linked since before movies even had talking.

That said, a star turn in a movie can completely change the fortunes of an ailing song.

Take, for instance, the Leonard Cohen song "Hallelujah." A very pretty song about a biblical sexual encounter, the song was released on the 1984 album *Various Positions* and was greeted with nearly no recognition or chart success. His record label initially refused to release it. A 1991 tribute album by John Cale would be a break for the song, but still not for the better part of a decade. However, in 2001, the animated film *Shrek* used the Cale composition during a pivotal sequence in the story, playing it pretty much unabridged for several minutes of the film immediately preceding the climax.

The popularity floodgates opened almost immediately. The song was a hit. The Rufus Wainwright version appears on the soundtrack, and suddenly licensing teams from *Scrubs* to *Cold Case* were bringing in "Hallelujah" for bummer moments that required the right kind of tender yet intense pathos.

The song has since gone on to be among the most popular songs in the canon, a staple of talent shows and a classic cover. Cohen's fans cataloged nearly six hundred covers of the song from 1985 to 2013, with the overwhelming majority—95 percent, to be precise—made post-*Shrek*.

"HALLELUJAH" COVERS

Shrek put the song ogre the top in popular consciousness

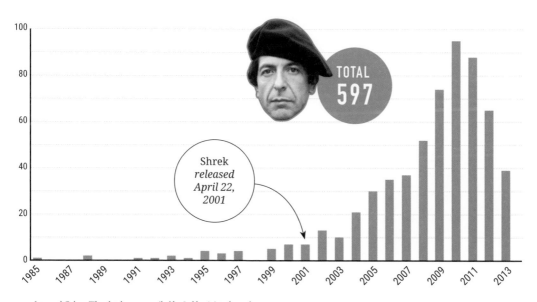

TOTAL
597

Shrek
*released
April 22,
2001*

Leonard Cohen Files database, compiled by Jarkko Arjatsalo et al.

SONG INFLUENCE IN MOVIES | By weekly Billboard Hot 100 rank

"Life Is a Highway"

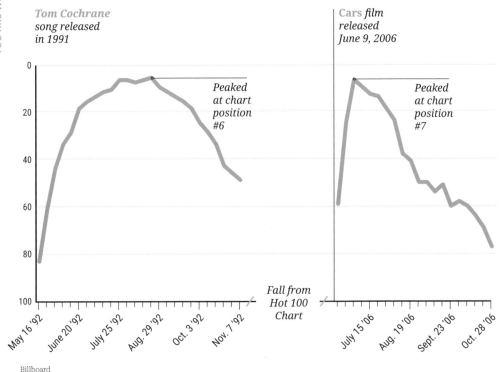

*Tom Cochrane
song released
in 1991*

*Cars film
released
June 9, 2006*

*Peaked
at chart
position
#6*

*Peaked
at chart
position
#7*

*Fall from
Hot 100
Chart*

Billboard

Although "Hallelujah" may be an especially striking example, given that a hideous ogre was responsible for its elevation to the status of a standard, songs that were forever boosted by movies are common once you know where to look.

They're also great for aging rockers in need of royalties. AC/DC's "Back in Black" hit the top ten of catalog albums in the weeks after it was featured in *Iron Man*. The *Cars* soundtracks breathed new life into Tom Cochrane's "Life Is a Highway." Guns N' Roses' "Welcome to the Jungle" was the sixth-best-selling rock song digitally the week after *Jumanji: Welcome to the Jungle* hit cinemas.

The Deadpool films are oddly good at elevating songs featured on their soundtracks.

DMX's "X Gon' Give It to Ya" peaked at number seven on the Rap Digital Sales chart after being featured in the first movie. It would remain on that chart for twenty-two weeks of 2016. Likewise, Juice Newton's "Angel of the Morning," which first charted on the Hot 100 upon its release in 1981 but appeared on the Country Digital Song Sales Chart for a week after its appearance in *Deadpool*'s opening title sequence.

And although a Bond song wouldn't hit number one in the UK until "Writing on the Wall," only two of them have ever missed entirely—"Moonraker" and "The Man with the Golden Gun" failed to seal the deal and chart at all. But every song of the Daniel Craig era managed to get to the top ten.

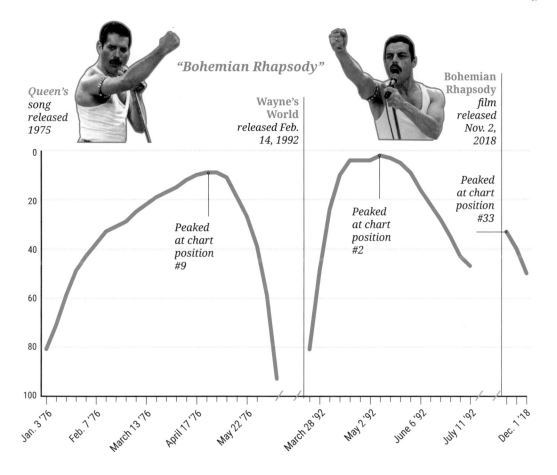

"Bohemian Rhapsody"

Queen's
song
released
1975

Wayne's
World
*released Feb.
14, 1992*

Bohemian
Rhapsody
*film
released
Nov. 2,
2018*

*Peaked
at chart
position
#9*

*Peaked
at chart
position
#2*

*Peaked
at chart
position
#33*

0

20

40

60

80

100

Jan. 3 '76   Feb. 7 '76   March 13 '76   April 17 '76   May 22 '76   March 28 '92   May 2 '92   June 6 '92   July 11 '92   Dec. 1 '18

One of the best examples of the way a movie can permanently alter the trajectory of a song is "Bohemian Rhapsody" by Queen, which has had three separate runs on Billboard's Hot 100 chart: first in 1976, when it peaked shortly after its release at number nine, once again in 1992, when it peaked at number two after *Wayne's World*, and then for three weeks in late 2018, when it peaked at number thirty-three after the release of the film *Bohemian Rhapsody*.

A film can even elevate an entire genre or era of music. Since vinyl became trendy again, one album in particular has stubbornly remained in the top-twenty-selling vinyl records since its release in 2014: *Guardians of the Galaxy: Awesome Mix Vol. 1*. It's one of the most persistent things in all of music: From 2014 to 2020, it appeared in the top ten for at least a week. It managed to be the second-best-selling vinyl record for at least one week of 2015, 2017, 2018, 2019, and 2020, not to mention introducing an entire generation to bands like Blue Swede. The film's sequel managed to get Electric Light Orchestra's "Mr. Blue Sky" to Billboard's Hot Rock Songs list for eight weeks, the first time it charted since 1978, and boosted Fleetwood Mac's "The Chain" up to number seven on that same list.

GHOST IN THE MACHINE

As so much cultural consumption moves online, it's nevertheless naïve to think that memes and internet forces will entirely replace movies, television, and music as cultural touch points. Indeed, it doesn't even bear out when looking at memes. In late 2021, I scraped the 4,631 internet memes that had been verified by Know Your Meme. I then categorized the stated origin of each, be it a sui generis meme that arose from internet culture, something spawned from film or TV, an import (typically from Japan), or from music, gaming, or news.

Of primary interest were the memes from traditional pop culture outlets, things like movies and video games, book and comics, or television and cartoons. Of the 4,471 with some kind of verifiable origin, 1,452 of them, or around 32.4 percent, pulled from some element of traditional pop culture. Far from rendering typical forms of pop culture vestigial, internet culture is built on a foundation of SpongeBob, Leonardo DiCaprio expressions, and obscure gaming references.

MEMES

32.4%
Pop Culture Derived

67.6%
Non-Pop Culture Derived

Know Your Meme list of verified memes

Wrinkles in Time

Beyond the quixotic appeal of cute dogs and oddball sports, the simple act of consuming media versus not consuming media has significant consequences for people.

Those who are anti-TV tend to say things like "Television rots your brain" or that watching something can make you less smart. The reality is less complicated: Time is a limited commodity to humans and therefore valuable, and media consumption is but a single use of it. There are situations where the time spent on media is better than the alternative, like if the three hours you spent going to see a movie would otherwise have been spent eating high-cholesterol foods or binge drinking alcoholic seltzer. Conversely, there are

surely situations where time spent on media is worse than the alternative (like when you watch a bunch of Miyazaki movies instead of writing your book). But generally, when people critique media use, they make the fallacious assumption that the time spent consuming media would otherwise have been spent on something more noble or edifying, like feeding orphans, going to church, volunteering, or learning new skills. But that's an obviously false equivalence based on opinion or desire: To understand what media does to us, we need to contrast it with actual alternatives.

We tend to be particularly animated about this fallacy when we talk about what we think kids should be doing with their time.

For instance, playing video games is held up as wasteful, useless, and distressing for children. Inevitably, the time spent playing online games with friends is compared with time that could have been spent on schoolwork. But in reality, it's probably replacing not schoolwork but other social activities, or even nonsocial activities like watching television.

What's more, consuming media can have a positive impact on kids. We know this because, although we take it for granted now, there was a time when televisions were not in every home in the developed world. One study from around this time looked at test scores in Canada as different cities began to get television reception at different times as it gradually rolled out across the country. What the study revealed was remarkable: Rather than making kids less intelligent, there was strong evidence against the idea that television in any way caused cognitive harm or hampered educational development. Instead, they actually saw a slight increase in adolescent test scores, which researchers speculated could be attributed to each additional year of pre-K television.

The fear that the introduction of television will set kids back is not new, nor is it new knowledge that it's false: A 1961 study looked at two towns in Western Canada, one with television and one without. In the town with television, kids in first grade watched one hour and forty minutes of TV per day. Where'd the time come from? They spent 35 fewer minutes listening to the radio, 33 fewer minutes at play, 20 fewer minutes watching movies and reading, and 13 fewer minutes sleeping. Homework didn't take a hit.

To be sure, there are lots of specific ways that kids get changed by movies, and the depiction of various things within them can make a difference, some good and some bad.

At its very best, media can make people more sympathetic to those who are different from them. One study asked 1,142 people to weigh in about their views on torture, executing terrorists, and how they felt about Muslims, gays, and others. The number of Harry Potter movies seen was linked to more tolerant views toward minority groups and opposition to punitive policies, an effect that was even stronger when looking at the number of Harry Potter books that a respondent had read.

But it's also dreadfully hard to link some of those portrayals to cause and effect. For example, did the number of films with sexual content seen at a young age actually cause an observed increase in the average number of lifetime sexual partners? Or was the life experience of growing up in an environment where such films were permissible the cause? Sometimes the data all points in a clear direction: We do know smoking in movies is linked to adolescent smoking. The challenge is always getting beyond "linked to." Unless you're designing double-blind experiments where you show some kids only versions of movies with smoking and other kids versions of movies without it, and then counting up the number of smokers, getting to causation is hard.

We know that media can change or reinforce people's views based on their preconceptions and affinities for the views espoused, and make those inclinations stronger and more animated. We also know that consuming media takes time. That time can be spent on other things, but when you are sitting idly, being catered to, you cannot actually do those things. Recall, you are far too busy watching the thing that animates your views to act on your views.

What we spend our time on has a great impact on who we are. Sure, you can tune in every night to shows that make you mad about the news or scroll for hours on apps designed to make you do just that. But when it comes to pop culture like movies and shows and concerts and the people who deliberately and conscientiously go out of their way to engage with them, the results are rarely that grim.

A 2019 study looked at 6,710 adults aged fifty or older who first provided baseline data in 2004 and 2005. In general, the people who went to cultural events more often had better health outcomes: Of the 1,906 who attended some kind of performance every couple of months, 355 were dead at the end of the study, compared with the 1,762 who never went to such events, of whom 837 died over the same time frame.

When researchers controlled for demographic information, socioeconomic status, and health status, as well as several behavioral and social factors, they found that, yeah, regardless of those things, going out to consume culture was linked to better health outcomes. Those who went once or twice a year had a 14 percent lower risk of dying during the follow-up period. Those who went every few months had a 31 percent lower risk of death. And although time will always catch us in the end, "lifelong cinephile" sure sounds a lot better in an obituary than "committed social media user."

Crimefighters

Media exposure has one pretty obvious relationship to crime. Namely, it convinces people there's a whole lot of it.

Whether it's the "if it bleeds, it leads" style of local news, our very human obsession with the things that can kill us, or entire television shows and podcasts devoted to crime mysteries, it's a reliable conclusion of Americans that crimes are common and happening right around the corner, and that the crime rate is constantly going up.

But the thing is, it's not. The crime rate hasn't gone up substantially for decades. Nevertheless, most people think crime is always going up. It's entirely perception and not grounded in reality—and the media ecosphere bears some responsibility.

Pretty much annually since 1989, Gallup has asked Americans a simple question: "Is there more crime in the US than there was a year ago, or less?" And every single year a majority of Americans have said they believe crime is up. And we're not talking about a tiny majority, either; since 2010, the number of respondents who believe crime is rising has never been below 60 percent. And on average, 67 percent of Americans said crime was up, 19 percent said it was down, and 8 percent said it was the same.

Overwhelmingly, Americans were wrong. Of the twenty-six surveys across thirty-one years, the crime rate had actually gone up just five times.

We can probably blame "the media!" for making us think there's more crime than there is, but one thing we actually can't blame them for is violent movies and video games and violent everything else actually provoking violence.

In truth, violent movies *reduce* crime.

"We said, *I wonder if it's really true that watching a violent movie actually translates into worse behavior.*"

A pair of economists, Gordon Dahl from the University of California, San Diego, and Stefano DellaVigna at the University of California, Berkeley, decided to put a simple question to the test: Does watching violent movies encourage people to do actual violence? They collected movies released in cinemas from 1995 to 2004 and pulled in data from a group that advised parents about movie content by labeling films as nonviolent, mildly violent, or violent.

They had an early break in constructing their natural experiment, the kind where a researcher observes that real-world conditions have incidentally set up a control group and an experimental group and uses that for a study. The good news for them was that violent movies are not released on the same weekend every year. This allowed them to compare what happened in a weekend when there was a big release of a violent film with that same weekend in other years when there wasn't.

Looking at box office receipts, they were able to estimate that about 25 million Americans were fans of movies with mild violence in them, and about 12 million people liked strongly violent movies. Given the size of the audience, they thought, that kind of massive

PERCEIVED CRIME

Is there more crime in the US than there was a year ago, or less?

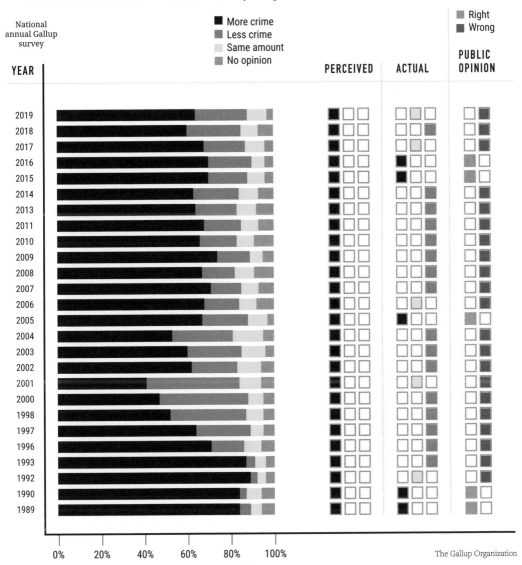

National annual Gallup survey

■ More crime
■ Less crime
□ Same amount
■ No opinion

■ Right
■ Wrong

| YEAR | | PERCEIVED | ACTUAL | PUBLIC OPINION |

The Gallup Organization

human arousal and aggression would surely show up statistically in crime data if indeed violent movies contribute to violent crime.

A multitude of factors make someone more likely to commit an assault, but they typically come down to three things: They are young, they are male, and they are drunk. This is why lots of crime prevention is designed to offer men who are young and possibly drinking another thing to do, like a night basketball league or a church or community event. Movies are another appealing option, because to watch one you have to sit in an alcohol-less cinema for three hours. And lighter fare isn't going to cut it with the target demographic. As a result, strongly violent movies are a great way to compel millions of people who would otherwise be out possibly getting into trouble to get their butts in seats.

"To be honest, we didn't know what we'd find," said Dahl. "Our idea was really 'Oh, we're probably going to see an increase in crime.' And that's exactly *opposite* of what we found."

The effect was, in fact, huge. Dahl and DellaVigna paired crime data with the releases of violent films and found a clear relationship between audience turnout for violent and strongly violent movies and marked decreases in crime. They determined that violent movies deterred about a thousand assaults on an average weekend, with no observed medium-term effects. (The effect of large releases for nonviolent movies was insignificant.)

Between the hours of 6:00 p.m. and midnight, for every million people watching a strongly violent movie, the number of violent crimes decreased 1.3 percent; for every million people watching a mildly violent movie, the rate declined 1.1 percent.

"When you're in a movie theater, it's actually a quite safe environment—there are other people sitting there. One of the things about assaults is they happen in environments that aren't as controlled," explained Dahl. "So, we thought, 'Oh, this is sort of like incapacitation,' if you put someone in a movie theater, they commit less assault because they can't really assault someone while they're in a movie theater."

Incapacitation is one of the central ideas in the economic theory of crime, which was partially developed by Nobel Laureate Gary Becker. It's pretty simple: When you put people in prison, besides any higher idea of rehabilitation, you do it in part because they are criminally incapacitated, and therefore unable to do more crimes outside their incarceration. But what makes Dahl and DellaVigna's finding so striking is that with violent movies the incapacitation is *voluntary*.

It goes further. The two economists then turned their attention to crime data between the hours of midnight and 6:00 a.m. after those movie nights. The idea was that there might

be an increase in violent crime once those moviegoers left the movie. This is, after all, what lab experiments about violent movies indicate: Violently primed people will do violent things.

"Turns out the opposite happens," said Dahl. "What happens instead is that violent crime goes down *a lot* from midnight to 6:00 a.m. following the movie."

For every million people who saw a strongly violent movie at the cinema, the rate of violent crime went down 1.9 percent in the six hours after midnight, and for every million people watching a mildly violent movie, the rate dipped 2.1 percent.

That larger decrease after midnight might be puzzling until you remember the risk factors of committing violent acts: young, male, and *drunk*. The scenario is easy enough to imagine: Two dudes, neither of whom have yet learned how to process strong emotions in a constructive way; one decides to see *Murdersuck 4: Buckets of Blood*, the other goes to the bar. They meet up after the movie at 11:00 p.m. for drinks. One has a blood-alcohol content (BAC) of 0.00, the other's is around 0.07. They both proceed to have four drinks over the next three hours. It's now 2:00 a.m., and someone walks into the bar and starts getting seriously rude to the people with whom these two guys have been talking. Our moviegoer now has a BAC of about 0.07; his buddy is clocking in at 0.14. Which dude do you think is gonna throw the punch?

We can link this to alcohol because the reduction in crime from midnight to 6:00 a.m. after a violent movie is two to three times larger among the group aged twenty-one to twenty-four compared with the group aged seventeen to twenty. The latter can't spend the alternative time in bars.

All this to say that in a given year, the release of strongly violent movies has a net effect of about 52,000 assaults just not happening. Besides the human impact, that saves about $695 million in averted victimization costs, all because 4 to 8 percent of the US population saw a violent movie *instead* of getting drunk and committing assaults.

Self-sequestration is the ideal: Given alternatives, people willingly choose to do the less risky thing. Ideally the movie's not a gorefest, but on net even that is better than the alternative.

"It looks like the incapacitation effect dominates any of what sometimes people call the arousal effect that gets you worked up," said Dahl. "It's not true that there's *no* arousal effect; it just turns out the incapacitation and choice of activity dominate any arousal effect."

By this metric, *Joker* is probably a better crime fighter than Bruce Wayne.

This applies just as much, if not more, to video games. Containing people with impulse control problems—young, drunk men—on Xbox Live makes them less likely to do something stupid to someone else and jeopardize their futures. From a public health standpoint, violent media is a service to their communities. It gets at the same idea behind why television is not all bad for kids—namely, comparing the violent media consumption not to, say, volunteering at a soup kitchen, but instead to the actual control group, which may be pounding whiskeys at happy hour.

Constant portrayals of violence in the media are likely a contributing factor to why a large majority of Americans think violent crime is up year after year. But the bargain, at least as it exists with Hollywood, is that they can make enormously successful violent movies and society as a whole will tense up a little about it and despair at the state of our collective morality. But at the end of the day those violent movies actually reduce the rate at which people commit violent acts. There are worse ways to spend a Friday.

The Big Guns

The filmmakers behind *One Hundred and One Dalmatians* likely didn't intend to fuss with the entire canine economy decades later, nor did the twisted mind of Wes Craven set out to reduce crime in major American cities. But sometimes, a movie comes around and fundamentally alters a real-world relationship via pop culture, so much so that the world itself begins to change, adapt, and pursue representations in pop culture to suit its aims.

And what better place to start than with what happened at the Pentagon after *Top Gun* came out.

The US military is not exactly a stranger in the movie business. They assisted in the first film to ever win an Academy Award for Best Picture, *Wings*. During World War II, the US military walked in lockstep with Hollywood—Donald Duck's stint with the navy had genuine homeland propaganda intentions—and Hollywood made all sorts of screwball comedies like *Caught in the Draft*, *You're in the Army Now*, and *Boobs in Arms* to make getting drafted seem like a good time. But after WWII, the military was chided by US senators after diverting resources to help film 1962's *The Longest Day*, a D-Day movie with extensive materials and personnel from the military, during the Berlin Crisis. Further, director Darryl Zanuck refused to delete dialogue the military found distasteful in the final cut. Taking flak from both sides, Pentagon brass licked their wounds and in 1964 rolled out a guide for all future collaborations between Hollywood and the Department of Defense, which mandated that the US Armed Forces wouldn't collaborate on films where they didn't also get full script approval.

Given the Vietnam War and the politics of a rising tide of Hollywood directors, the US military didn't end up collaborating on much for quite some time. And for the two decades afterward, the portrayal of the Pentagon was not particularly positive. They did help with the jingoistic John Wayne flick *The Green Berets* in 1968, but needless to say didn't collaborate with the makers of *The Deer Hunter*, *Apocalypse Now*, *First Blood*, or *Full Metal Jacket*.

Then came *Top Gun*.

In May 1984, Jerry Bruckheimer sent a script to the navy about a thrilling story of modern

TOP GUN RECIEPTS

Paramount spent more on Tom Cruise than every plane, carrier, and base in *Top Gun*

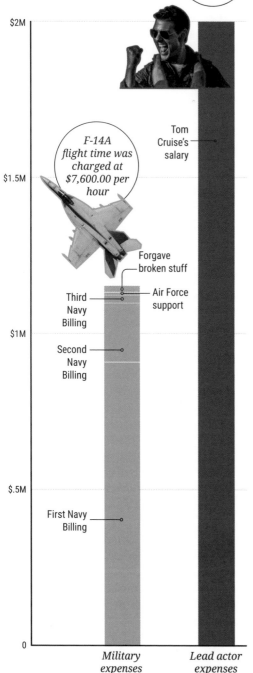

Top Gun box office was $357.1 million

F-14A flight time was charged at $7,600.00 per hour

Tom Cruise's salary

Forgave broken stuff

Air Force support

Third Navy Billing

Second Navy Billing

First Navy Billing

Military expenses | Lead actor expenses

Pentagon documents obtained by Tom Secker, SpyCulture.com

fighter pilots. The request: Planes are really expensive; boy, would it be great if we could borrow some of yours.

A November letter from John E. Horton, then the Pentagon's liaison with Hollywood, laid out the price.

"Generally, the reaction to the script is positive with the belief that produced with care and interpretation as a positive patriotic film that you have stated you desire, the film could be beneficial to the Navy," he wrote.

But there would have to be changes. The love interest of Tom Cruise, the female. There's concern that she's also in the navy, could they change that? The hard drinking of the fighter pilots, could that be toned down? Also, here are 22 specific changes on specific pages that we would like to change.

This wasn't the first bit of feedback, nor would it be the last. For instance, consider the nationality of the pilots flying the MiGs, Russian-made fighter jets. In the script, they're North Korean. A memo to the public affairs office from Wallace O. Knowles, then the assistant for Korea, on the subject of "Top Guns Movie Scenario" [*sic*] reads as follows:

"I have reviewed the attached scenario and because of ongoing efforts to reduce tensions between the two Koreas cannot concur in identifying North Korea in the film as the aggressor nation. The NESA region does not object to identifying Libya as the aggressor nation."

But the best part isn't the typed portion of this memo. Written in pen and ink, "does not object" has been scratched out. Below it, in handwritten script, reads, "No need to highlight Libya or give Qadhafi any ideas!! We don't want to highlight him or his actions, real or fictional," and it is signed by country director for Libya. A fictional country is recommended, and lo and behold, the bad guy in *Top Gun* is suddenly mysterious.

Satisfied, the US military then allocated aircraft carriers, planes, bases, even personnel to appear on-camera for weeks of shooting. They billed Paramount, but not excessively; often it was just the basic hourly rate. All told, Paramount paid the Pentagon $1,100,686.95 for every pixel of Department of Defense equipment on-screen. Tom Cruise, by comparison, made $2 million for his time.

But everyone got what they wanted. Paramount scored a hit and didn't have to buy any planes to get it. The navy experienced a recruiting bonanza: After the film's release, recruitment reportedly increased measurably. Beyond just a win, the Pentagon also got a playbook.

"For the first time in many, many years, you could make a movie that was positive about the military, [and] actors could portray military personnel who were well motivated, well intentioned, and not see their careers suffer as a consequence," said Phil Strub, the now-retired longtime liaison between the Pentagon and Hollywood, in a 1997 documentary.

Suddenly, Hollywood was eager to work with the Department of Defense because it meant they could slash a fortune off their budgets for prestige war movies. The Pentagon was likewise thrilled, because they now had

leverage over the studios and could rewrite how they were represented on-screen.

It's now incredibly common for the Pentagon to impact scripts.

"Before we did this work, most academics I knew estimated about 200," said Roger Stahl, a University of Georgia researcher who studies the military's influence on movies. "But now we know it's around 4,500, and the numbers [are] probably going to go up if we count individual television episodes. The estimate [including TV] is 10,000—it might be higher than that."

But why?

"The Pentagon claims that it does not do effects-based research on its public relations activities with regard to television and Hollywood," Stahl said. "They've said this over and over again, and actually when we go into the archives and make FOIA requests for this kind of thing, nothing comes up. After *Top Gun*, they did one study, and this is the one they will cop to, not because they know it's available, because they didn't really know it was available. But it's probably the only one they ever did."

There are a number of advantages to weighing in on movies. The Pentagon has long claimed that it doesn't do research on the impact of military films it helps make, but on the most basic level, it increases accuracy. It can also help the military change the narrative around missions: Stahl points to *Black Hawk Down*, which centers on a controversial incident that resulted in the deaths of a number of US service members in a botched mission in Mogadishu, Somalia. The movie reframes it as a successful rescue. Movies can similarly downplay or reinterpret other historical incidents that negatively define the actions of the US military, like a request to remove references to the bombings of Hiroshima and Nagasaki in the 2014 *Godzilla* film. As with *Top Gun* or any number of Transformers movies, they can also drum up recruitment. Stahl added that the conditional offer of support lets the military stymie references to things like PTSD, suicide, and sexual assault in media it officially supports.

MILITARY BACKING OF MOVIES
Films and what the Pentagon said about them

■ No Assistance Requested
■ Assistance Declined
■ Assistance Approved
■ Assistance Enthusiastically Approved

COCOON

"THE FILM PORTRAYED THE AIR FORCE
UNREALISTICALLY, THE IMAGE OF THE AIR FORCE
WAS PORTRAYED UNPROFESSIONALLY, AND THIRDLY,
THE BASIC STORYLINE IS CONTRARY TO AIR
FORCE POLICY ON UFO'S-THE AIR FORCE HAS
ALWAYS REFUSED TO PROVIDE ASSISTANCE TO
STORIES THAT SHOW UFOS AS REAL INCLUDING
CLOSE ENCOUNTERS OF THE THIRD KIND AND *STAR
MAN*.

ROCK, THE

"JERRY BRUCKHEIMER AND MICHAEL BAY PROBABLY
KNEW THEY COULD NOT OBTAIN ASSISTANCE FOR A
SCRIPT WHICH SHOWS A RETIRED MARINE GENERAL
THREATENING TO DESTROY SAN FRANCI5CO WITH
A ROCKET LAUNCHED FROM ALCATRAZ. FULL OF
HOLES. AS WITH *TWILIGHT'S LAST GLEAMING*,
ABSURD TO THINK A GENERAL WOULD PUT HIMSELF
IN A POSITION WITH NO WAY OUT. ABSURD, BUT
SOMETIMES EXCITING. NEGATIVE, INACCURATE.
IMPOSSIBLE TO ALTER BY ANY MEANS OTHER THAN
TOTAL REWRITE AND COMPLETELY NEW FILM."

FIRST BLOOD

"DECLINED TO ASSIST BECAUSE MILITARY
PORTRAYALS WERE TOTALLY NEGATIVE AND
INACCURATE."

SEVEN DAYS IN MAY

"THE PENTAGON DENIED ALL ASSISTANCE IN
LIGHT OF STORY OF CHAIRMAN OF THE JOINT
CHIEFS OF STAFF PLANNING A COUP BECAUSE
PRESIDENT SIGNED A DISARMAMENT TREATY.
HOWEVER, FILMMAKERS TALKED THEIR WAY
ABOARD AN AIRCRAFT CARRIER IN SAN DIEGO TO
OBTAIN SHOTS TO CREATE AMBIANCE OF CARRIER.
PRODUCER ADMITTED BUT CLAIMED NAVY SHOULD
HAVE INFORMED ALL SHIPS NOT TO LET HIM."

HONEY, I BLEW UP THE BABY

"DOD ATTEMPTED TO REMOVE THE DEPICTION OF
MILITARY HELICOPTER PILOTS FOLLOWING THE
MURDEROUS ORDERS OF A CIVILIAN SCIENTIST BAD
GUY. HOWEVER, DOD ABILITY TO INFLUENCE THE
SCRIPT WENT AWAY WHEN IT WAS INFORMED THAT
ITS ASSISTANCE WAS NO LONGER REQUIRED."

OFFICER AND A GENTLEMAN, AN

"THE NAVY DECLINED BECAUSE OF DAMAGING
PORTRAYAL OF NAVY SINGLE PARENT LIFESTYLE,
NEGATIVE PORTRAYAL OF WOMEN LIVING AROUND
AIR STATION, AND A FIGHT BETWEEN OFFICER
CANDIDATE AND DRILL INSTRUCTOR. FILMMAKERS
WOULDN'T CHANGE THESE SCENES, SO ASSISTANCE
BECAME IMPOSSIBLE."

SAVING PRIVATE RYAN

"TECHNICAL ERRORS INCLUDING REALITY THAT
THE PENTAGON COULD NOT HAVE LEARNED TWO
DAYS AFTER D-DAY THAT TWO RYAN BROTHERS
HAD DIED ON D-DAY. ARMY HAD NO EQUIPMENT
DATING FROM WORLD WAR II. SPIELBERG USED
IRISH ARMY FOR LANDINGS AND SUBSEQUENT
SCENES SHOT IN ENGLAND."

STAND, THE

"THE PRODUCER HOPED THAT THE NATURE OF
THE STORY, WHICH DEPICTED THE ARMY
ACCIDENTALLY RELEASING A GAS THAT ALMOST
KILLS EVERYONE IN AMERICA, WOULD NOT DETER
THE DOD FROM FAVORABLY CONSIDERING HIS
REQUEST FOR ASSISTANCE. DECLINED ASSISTANCE.
NO FILE EXISTS."

INDEPENDENCE DAY

"NO COOPERATION DUE TO IMPLAUSIBLE PORTRAYAL
OF MILITARY AND STORY CENTERED ON ALIENS
ATTACKING FROM SPACE AND ANEMIC US MILITARY
RESPONSE. BECAME OBVIOUS THAT THE COMPANY
WAS GOING TO GO ITS OWN WAY AND MAKE THE
PICTURE WITHOUT US."

Pentagon documents obtained by Tom Secker, SpyCulture.com

FORREST GUMP

"EARLY SCRIPT HAD NIHILISTIC VIEW OF
MILITARY & VIETNAM EXPERIENCE ARMY & WE SAID
NO THANKS. THE FILMMAKERS DID MAKE ONE VERY
IMPORTANT CHANGE SUGGESTED BY THE ARMY;
ORIGINAL SCRIPT HAD A ENTIRE COMPANY OF MEN
LIKE FORREST AND BUBBA; ARMY POINTED OUT THAT
THE ACTUAL PROGRAM DISTRIBUTED SOLDIERS LIKE
FORREST AMONG 'NORMAL' SOLDIERS IN
MANY COMPANIES."

SLEEPLESS IN SEATTLE

"PRODUCTION COMPANY REQUESTED USE OF NAVY
HANGAR IN SEATTLE AREA, FOR USE AS A
PRODUCTION FACILITY. CONSIDERING HANGAR WILL
SOON BE TURNED OVER TO THE STATE, WE AGREED,
ALTHOUGH THERE IS NO MILITARY THEME TO THE
PICTURE AT ALL."

STAR TREK IV

"APPROVED US OF NAVY'S *U.S.S. RANGER*. IN THE
BEST INTEREST OF THE DEPARTMENT NAVY HAD SOME
CONCERN ABOUT *ENTERPRISE* CREW MEMBERS GETTING
INTO SECURE LOCATIONS UNTIL REMINDED THAT A
TRANSPORTER WOULD DELIVER CREW AND SO NOT BE
A SECURITY VIOLATION."

JURASSIC PARK III

"SCRIPT FEATURED A 'BAD' MILITARY FORCE
THAT EVENTUALLY FOUGHT DINOSAURS OR ATTEMPTED
TO DO SO. SCRIPT REWRITTEN AT OUR SUGGESTION
TO ELIMINATE ALL MILITARY REFERENCES, SINCE
NO POSITIVE MILITARY PORTRAYAL SEEMED
FEASIBLE. THEN THE PRODUCTION COMPANY
EXPRESSED AN INTEREST IN WRITING A MILITARY
RESCUE SCENE. ULTIMATELY WE CAME UP WITH A
MUTUALLY AGREEABLE SCENARIO. DOD APPROVED
FILMING IN HAWAII WITH NAVY HELICOPTERS,
MARINE CORPS AMPHIBIOUS ASSAULT VEHICLES,
AND MILITARY EXTRAS."

GOLDENEYE

"APPROVED REQUEST FOR MARINES AND NATL GUARD
HELICOPTERS TO COME TO THE RESCUE OF JAMES
BOND AT CONCLUSION OF THIS FILM. NO FILE.
REASONABLY REALISTIC & POSITIVE, IF BRIEF."

HAIR

"ARMY ORIGINALLY REFUSED TO EVEN CONSIDER
COOPERATION, EQUATING FILM SCRIPT WITH
ORIGINAL PLAY. IN FACT, SCRIPT ENTIRELY
DIFFERENT. PRODUCERS REFUSED TO TAKE NO FOR
AN ANSWER AND APPROACHED THE SECRETARY OF THE
ARMY FOR HELP. DOD (NORM HATCH) SAID STORY
WAS VERY 'RELIGIOUS.' ULTIMATELY CALIFORNIA
NATIONAL GUARD PROVIDED A CLOSED BASE AND A
PLANE FOR A FEW SCENES."

SILENCE OF THE LAMBS, THE

"IT WAS THOUGHT THAT THE DEPICTION OF A
PRISONER TRANSFER IN A MILITARY HANGAR FOR
SECURITY PURPOSES WAS REASONABLY ACCURATE AND
POSITIVE. AIR NATIONAL GUARD ASSISTED."

HUNT FOR RED OCTOBER, THE

"THE SCRIPT WAS VERY POSITIVE FOR THE NAVY.
ASSISTANCE INCLUDED USE OF AIRCRAFT, AN
AIRCRAFT CARRIER, A SURFACE WARSHIP (USED
TO DEPICT THE *RED OCTOBER* ENGINE ROOM) AND
A NUCLEAR ATTACK SUBMARINE."

CAPTAIN AMERICA: THE WINTER SOLDIER

"THE NATIONAL GUARD ALLOWED MARVEL TO BUILD
A FEW SETS IN A SECLUDED AREA OF THE 22,000
ACRE ARMY NATIONAL GUARD BASE. IN RETURN, THE
GUARD RECEIVED SIGNIFICANT PORTRAYAL IN THE
FILM. AS ALWAYS, THERE WAS NO COST TO THE
GOVERNMENT, AND WHEN FILMING WAS COMPLETED,
MARVEL TORE DOWN THE SETS AND RESTORED THE
INSTALLATION BACK TO ITS ORIGINAL CONDITION."

BLACK HAWK DOWN

"ULTIMATELY THE DEPLOYMENT WAS APPROVED
PERSONALLY BY THE CHAIRMAN OF THE JOINT
CHIEFS OF STAFF (GEN. HENRY SHELTON) AND THE
SECRETARY OF DEFENSE (HON. DONALD RUMSFELD).
THE 8 AIRCRAFT CAME FROM THE US ARMY SPECIAL
OPERATIONS COMMAND AND CONSISTED OF 4 MH-60
AND 4 AH/MH-& LITTLE BIROS, THE RANGERS, AND
UP TO APPROX. SIXTY SUPPORT AND COMMAND AND
CONTROL PERSONNEL DEPLOYED FOR
APPROX. 2 MONTHS."

This can manifest in ways large and small.

In *Iron Man*, for instance, Phil Strub and director Jon Favreau reportedly got into a heated argument after an actor playing a general told Colonel James Rhodes, future War Machine, "Any one of those guys would kill themselves for the opportunities you have."

"They don't want any suggestion of suicide," said Stahl. "They just don't want to bring it up."

Sometimes, issues can lead them to forgo any support whatsoever. Ridley Scott wanted the Pentagon help to make *G.I. Jane*, but the film posed an issue for the navy, specifically some language they considered sexist coming from a commanding officer.

And it's hardly just the Pentagon. The CIA, though late to the game, began to advise on movies in the 1990s, after the conclusion of the Cold War. The timing was not a coincidence: The '90s were a time of turbulence for the agency, which had long been defined in opposition to an enemy that no longer existed. Seeing advantage in collaborating with Hollywood but lacking the spiffy hardware that served as the Pentagon's chief bargaining chip, the CIA went a different route: They started pitching.

Tricia Jenkins is a professor at Texas Christian University who studies how different

Ben Affleck as CIA Agent Tony Mendez (Argo, 2012).

government institutions, including the CIA, work with the movie business.

"The CIA was pretty much the last major governmental organization to develop an entertainment industry liaison program," said Jenkins. "FBI has been doing this stuff since like the '30s and '40s; DOD, pretty much since the inception of the film industry. But the CIA doesn't develop a formal mechanism to work with film and television makers until 1996."

Obviously the CIA was, shall we say, somewhat more hands-on in terms of mass media in other countries. Yet lacking the military's leverage in hardware, the agency's liaisons would scour the film trades—*The Hollywood Reporter*, *Variety*—looking for references to movies entering production that might have something to do with intelligence or spycraft. Then the agency would reach out, explain what the office did in connecting actual spies with the production to up the veracity, and try to get a conversation going.

When Kathryn Bigelow began planning *Zero Dark Thirty*, the CIA suddenly volunteered people associated with the Osama bin Laden raid, offering the kind of information that hadn't yet hit the press. Chase Brandon, the agency's first entertainment liaison officer, reportedly worked closely with Robert Towne, who wrote early Mission: Impossible scripts.

And although recruitment is certainly part of it, Brandon once quipped, "What really drives us, more than anything else, is that we finally got tired of being universally cast as bad people."

Consider, for example, why the agency was so helpful on a movie like *Argo*. Across thousands of emails between the production staff—including Ben Affleck himself—and the CIA, they offer consistent and rather forthcoming feedback on the props, settings, and actions of those involved. Part of this, no doubt, is that *Argo* makes the agency look brilliant. But all the cooperation is also in no small part surely because of the movie's starting point, which is immediately *after* one of the most disastrous intelligence failures in the history of American foreign policy, the one that allowed the US embassy in Tehran to get overtaken in the first place.

The perks for the CIA in being on-screen are not just about highlighting its successes. In a 2010 interview, Michael Frost Beckner, who created the show *The Agency*, related that Brandon, the agency's entertainment liaison, would call to offer ideas about biometric identification, futuristic technology that was, admittedly, a little too high-tech for the era.

"Put it in there, whether we have it or not," Brandon reportedly said. "These people [terrorists] watch TV, too. It'll scare them."

This is not to say that the relationship flows only in one direction.

When interviewing CIA legend Tony Mendez—the agent Ben Affleck plays in *Argo*—for her dissertation, Jenkins wanted to know if the agency ever got any ideas from movies. Mendez recalled that, after the Bond flick *A View to a Kill* came out in 1985 and featured then-fictional facial recognition tech, CIA Director Bill Casey asked his technicians to whip it up for him.

Robert Wallace, who retired from the CIA Office of Technical Service, once recalled, "Whenever a new Bond movie was released, we always got calls asking, 'Do you have one of those?' If I answered no, the next question was 'How long will it take you to make it?'"

Not Quite Rocket Science

Felicity Mellor is a theoretical physicist in the UK. In graduate school, as part of her doctoral research she was looking at the internal structure of black holes. When her adviser, a Star Trek fan, described the work to a journalist at *New Scientist*, he mentioned that there was a time travel implication. Naturally, this was at a theoretical level, in the sense that the internal math of the objects Mellor was studying didn't yet rule out time loops.

New Scientist wrote up the time travel bit, then newspapers picked it up, and then suddenly Mellor was beset with callers asking about the time machine she'd built in her lab.

"I've just shuffled around a few equations," she said. "And it had nothing to do with the real world whatsoever."

Mellor now studies and teaches how scientists communicate with the general public. And so much of that communication relates to pop culture, she says, because it can be a struggle to communicate the fantastical to a lay audience.

This tenuous relationship between the scientific community and the entertainment world is one of the most consequential information flows in all of media. For all their many faults, movies are incredible platforms that are able to raise awareness about under-covered scientific issues, scare up funding for research, and act as vehicles to argue for your views and beliefs as a scientist. How researchers and scientists navigate that need to be straightforward about science while also making their work appealing to a wider audience has implications not only for how science works in the cinema, but the very future of the fields represented on screen.

* * *

The history of space exploration is told in daring rocket launches, life-or-death problem solving, and heroic touchdowns on foreign objects moving at incredible speeds, but the prehistory of space exploration was won in the minds of the public. Even before there was a NASA, popular culture and science fiction was absolutely central in getting Americans to think of space exploration as a feasible and worthwhile goal. In the 1940s, rockets were best known for their work leveling large portions of London. The prospect of using intercontinental ballistic missiles to get human beings into space? It wasn't an entirely attractive prospect, and to call Americans skeptical was an understatement. A 1949 Gallup Poll

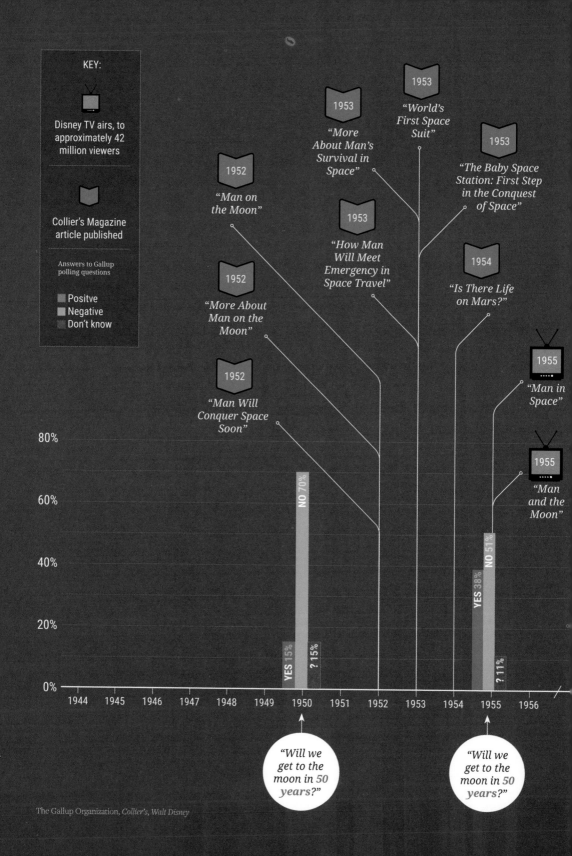

Sputnik 1 launches

Apollo 11 reaches the moon

ROCKET LAUNCHES DIDN'T GET AMERICA TO BELIEVE IN SPACE EXPLORATION, MEDIA DID

Before the US successfully launched rockets into orbit, magazines and television shows got the country to believe in the possibilities of space

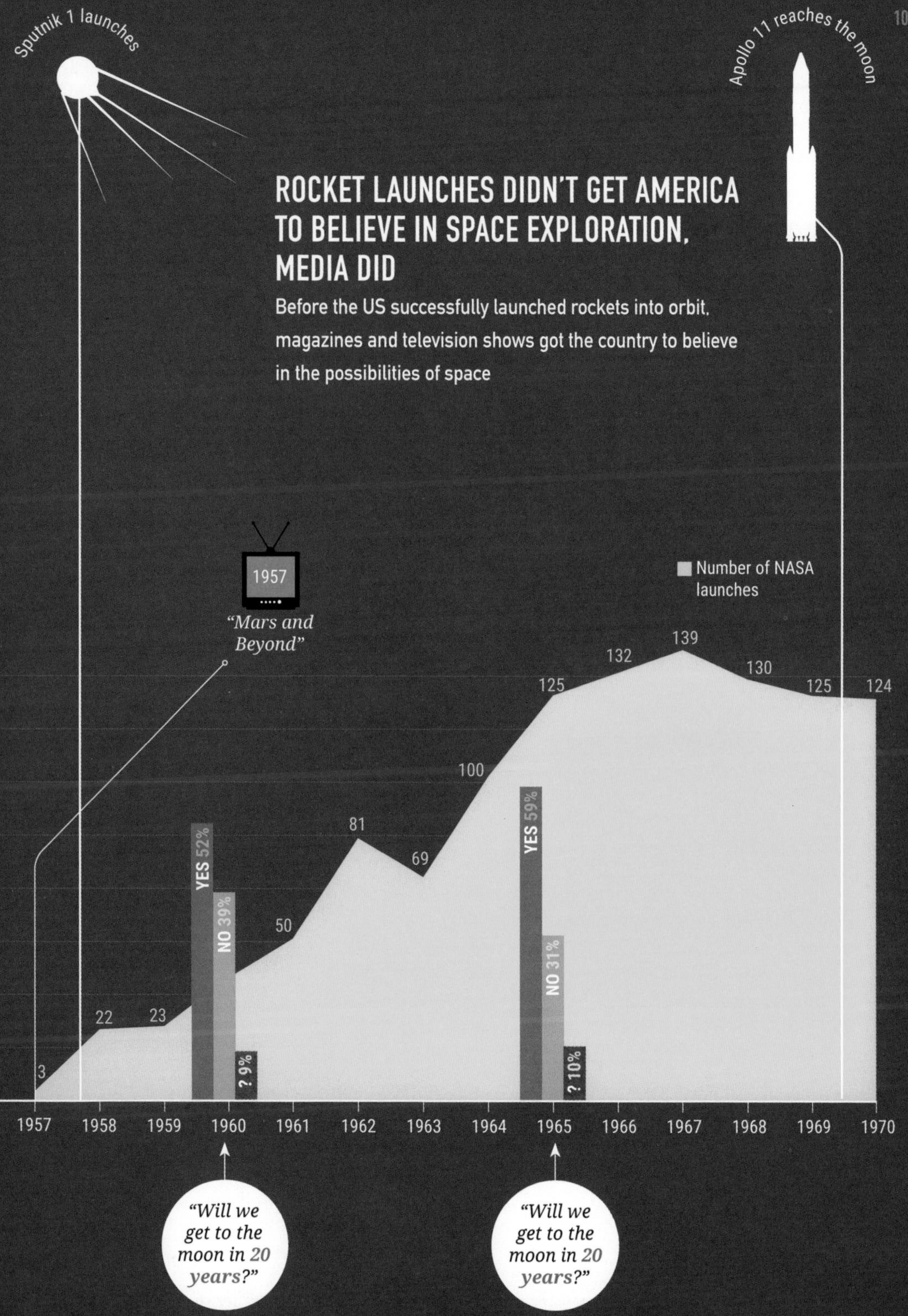

1957

"Mars and Beyond"

■ Number of NASA launches

139

132

130

125

125

124

100

81

69

50

YES 52%

NO 39%

? 9%

YES 59%

NO 31%

? 10%

22

23

3

1957 1958 1959 1960 1961 1962 1963 1964 1965 1966 1967 1968 1969 1970

"Will we get to the moon in 20 years?"

"Will we get to the moon in 20 years?"

of 2,810 Americans asked, "Do you think that men in rockets will be able to reach the moon within the next 50 years?" To which 70 percent of people responded "No."

This public opinion issue grated on the scientists who believed that it was not only possible but, with adequate funding, absolutely feasible. Paramount among them was Wernher von Braun, the German émigré who designed Nazi Germany's rocket program but was brought to the States for Operation Paperclip, where German scientists were put to work for the American government in the Cold War. At the time, he was working for the US Army but had a vision for a civilian space program.

At a 1951 scholarly conference at the Hayden Planetarium in New York, Cornelius Ryan, then an associate editor at *Collier's*, attended to learn about the plausibility of spaceflight. While there he met von Braun, who explained his vision of how America could viably pursue space exploration.

Ryan was convinced, and he pitched his editor on a high-concept series of special issues that would explore von Braun's argument that space exploration was not only possible but going to happen far sooner than the public imagined.

The first issue came out in October 1952 and it was a smash hit. *Collier's* circulation at the time was 3 million, but the estimate is that the first issue circulated to over 10 million people. It featured elaborate concept art and clear explainers about how rocketry worked and the potential space held for scientific discovery, including ambitious depictions of space stations, space shuttles, and more that were at least decades ahead of their time. The issue made a conceptually intimidating thing—riding a missile to space—into a conceivable trip. More *Collier's* issues on space exploration would follow, and public perception began to move, but von Braun's vision had already reached a patron who would bring his ideas to an entirely new medium: Walt Disney.

Disney had a Sunday night television program called *Walt Disney's Wonderful World of Color*, and it was one of the most popular shows in the nascent medium of TV. Disney launched a series of specials talking about trips to the moon and the development of space stations with von Braun featured in all of them, including televised depictions of weightlessness and the logistics of such a trip.

"The whole point of all this was this is *real*, this is going to *happen*, and it's going to take place within a very short period of time," said Roger Launius, NASA's official historian for decades. "All pre-NASA, all of it."

There were three space-specific issues of *Collier's* in 1952, four in 1953, and one in 1954. Disney's *Man in Space* aired in March 1955. With an estimated 42 million viewers, it was one of the most-watched television programs *ever*. *Man and the Moon* would follow in 1955, and *Mars and Beyond* came out in 1957. The first successful orbital launch didn't happen until 1957, with Sputnik I, launched by the Soviet Union. The bill to create NASA would be signed into law a year later.

When Gallup surveyed Americans again at the beginning of 1955, after the *Collier's* pieces but before the Disney shows, the percentage of Americans who said "yes" to being able to land on the moon in the next fifty years had jumped to 38 percent, "no" was down to 51 percent, and "no opinion" was at 11 percent. That's a 23 percentage point jump in six years when there were zero orbital rocket launches, but there was the strong beginning to a pop cultural campaign to woo Americans to space.

NASA was in its infancy, but a decade of persuasion from Disney and *Collier's* successfully built a fandom around space: In 1959, when Gallup asked if man will have landed on the moon by 1980, a 52 percent majority said yes.

"The public relations campaign of the 1950s really proved to be remarkably successful," said Launius. And the space community had learned a valuable lesson: They had a true ally in pop culture.

In the 1960s, Fred Ordway was working at Marshall Space Flight Center in public affairs. When a director named Stanley Kubrick reached out to NASA for help on a forthcoming project, he asked for Ordway, who was personally recommended by von Braun. Ordway then quit his job and moved to England for three years to serve as the technical adviser for *2001: A Space Odyssey*. NASA was typically quick to respond to requests from Hollywood. If James Bond was going to escape in a moon buggy in *Diamonds Are Forever*, NASA was happy to send over photos and schematics. The relationship was handled somewhat informally until the 1990s, when NASA got a designated entertainment industry liaison, Bobbie Faye Ferguson.

Apollo 13, a film that delved deeply into NASA history, enjoyed peerless access to the administration's facilities, including the Launch Control Center at the Kennedy Space Center, Apollo 13's launchpad 39A, NASA's Houston training facilities, anything.

"It paid off beautifully," said Launius. "If there were ever a film that made NASA look great, it's *Apollo 13*."

But esteem isn't the only thing NASA gets from films, nor is technical knowledge the only thing Hollywood gets back. Much is made of the twin films *Armageddon* and *Deep Impact*,

each about a team sent to destroy an incoming projectile that threatens to wipe out all life on Earth. Both movies came out in 1998, and although the looser, cooler *Armageddon* enjoys more longevity, that the separate productions happened simultaneously is not mere coincidence.

In 1994, a comet called Shoemaker-Levy 9 passed by Earth and continued on its path through the solar system. It was then captured in unprecedented detail by the Hubble Space Telescope as it smashed into Jupiter, a moment of cinematic destruction that would raise the alarm of the possible dangers of space rocks not only at NASA but also in Hollywood.

Another major scientific discovery in the 1990s, or rather confirmation of a giant asteroid impact, also came into play. What was known as the K-T event, or the asteroid that killed the dinosaurs, was confirmed. One discovery in the depths that an asteroid nearly wiped out life on Earth, one discovery in the heavens that comets were still hitting planets so often we can film it.

Armageddon (1998)

It wasn't only Hollywood that got startled by Shoemaker-Levy 9. The US Congress soon grew interested, holding hearings about the potential difficulties posed by near-Earth objects in May 1998. Dr. Clark R. Chapman of the Southwest Research Institute was called to testify. After alluding to the recent exploration of the large asteroid Eros, he communicated the threat in a way even a member of Congress could understand.

"I wish to talk with you not about the probability of impacts millions of years from now, but about the slight possibility that an asteroid or comet might strike Earth in our lifetimes, perhaps destroying civilization as we know it," he said.

After explaining the relatively low risks of extinction-level collisions, but the distressingly possible risks of smaller but still destructive collisions, eventually he made a pitch so well suited to the House of Representatives Oversight Committee, he should have been invited to play in the congressional baseball game.

"The cost is not large. I believe that *Deep Impact* has already taken in more money at the box office than the cost of the entire Spaceguard Survey, from beginning to end. Astronomical programs are comparatively cheap."

By June 1998, NASA's Near-Earth Objects Observation Program office had opened for business.

* * *

In 1843, a British writer was so disgusted and distraught at the state of the world around him—the needless poverty, the greed of the ruling class, the absence of accountability, the callousness of the wealthy toward the indigent—that, full of bile, he pitched his publisher on a political pamphlet to be called *An Appeal to the People of England, on behalf of the Poor Man's Child*. The work would use figures and facts, reportage and rhetoric to sway minds to act, to care about the poor.

But at a fundraising speech, the writer's lectures fell on deaf ears. His argument for education reform didn't light up the crowd, so he gave up on the *Appeal*.

Then, over the course of six weeks, Charles Dickens wrote *A Christmas Carol*.

All that vinegar turned to mulled wine, and the story sold out in three days, becoming a fixture in the English literary canon, an annual Christmas morality tale, and the inspiration for hundreds if not thousands of adaptations. All the ideas Dickens wanted to include in his scholarly treatment are in *A Christmas Carol*—the dignity of human life, the senselessness of greed, the culpability of the ruling class. The difference is that *A Christmas Carol* is pop culture, which is often more effective at moving social change than reasonable, well-researched arguments supported by unimpeachable data.

In the mid-2000s, two films took aim at the catastrophic impacts of climate change, both attempting to use their platform to tell the story.

An Inconvenient Truth became very well known and revered, received critical acclaim, and featured the former vice president of the United States. It was honored with two Oscars and became a darling of the intelligentsia, the glitterati, and the scientific community.

The other film, *The Day After Tomorrow*, was an implausible Roland Emmerich disaster movie. It won zero Oscars, featured Jake Gyllenhaal, has a 45 percent score on Rotten Tomatoes, and fueled weeks of "well, *actually . . .*" moments from the lab coat crowd.

One of these movies had an opening weekend of $68.7 million at the domestic box office; the other made $281,330. One maxed out in 3,444 cinemas domestically, the other in 587. One had a $125 million production budget, the other had $1 million to work with. And, finally, one of them made more than half a billion dollars worldwide, while the other earned just $53 million.

Money aside, here's the more pertinent question: Which one raised more awareness about climate change?

Anthony Lieserowitz directs Yale's program on climate change communication. He studies how best to communicate the threat of climate change. Lieserowitz was well aware

THE DAY AFTER TOMORROW POLLING

Lieserowitz survey taken three weekends after the movie hit theaters,
after 21 million people had seen it

The Day After Tomorrow was released May 24, 2004

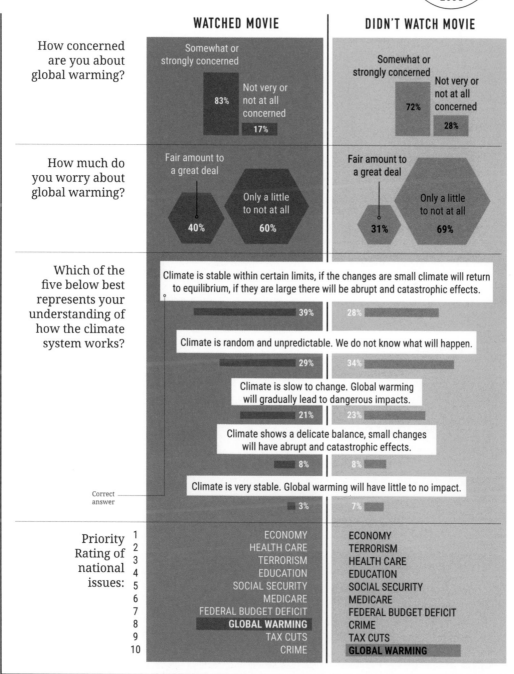

WATCHED MOVIE   **DIDN'T WATCH MOVIE**

How concerned are you about global warming?

Somewhat or strongly concerned
Not very or not at all concerned
83%
17%

Somewhat or strongly concerned
Not very or not at all concerned
72%
28%

How much do you worry about global warming?

Fair amount to a great deal
Only a little to not at all
40%   60%

Fair amount to a great deal
Only a little to not at all
31%   69%

Which of the five below best represents your understanding of how the climate system works?

Climate is stable within certain limits, if the changes are small climate will return to equilibrium, if they are large there will be abrupt and catastrophic effects.
39%   28%

Climate is random and unpredictable. We do not know what will happen.
29%   34%

Climate is slow to change. Global warming will gradually lead to dangerous impacts.
21%   23%

Climate shows a delicate balance, small changes will have abrupt and catastrophic effects.
8%   8%

Correct answer

Climate is very stable. Global warming will have little to no impact.
3%   7%

Priority Rating of national issues:

	WATCHED MOVIE	DIDN'T WATCH MOVIE
1	ECONOMY	ECONOMY
2	HEALTH CARE	TERRORISM
3	TERRORISM	HEALTH CARE
4	EDUCATION	EDUCATION
5	SOCIAL SECURITY	SOCIAL SECURITY
6	MEDICARE	MEDICARE
7	FEDERAL BUDGET DEFICIT	FEDERAL BUDGET DEFICIT
8	**GLOBAL WARMING**	CRIME
9	TAX CUTS	TAX CUTS
10	CRIME	**GLOBAL WARMING**

Leiserowitz et al.

that for years, climate change was described as a slow, gradual process, but in the last decade or so before *The Day After Tomorrow* came out, the field had undergone a major revolution in that thinking.

"As a complex system, you pass certain thresholds and the [climate] system reorganizes," explained Lieserowitz. "And there's no just going back. It's in a new state—you can't reverse it."

The screenwriter for *The Day After Tomorrow* was fully aware of this concept—he'd seen the shift in climate literature and was directly informed by the thermohaline circulation system, the breakdown of which is the very thing that kicks off the plot of the movie. When Lieserowitz saw this movie was coming soon and that the price tag meant it was slated to be a blockbuster, he immediately set about pitching a study. He drafted a proposal to the National Science Foundation, who then agreed to fund it.

His idea: Lieserowitz wanted to see how a blockbuster movie would influence public opinion.

"The bottom line is, we found that the film did have a very significant impact on those that saw it, they became more convinced that climate change was real, was human-caused, they became more worried about it, and their underlying mental model—which is really the core thing I was trying to get at—changed from seeing it purely as this slow, gradual thing, to actually being this tipping-point-type model, that things can change dramatically," he said.

The cruddy science in the film didn't make much of a difference. That extreme weather would not happen on a nearly instantaneous timeline didn't matter as much as getting across that extreme weather would happen on a timeline if climate change was left unaddressed.

Leiserowitz's research has managed to identify the five key ideas that an effective message about climate change, whether it's a scientific paper or a blockbuster movie, has: "Scientists agree. It's real. It's us. It's bad. But there's hope."

The decisions that producers of entertainment make can have implications for not just the portrayals of science but the processes as well. Scientific understanding is a continuously evolving debate, where consensus is built out of a general understanding of the evidence as it exists at a given moment. When movies

Jurassic World: Dominion *featured an interpretations of pyroraptors that factored in the latest theories on dinosaurs and feathers.*

PALEONTOLOGY AND JURASSIC PARK

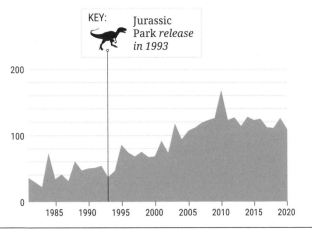

KEY: Jurassic Park *release* in 1993

Annual papers

Journal of Vertebrate Paleontology

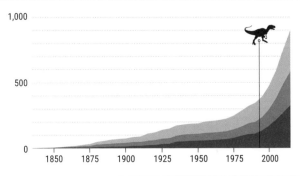

New taxa of dinosaurs described

- Ornithischians
- Sauropodomorphs
- Therapods

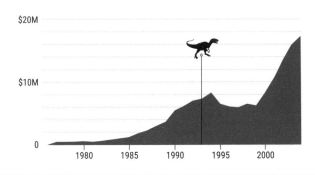

Grants awarded

Value of National Science Foundation grants that mentioned dinosaurs

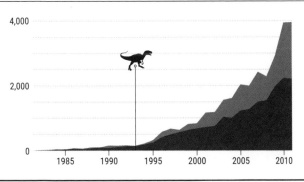

Annual citations

- *Journal of Vertebrate Paleontology* citations
- Citations of the journal *Palaeontology*

Author's analysis, National Science Foundation, Scopus, Tennant, J. P., et al., 2018

integrate science, they tend to pick a theory and call it a winner. We may not know if dinosaurs had feathers, for example, and that may be a matter of profound scientific debate, but, well, the show must go on, and these decisions—and the advisers who get consulted before making them—stick in the public consciousness.

Today, Hollywood is home to a generation of filmmakers who grew up watching scientific innovation change the world around them, from space to biology to weather and more. And the scientific world is full of researchers who were initially introduced, if not seduced, to their profession not through a college but through a movie.

And that's the generation of filmmakers *and* scientists now working together. Because when done right, a single blockbuster film doesn't just advance a scientific theory or add another round to some fight among PhDs. Some movies can permanently change the face of a scientific field forever.

"I think *Jurassic Park*, the original film in '93, was probably the single most important thing that happened in paleontology in a really long time," said Steve Brusatte, a paleontologist at the University of Edinburgh.

Originally a 1990 science fiction novel by Michael Crichton, *Jurassic Park* was adapted by Steven Spielberg into one of the most enduring movies ever made. The state of paleontology when the book was published, when the total variety of dinosaurs believed to exist was somewhere between 900 and 1,200 genera, was vastly different fifteen years later, when an update to the estimate increased that number to 1,850 genera, of which 71 percent were still unknown.

The early 1990s saw new parts of the world open up to research. New techniques emerged, and a new understanding of how life ended for the dinosaurs became established fact. It was a promising time. However, *Jurassic Park* poured gasoline on that fire, leading to an explosion in interest that would reshape the field of paleontology.

After *Jurassic Park*, university physical science departments were mobbed. One 1998 article in *Science* by Erik Stokstad observed that "Students are crowding into paleontology classes, corporations and philanthropists are pledging support, money is flowing into the field from movies and spinoffs."

It was more than just people taking classes; an entire economy around dinosaurs emerged in the 1990s that would change the finances of the field. Popular interest fueled by *Jurassic Park* vastly increased demand for dinosaur museums, traveling dinosaur exhibits, and dinosaur merchandise. The money spent at those exhibits, and the jobs that they created, was a huge infusion of resources into a science otherwise defined by how stagnant its subjects have been.

"I do know certain colleagues, people that are a bit older than me, people who were hired explicitly in the '90s because a university was putting out a new dinosaur course or a museum wanted a new dinosaur exhibit," said Brusatte. "This was a real impact on the science, which was a great thing."

The money and the jobs and the newfound resources did wend their way from the pockets of pop culture consumers through a few charitable organizations set up to direct the largesse of the media properties that thrived on dinosaurs to the people actually doing dinosaur science.

In the 1980s, only about one in ten papers in the *Journal of Vertebrate Paleontology* was on dinosaurs. But by 1997, a quarter of the papers in the journal were about dinosaurs. One reason for that was brand-new financial support.

A fair amount of largesse in the field came from the Dinosaur Society, which by 1997 had doled out just shy of a million dollars. Some funding had a direct link to the films. From 1997 to 1998, the Jurassic Foundation—founded by Universal Studios and Amblin Entertainment, Steven Spielberg's production company—was seeded with $150,000 in funding from the proceeds of the Lost World exhibit, an exhibition about dinosaurs that was inspired by the film. It may not sound like all that much for a scientific research grant, but paleontology is notoriously cheap. Brusatte himself got a grant from the Jurassic Foundation that enabled him to go to China to investigate a find.

"That amount of money produced several publications; it launched a few very important collaborations," Brusatte said. "The big thing for my career, just those small bits of money, and that all stemmed initially from *Jurassic Park*."

After publishing his book—*The Rise and Fall of the Dinosaurs*—Brusatte got his own opportunity to pay it forward when director Colin Trevorrow, the architect behind the Jurassic World franchise, brought him on as a paleontology consultant for *Jurassic World: Dominion*.

Paleontology now looks different from a lot of other sciences, too. In fact, it looks a lot different from the rest of academia, which often rewards and empowers longevity. In 2018, the Palaeontological Association, a UK society of paleontologists, conducted an internal diversity study. They found that, all told, 71 percent of respondents were born in either the 1980s or 1990s, a disproportionately young skew for an ancient field. The younger generation was also majority women, a rarity in the physical sciences.

Jurassic Park, a single movie that birthed a franchise, brought vitality to a field that desperately needed it. Today's paleontologists grew up in a world where their kind were not staid hobbyists but daring heroes, and where dinosaurs were not mere rock and bone, but creatures of flesh, and claws, and teeth, and blood.

* * *

Michael Graham is a professor at the Moss Landing Marine Laboratories at San José State University. He's a phycologist, someone who studies algae—in his case, seaweeds. He's one of the world's foremost experts on the ecology of kelp forests in particular. Rewatching *Jaws*, which had a profound impact on his decision to pursue marine science in college, he got his first taste of scientific consulting. He noticed the shark is swimming through kelp off the coast of Massachusetts. But that species of kelp doesn't grow in the Atlantic, so the scene must've been shot in the Pacific.

"So here it is, the opening scene of my favorite movie is completely scientifically wrong," said Graham.

When he was a postdoctoral student in 2000, he got a call from a colleague about a film studio that wanted a marine scientist to make sure the shots they were using for background images made sense, that the species they were shooting were where they needed to be, and that the environment they'd designed was up to ecological snuff.

That is how Graham found himself in an auditorium addressing a team from Pixar.

The studio was still smarting from the scientific reaction to *A Bug's Life*, which features insects with four legs. They wanted to bring in experts early to avoid that kind of pitfall. Toy experts don't send angry letters about the representation of Mr. Potato Head, but the ant people, they were not so generous. Graham was game: He got a couple hundred bucks to give a talk and field some questions.

"They told me when I was at Pixar, 'Hey, you got to be careful, I mean, don't start getting too detailed here, because the fish will talk. And their eyes are in the front of their heads. Because if they're on the side of their heads, like they're supposed to be, that makes for a horrible movie,'" he explained.

The first day, they said they wanted to talk about corals. Graham launched into an hourlong lecture for more than a hundred Pixar storytellers about how to make sure they were pointed in the right direction and how the water moves in a coral reef, fielding seemingly endless questions from animators who had been staring at a digital reef for god knows how long.

And at the end of the hour, someone up front asked, "Of all the things we could possibly do, what would be the one thing that would make your stomach cringe?"

"I said, 'Well, the worst thing you could possibly do is put kelp—you know, big glorious kelp that grows in the cold climates—*right* next to your corals, which grow in the warm climates, because even the kindergartners at the Monterey Bay Aquarium know that.'"

He heard a laugh from the top of the auditorium.

"Well, you better not see the movie then!"

Lo and behold, in the very first trailer for *Finding Nemo*, which features Marlin and Dory swimming through the coral, in the near distance you can see some meticulously animated, lifelike, ebbing and flowing, glorious cold-water kelp. Right next to the reef.

Because whether a moviemaker consults with a scientist or not, movies have power. Since the release of *Jaws* in 1975, the shark population is down 90 percent. If I showed you that on a chart but didn't label the animal, you'd think it was a plague. The movie prompted a surge in trophy-hunting for sharks, and when overfishing began to decimate shark populations caught up as bycatch, well, let's just say they lacked the good press of *Free Willy* or *Flipper*. Peter Benchley, the author of the book *Jaws*, felt enormous guilt for his accidental role in the decimation and spent the rest of his life calling for conservation.

And while science impacts movies, it's worth noting that movies have often been what led many viewers to become scientists.

"I mean, *Jaws* is the reason I became a marine biologist," said Graham. "It was Hooper I idolized. He had his fear he had to deal with, but for the most part he just found this man-eating shark fascinating. He was using his science throughout the movie, to insert reality, but also a sense of the mysticism to the fisherman who had no science in him."

* * *

What does it all mean?

The time we spend watching things and hearing stories is immensely valuable. Although it's not perfectly good or bad, access to media, television, movies, and theater can benefit the developing minds of kids, the behavior and opportunities of young adults, and the health and bodies of older adults. Yes, there are downsides to how media and culture can influence society, but focusing on them would mean deliberately ignoring the vast social benefits of culture. Seeing representation and opportunities on screens has the power to inspire people to change who they are in new ways, whether they're trying a sport they never thought was *for* them or adopting a puppy they'd otherwise leave at the pound.

How we individually see and think and feel matters—but when it happens to us as a society, it can change the world.

CHAPTER 5

COMMERCE & CULTURE & COMMERCE

Creativity doesn't just make movies, it also funds them.

The birth of the blockbuster allegedly took place in June 1975 when director Steven Spielberg blew the doors off the world with the smash hit *Jaws*. Swimming into theaters and springing on unsuspecting audiences, that movie's success permanently changed how the movie industry worked. It did this primarily by choking out the independent scene and setting a course where big studios bet the farm year after year on stunning summer spectacles, then backed them with splashy, nationwide same-day simultaneous film rollouts and huge ad pushes ahead of release. No longer were studios content to play wait-and-see with experimental wares; instead they would put up big budgets for big hits, and big misses. The business model of an earlier age died in a shock of blood beneath the waters of Amity Island. *Jaws* was the start of a new era, one in which smaller and independent production houses struggled to keep up and survive.

Most film buffs have probably heard this story before. But it is wrong. Compelling, but wrong.

I'm not saying *Jaws* didn't have an impact or didn't change the world (see the previous chapter and all the dead sharks)—the movie's success absolutely showed how to properly turn a film into an event. But a new and promising business approach isn't really enough to wipe out just about all the other approaches. No, to bury a decade of American cinema where the future titans of the box office—Spielberg, Scorsese, Lucas, Coppola—made their bones, that took a piece of legislation.

The Blockbuster Loophole

Blockbusters were actually born with the stroke of a pen from President Gerald Ford, with the passage of the Tax Reform Act of 1976. And although the story doesn't contain any moments where the water bursts with blood, it holds its own.

In 1973, the only real avenue by which to invest in film was to acquire completed movies for a fee and then roll the dice on distribution, hoping to make that fee back through box office admissions. But what an enterprising accountant by the name of Burton W. Kanter realized around then was that you could structure an investment deal so the losses on paper looked large enough early on that an investor would turn their true profit not at the box office but at tax time. Any actual returns on the investment would be pure upside.

The process involved a guy called a film packager who connected moneymen in search of lowering their taxes to young, scrappy producers and directors. The film packager gets "investments" from a number of other wealthy, tax-averse men and invests them in a production services corporation. The packager then approaches a lender with the investors' money and uses it as a down payment for a loan four times the size with the debt levied against future box office receipts. There are banks—large, publicly held banks—that are delighted to put up this money, which then becomes the movie's budget.

From a tax perspective, what just happened is that you invested $100,000 in a business, but the business "lost" $400,000 this year after financing the budget. So, for $100,000, you're able to reduce your income by $300,000, which, given the top tax bracket of 50 percent at the time, translates to $200,000 in savings. If the movie makes money, you have to pay taxes on that, but in 1973 you probably just buy treasuries, on which you don't have to pay taxes.

Two years later, the movie gets released and one of two things happens: About a third of the time, you don't make any money. The production company can't repay the bank

loan and goes bust, and the bank eats the loss. However, on the off chance your investment pans out—as it then did about seven out of every ten times—great work! You made a little on top *and* you dodged taxes.

Now, let's say you get real lucky and the movie in which you invested was *Taxi Driver*. Well, now you've got to pay some income taxes. But that's okay, because you already know a film packager, and . . . the cycle repeats.

More impressive even than the audacity of the scheme was its scale: The studios were hit hard with the onset of television, with theatrical receipts in decline and pressure from their investors to stop developing so many films in-house, where the risks were simply not paying off. The studios went from producing sixty movies in-house annually to an average of six, with the rest coproductions. Banks wouldn't lend the studios money unless they reined in costs, but audiences didn't want to see cheap movies. The only way to make the kind of films that put butts in seats was to distribute films that were developed by other outside investors with a higher appetite for risk than the studio backers. The first such film to be released in this way was *Payday* in early 1973, starring Rip Torn.

An illuminating example of how this new setup played out happened at Columbia Pictures, which was wrestling with a mountain of debt that they, like most distributors, had racked up throughout the 1960s. Columbia was able to stay in business through the early '70s only by tapping into those outside reservoirs of cash. In 1976, one packager estimated that the major studios got $60 million in financing from these production deals the prior year, the independents got another $15 million, and another $150 million was invested in the illegitimate market (movies that were not *actually* movies and maybe ran for a day or two in New York for tax purposes but were basically created to fleece the IRS). In 1975 dollars, the $75 million raised legitimately would be worth $360 million in 2020 dollars, and the balance, $225 million, is just north of $1 billion in 2020 dollars. And that's the money being *put up* by investors—the IRS could have absorbed a loss of revenue *three times that*, depending on how the individual scheme was constructed.

And now consider one package of movies funded by a pool of rich people attempting to minimize their taxes, each of whom put in $160,000: *Shampoo*; a Charles Bronson action flick called *Breakout*; a western, *Bite the Bullet*; a Streisand sequel called *Funny Lady*; and a war flick named *Operation Daybreak*. *Shampoo*, the first on-screen role for Carrie Fisher, became the third-highest-grossing film of 1975. *Funny Lady* came in as the seventh-highest-grossing film of the year, *Bite the Bullet* got two Academy Award nominations, and *Breakout* finished as the twenty-first-highest-grossing film of the year. *Breakout* was also one of the first studio films to attempt saturation booking, where 1,300 prints were released all at once. This strategy would be imitated two months later to significant success with *Jaws*.

Using films as tax dodges turned out to be a great way for nascent directors to get money to prove their chops. When James Cameron wanted to make a short film to show what he could do behind the camera, he enlisted some California dentists looking for a quick and dirty tax dodge. The short *Xenogenesis* got made, and the dentists pulled the rest of the funding, but Cameron got noticed by Roger Corman, who gave him a job as a special effects supervisor. (No tax dodgers, maybe no *Titanic*.)

In 1975, more than half the films produced in the United States were financed through tax evasion. By 1976, the party was over. Fed up with all manners of tax subversion, the federal government killed the write-off in the spring of that year. And they didn't just kill it by way of a 1976 tax reform bill; the IRS started directly threatening to investigate film productions. The jig was up.

By signing the Tax Reform Act of 1976, Gerald Ford set the stage, literally, for the domination of the blockbuster. With the indie financing wiped out, the only kind of movie that made sense anymore was a completely studio-financed and studio-controlled film—the kind that *Jaws* showed could result in an ocean of money.

We like to believe that films become popular because, like *Jaws*, they are inherently good. We sometimes think that the evolution we see on-screen is caused by the stories being told, the ways that the films resonate with the viewers, and how they can achieve an artistic impact. And that is definitely true, but it's not the whole story.

Like it or not, art has always been defined by commerce. But in many ways, commerce can also be defined by art.

Everlasting Lust

A plurality of paperback books are romance fiction. Surprised? Yes, the genre is formulaic, but formulas are great. And formula has *always* worked in romance fiction.

The plot of romance novels is simple enough. They are, in fact, just science fiction stories where the reader is transported to a magical realm of fantasy and wonder. In this realm, just about every single thing is the same as in our reality, with the sole exception that several men are not terrible.

To make successful books about desire, one must understand what is actually desired. And if anything, it is more books on romance, which as a genre is wildly successful. With $1.08 billion in sales and 23 percent of the consumer book market in 2016, romance is the undisputed juggernaut of fiction.

Determining the precise desires of the American consumer is a central effort of the loose-knit, often independent-minded romance fiction industry, which is composed of many independent authors who avoid literary agents and traditional publishing altogether and instead publish their e-books on Amazon's direct-to-consumer Kindle marketplace.

Alex Newton consults with romance authors about the state of the market and monitors the Amazon rankings across thirty main book categories (Amazon's word for "genre") and up to seven thousand subgenres. He's got a front-row seat to the ebbs and flows of consumer reading tastes. He also sees how those shifts in demand can spur swift changes in supply from authors. It can be as simple as one book, a single hit—take billionaire romance, the kind of book that swims in the wake of *Fifty Shades of Grey*, or period romance, works that follow the *Bridgerton* model—to shake up the entire ecosystem.

Subgenres that were once nonsellers can pop overnight and become hot, with the average sales rank of the top books within that niche spiking as readers find not only something they like but a whole new topic or a take they want to explore. Authors notice the shift,

move in, and soon enough you're looking at thousands of new books in a given genre or subgenre in a given year.

Take, for instance, a romance subgenre known as "clean and wholesome." Clean and wholesome is romantic fiction that doesn't include sex scenes, innuendo, or raunchy language. It emerged as a category from Amazon as a counter-trend when *Fifty Shades of Grey* was spawning countless Christian Grey imitators. It's often targeted for a Christian audience and has grown to be a dominant performer over the last decade.

In February 2016, there were fewer than 500 titles in the subgenre for sales on Amazon. By December 2016 there were 1,596 titles in the clean and wholesome category on Amazon, according to Newton, and the average Amazon sales rank of the top twenty titles in the subgenre was 1,807. At that point, the niche was off to the races: A year later, the number of titles had more than doubled, with 3,597 titles and an

GENRE TASTES ARE CONSTANTLY CHANGING

Genres rise and fall based on all kinds of trends, within literature and beyond

AVERAGE AMAZON KINDLE SALES RANK OF TOP 20 BESTSELLER POSITIONS OVER TIME

NUMBER OF ROMANCE TITLES IN "CLEAN AND WHOLESOME"

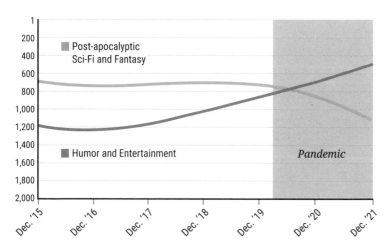

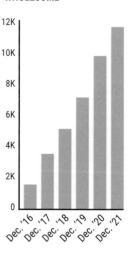

average sales rank of 1,055. Still pretty niche, but given the sales rank, it certainly qualifies as a bustling one.

By December 2020, there were 10,001 titles in the subgenre, with an average sales rank of 584. By then, clean and wholesome had made it: Ten thousand titles and you're not a niche anymore, you're in the mainstream. That kind of title growth, jumping from fewer than 500 titles to more than 5,000 in two and a half years, demonstrates just how much romantic fiction is subject to the desires of its readers, and how readily authors can flood a genre when those readers really, really love it.

The thing about demand is that it's possible to satisfy it. Desire can indeed be quenched. The data is already revealing a slowdown: From December 2020 to December 2021, 1,888 titles were added to the subgenre on Amazon, and the average sales rank declined from 584 to 929.

The surge of clean and wholesome is just one example of how quickly tastes can change. Sometimes it's not necessarily a blockbuster book or the counter-movement it spawns. Sometimes larger factors, like a pandemic, can send the sales needle swinging.

"The category of romantic comedy for the first time overtook the big umbrella category of contemporary romance, which had always been trending number one," said Newton, about what happened when the pandemic brought lockdowns across the United States. "We saw things like clean and wholesome rise versus all the darker stuff, horror going down, obviously post-apocalyptic fiction going down."

The pandemic also prompted swift shifts in genres that had been flailing. The paranormal romance genre had been in decline since the heyday of Twilight. The vampire romance genre had been slipping constantly since 2015, but the pandemic sent readers searching for the nostalgic and familiar, leading to soaring sales.

The Long Tail

Romance has a deeply loyal audience that makes fans of other book genres look fickle by comparison. Those who publish into the category know what readers want and give it to them. Among the broad contours of the pop culture industry, books more than many other mediums are subject to the whims of broader market forces. This is largely because there are simply more books made each year. Major Hollywood studios produce usually in the ballpark of 100 films per year that are released in cinemas. Even accounting for all other nonstudio releases, probably fewer than 1,000 films are released in the United States each year. Approaching the peak of peak television in 2022, there were just over 550 original scripted series on broadcast television, cable, and streaming services. Meanwhile, in 2018 around 1.7 million books were self-published, in addition to the 300,000-ish that came from traditional publishers. It's multiple orders of magnitude different from any other medium, and that requires far more sophisticated analysis of data.

Kristen McLean, an industry analyst for NPD Group, is a book industry veteran who has been researching the market since the mid-2000s. According to her, trends are simply getting faster, no doubt fueled by the independent creators who can get an e-book to market in weeks compared with the significant production cycles even a crash title, or one made on a very short schedule, can require at a traditional publishing house.

Another factor to consider is that many sales are increasingly "backlist" driven, meaning book sales for works that came out more than a year prior. Some niches have always been backlist driven, chief among them children's literature. New kids come into the world every day, and sometimes a hit is a hit no matter what decade it was published. Parents also tend to buy books for their kids that they enjoyed as kids. As a result, in the children's market about 75 percent of sales are backlist, compared with around a 50-50 split historically in the adult market for books.

BOOK SALES BY BACKLIST STATUS

The rise of online booksellers is changing what people read

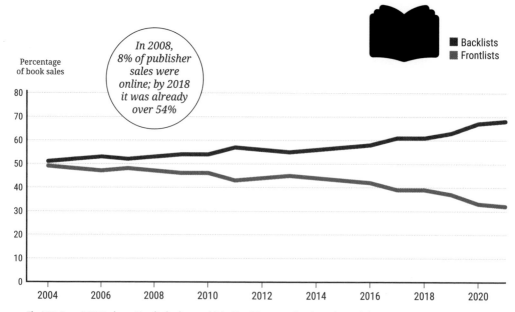

Backlists
Frontlists

Percentage of book sales

In 2008, 8% of publisher sales were online; by 2018 it was already over 54%

The NPD Group/NPD Bookscan. Frontlist books are published in rolling 12 months prior to data period.

That backlist power has begun to spread to other genres in the past decade or so. In 2006, 53 percent of sales in the adult market were backlist. But by 2021, 68 percent of sales were backlist, with frontlist books accounting for just 32 percent of sales. And although publishers' backlists are always going to get bigger, the reason for the shift of that magnitude was online book sales supplanting frontlist-driven brick-and-mortar shops. When algorithms place books before consumers' eyeballs in lieu of Barnes & Noble, high rankings translate to high sales, so popular books can remain in demand much longer than they once did.

"Online book buying doesn't favor frontlist," said McLean. "It's really hard for new books to be discovered on an online purchasing environment unless you know exactly what you want."

Whereas the pandemic nuked the movie theater business, the impact on the book market could reverberate for decades. The market for print books alone was up 8 percent in 2020 versus 2019, and it appeared to finish another

7 or 8 percent higher in 2021 over 2020. That's a difference of 70 to 100 million units sold, an absolutely massive number that the publishing world simply wasn't accustomed to.

Normally, although different publishing categories rise and fall, the overall sales pie is stagnant, with the difference between a good year and a bad year being a few percentage points. The pandemic created tens of millions of new readers, and although that will almost certainly decline somewhat, what McLean argued is that there are simply not enough marketing dollars to spur an increase of that magnitude without a pandemic.

"It's not like you discover 10 million more readers or anything; it's a pretty stable market," said McLean. "But what really did make people read more and engage with books more was the external forces that were acting on changing behavior across the board, the things that were making us stay home. That was profoundly interesting for me. You don't get to really run that experiment unless something really radical happens."

Emotional Roller Coasters

Ever since he was a kid, David Kennedy delighted in seeing how pop culture could make people happy.

"If the TV was on at my grandparents', I had my back to the TV," explained Kennedy. ". . . That would be the one time where people would sit and enjoy something together in harmony, more than they would even a meal. I always found that to be very moving, very powerful."

Kennedy eventually moved to Los Angeles and got a job working as a production assistant, gradually moving up the ranks making movies. He was working on a Star Trek movie in 2002 when he was asked to shoot some content that would later be bundled into a theme park attraction. He was then tasked with bringing the whole project to completion. The result was Star Trek: The Experience at the Las Vegas Hilton, an attraction that opened up in 1998 and would be followed in 2004 by the launch of Kennedy's Borg Invasion attraction at the same hotel.

"It started off with a full-fledged bar, a food and beverage area before you even went into the attraction, where certain people that were cleaning dressed up as Klingon and they spoke Klingon. They were rude, just like Klingons are depicted in the movies," he explained. "You could order crazy drinks, you could actually physically be engaged with a beverage from that universe, in full hair and makeup and costume from a show."

Working on that sprang Kennedy out of the two-dimensional arena of film and into the three- and four-dimensional world of theme parks, the kind of place where a creator can have complete mastery over the senses experienced by a viewer, who can engage on a level that a film or television director can only dream of.

Theme parks are a creative medium, and one that can teach us unique ways in which its consumers can be affected. Theme parks are a way of telling stories developed almost exclusively to achieve commercial ends, because the expense involved in writing a story or even shooting a film is dwarfed by the cost of building and operating an amusement park. Studios might take risks on money-losing films, or a publisher might gamble on an unproven novel, but nobody's making little indie amusement parks that may or may not turn a profit. No, they're explicitly and from day one designed to be businesses, but in spite of that, in spite of their pursuit of profit, we've nevertheless been able to learn outstanding things about how to emotionally grab and impact an audience.

Large, modern amusement parks are in fact profit engines explicitly designed to pull in money every minute they're open. They are the descendants of carnivals made permanent, but also works of popular culture themselves, creative expression designed not for celluloid or paper but rather in the physicality of the spaces they inhabit. And the creatives who shape them are no less auteurs than film directors.

The queue at Indiana Jones Adventure in Disneyland.

The ancestor of theme parks is the European pleasure garden, where carousels and wheels were about the best they had on offer. It was essentially a place of public relaxation and entertainment. Carousels, originally a horseman game of skill, were created sometime before 1673. At first they were wooden horses suspended from a central pole that rotated and moved riders outward using centrifugal force, which is insane. The roller coaster was unveiled in Coney Island in 1884, the Ferris wheel debuted in 1893 at the World's Columbian Exposition, the World's Fair in Chicago, and the loop-the-loop was first built in 1902.

These carnival attractions were great fun, but it wasn't until after World War II that the potential to combine storytelling techniques with environmental attractions was pioneered. Built for $17 million and opening in 1955, Disneyland was an interactive park built on several acres of Anaheim that was itself a special effect, a way for Walt Disney to construct a place that simultaneously offered innovative thrills for kids and nostalgia for their parents. This magic trick was perfected in the follow-up park in Florida, which is an illusion itself: The entire park was built atop a labyrinth of supply rooms and tunnels that allowed workers to travel all over under it with food and supplies and for garbage to be extracted from the park discreetly and with ease. Constructed by Navy Rear Admiral Joseph W. Fowler, Disneyland and, later, Walt Disney World were technological feats for a creative end, not unlike the films and the characters they brought into a three-dimensional space.

Theme parks are a medium, the same as television or novels. Their motivation is obviously commercial at the outset, but unless there was some kind of appeal or fun to be had, people wouldn't go to them. The evolution of theme parks as a business mirrors their evolution creatively. When attractions cost a penny a ride, the goal was to improve the ride—that's one reason you saw such an engineering renaissance in the late nineteenth and early twentieth centuries. The goal was to make a machine that could make someone so thrilled they would pay the same amount of money a second time to experience it again.

But thrill rides get boring eventually, and so the next innovation—a flat entry fee,

merchandising, food and beverages inside the park—fundamentally evolved the vision and the value of an amusement park. This change was based on optimization research that determined that if you want to maximize profits, you need to maximize the time guests spend in the park and the length of their overall stay. This shifted the goal to "How do we engage guests for long periods of time?" which is why parks began allying with media enterprises—movies, television, characters—to get people to stick around and do stuff besides wait in lines for rides.

Full-Body Experience

With amusement parks, detail is everything. A film director can get away with paint for some props and sets, but for a space used by thousands or millions of probing, curious, independent people, the depth of authenticity is a must.

Fred Bode, who served as the creative director of Warner Bros. Abu Dhabi, the latest park built by Warner, is one of the few people who have gotten the chance to sculpt one from scratch. The effort requires the work of hundreds, if not thousands—an army of people working to build as visceral an experience as possible. This means not only employing the tools in the arsenal of film directors but taking them a giant step further and building an immersive environment that includes engaging a guest's senses of taste, touch, and smell.

"I remember a situation [where] we were doing a Wile E. Coyote coaster ride," said Bode, "and there was a lot of sculpted rockwork that went into that. I literally would be on the job site when we were painting and sculpting this rockwork . . . and I would do everything in my absolute power to make sure that that 3D physical experience was authentic to the cartoon."

The obsession of the engineers and designers behind theme parks is deep, and in this case, that meant everything from counting the hairs of Fred Flintstone's head to crafting the meticulous art deco details in the cityscapes of Metropolis and Gotham City to creating flows of landscapes that subliminally enticed people to keep going, keep moving.

"It was really important in the DC [Comics] areas to make sure we saw big cityscapes behind things, things that would draw you in, and lighting that would make you want to go past where it was you were," Bode said.

The tools at a creator's disposal in crafting spaces, from DC Comics Gotham City to Metropolis, are myriad. Theme park designers have long known that even if people don't specifically notice that they're pumping vanilla smells on to Main Street, U.S.A., their brain certainly does, and a swift change in temperature might not mean much to a parkgoer beyond a slight shift in comfort, but it certainly draws the attention of their nervous systems.

"If you're in a wharf area and there's water, there's a smell that comes from the water and there's a temperature change," Bode said. "You get this feeling that you're actually outside, even though you're inside a million-square-foot building in the middle of the Arabian Desert."

Two decades after coordinating the Borg's invasion of the Las Vegas Hilton, David Kennedy was one of the designers who worked on the Abu Dhabi park. After returning briefly to films, he came to long for the challenge of themed entertainment, the thrill of bringing together engineers and designers and people at the height of their craft to build fully immersive environments. Hundreds of commercials, television shows, and dozens of attractions from Epcot to Shanghai later, he found himself in Abu Dhabi, laboring for three and a half years to bring his full knowledge to bear in the new park.

When you design a railing for a Batman ride, it can't just be a railing from Home Depot, it needs to be the kind of railing that Bruce Wayne would specifically design for the Batcave. When you're outside the Justice League attraction in Metropolis, today's paper in the newsstand has a cover story that, little do you realize, sets up the story within the ride. The goal is to create the universe and a false sense of reality to pull people in, whether they're ambling through the park, in a line, or in the attraction itself.

Lines, in fact, can be an outstanding opportunity to pluck guests out of Abu Dhabi or California and into a fantastical place.

"Do we want to encourage anxiety?" Kennedy said. "Maybe we make a pinch point where the walls come closer together, or they appear to come closer together, and then the walls can be very cold, and maybe we adjust the lighting to be cold. On another hand, if you want to support something like Looney Tunes, this has to be just a joy-driven experience. You might have a surface that they touch be extremely smooth, maybe nothing would have a right angle at all, it would almost undulate, as if your hands were going over a cloud."

Indeed, a great way to make an attraction more immersive has nothing to do with the attraction at all; it all comes down to the approach to the ride.

"One of my favorites is the Indiana Jones attraction in Disneyland," said Kennedy. The queue for Indiana Jones Adventure is renowned for its depth. The feeling is of entering a jungle, and then entering a secluded part of a jungle, and then delving deeper and deeper underground, disorienting the rider and pushing them out of California and into the ancient maw of Adventureland, where the ride itself is the destination.

To illustrate how a queue can prime a guest well before they get to the ride itself through sense alone, Kennedy offered a hypothetical attraction about a volcano, or something similar to Universal Studios' retired fire special-effects show *Backdraft*. In it, you'd have guests travel downward and would make the railing increasingly warm every ten feet or so. Then maybe the audio starts as a low rumble but gradually becomes more pronounced, to the point where you go from subconsciously noticing it to consciously perceiving it. And it doesn't even have to be *every* railing or every room, rather just enough to get the point across: After all, our brains are pretty good at filling in the blanks—they'll do enough of the work if a design gets it going. Finally, a quick

DISNEY WORLD WAIT TIMES INCREASE AFTER RIDES ARE FEATURED IN MOVIES

Wait times in minutes 2015-2019

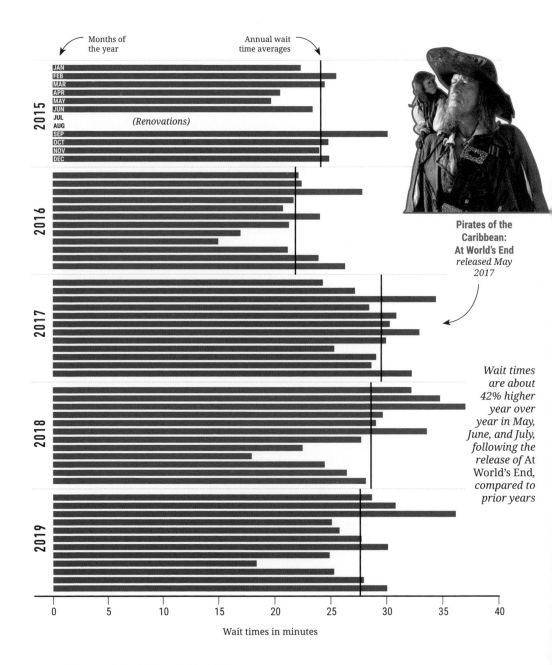

Months of the year

Annual wait time averages

JAN
FEB
MAR
APR
MAY
JUN
JUL
AUG
SEP
OCT
NOV
DEC

2015

(Renovations)

2016

2017

2018

2019

Pirates of the Caribbean: At World's End *released May 2017*

Wait times are about 42% higher year over year in May, June, and July, following the release of At World's End, *compared to prior years*

0   5   10   15   20   25   30   35   40

Wait times in minutes

touringplans.com, "Disney World Crowd Calendar" data

blast of warm air will tip the mind into a full state of alertness and immersion, leading to a far more interesting ride experience than if a guest just hopped into the ride car next to a cotton candy stand.

And the experience doesn't stop when you're in the attraction. Kennedy recalled working on a flying theater attraction for a Wanda park in Hubei, China. Flying theaters put guests in seats, then raise them up and put on a three-dimensional show that provides the sensation of flying, the classic example being *Soarin'* in Disneyland's California Adventure. It doesn't take all that much to fool our brains into feeling like we're flying; a little elevation, a little airflow, and a moving visual field is enough to provoke the sensation of flight. In one majestic scene, the guests fly over a field full of flowers that are only from the Hubei province of China. Kennedy remembered that it reliably made the older riders burst into tears.

Something particularly powerful about immersive attractions is how universal they are. Every human, whether the park is in California or Abu Dhabi or Hubei, responds to temperature, touch, smell. It speaks to the same reason why action movies usually travel far better than comedies, which require cultural context. Theme parks affect people regardless of where they're from because the sensory tool kit available to designers is not constrained by language or place. Where the earliest amusement parks and thrill rides were working toward a limited emotional end, the ambitions of today's designers include working with a complicated emotional palette.

The future of theme park attractions appears to be heading toward the personalized. If you're a frequent guest, and the park has a way of identifying you, why *not* make new ways of engaging with repeat guests to advance the story that's been carried on in their absence? No longer are theme park designers content with just instilling excitement, or fear: They're moving on to the other emotions. Movies begin and end, but a theme park by definition persists. The things you experience there will go on in your absence. If that stokes your fear of missing out, well, that was always the plan. Do come back again. Oh, and visit the gift shop on your way out.

The Gift Shop

People watch what they enjoy, but they buy what they love and what they think defines them on a personal or identity level. Through merch, we can learn about the deeper relationships that people form with pop culture, their place in fandoms, and how pop culture can really define someone's character. As a result of a number of changes that happened in the 1990s and early 2000s, engaging with pop culture means not just watching a thing once but buying ancillary objects related to that thing that identify characteristics that help define the buyer.

Merchandise based on film and TV characters has existed in one form or another since the 1920s, with comic strips and animated characters like Felix the Cat finding their way to all manners of product. Disney began merchandising Mickey Mouse in 1929. The next year, they'd signed a contract with Geo. Borgfeldt & Co. to merchandise Mickey abroad. By 1932, there was a whole division dedicated to creating merch. It became central to Disney's business, yet no competitor in the toon space really followed suit for decades. Warner Bros.—home of Looney Tunes—did not have a merchandising division or a real plan until the 1970s.

Outside of Disney, character merchandise existed, but it was auxiliary to the studios producing the works. That changed in 1977 when George Lucas released *Star Wars*. For those unfamiliar with the film's history, *Star Wars* was made for 20th Century Fox with a small budget in the interest of popularizing a promising toy business conceived by George Lucas, a now-famous toy salesman.

This deal has been well documented, but the gist is as follows: Lucas was offered flat fees by Alan Ladd Jr. at Fox to make the original 1977 film—$50,000 to write it, $50,000 to produce it, and $50,000 to direct it. Then Lucas' *American Graffiti* came out and it was a big hit that cost $750,000 to make but earned $100 million. This gave Lucas serious leverage at the negotiating table. Rather than fight for higher fees, he asked to retain sequel rights, with Fox getting the first chance to distribute the movie. When *Star Wars* became a big hit, Lucas had all the leverage he could want surrounding the sequel. So, in exchange for letting 20th Century Fox distribute the self-financed *Empire Strikes Back*, Lucas got the merch rights to the franchise back.

Star Wars had cracked a puzzling question. There were stringent rules on advertising to children, so toys for kids and entertainment for kids were actually kept pretty distinct. The top-selling toys in the '60s and '70s (stuff like Slip 'N Slides and Nerf Balls) weren't anchored to any of the big kids' movies or franchises, in part because it was against Federal Communications Commission regulations for a kids' show to exist mainly to pitch products. *Star Wars*, and especially the sequel *Empire Strikes Back*, with its evocative and imaginative characters and overnight canonization, didn't need a television show to pitch kids on buying toys. It was itself a pitch.

Star Wars achieved staying power by just being a really, really good movie that children liked, and the merch sales flowed organically. Compared with *Empire*, *Star Wars* is a fairly sparse movie. But *Empire* explores a dozen locales and introduces a host of visually striking characters. *Star Wars* was almost entirely set on a Rebellion cruiser, the planet Tatooine, the Millennium Falcon, the Death Star, a rebel base, space, and a large room used to give medals to nice boys. However, *Empire* was made by a man with the rights and know-how to forge every new side character into plastic, and

therefore, dollars. For proof, look no further than Boba Fett, who was *obviously* made by a man who intended to make him into a very cool toy.

Lucas's deal to own the sequel rights was never replicated by anyone else. He and Spielberg tried the same pitch at Paramount for *Raiders of the Lost Ark* and were told to pound sand. Because when *Empire* came out, it pushed toy sales to hyperspace. Afterward, no film was released without a specific plan to merchandise it.

The reason for this had to do with yet another legal change: In 1981, FCC chairman Mark Fowler oversaw the elimination of the restrictions that had formerly prevented children's television from simply becoming twenty-two-minute toy commercials. This meant that existing toy brands—My Little Pony, Transformers, He-Man—had the all-clear to develop television shows that highlighted their lines. And other shows—like *The Smurfs* and, later, *Care Bears*—were designed explicitly to launch alongside a line of collectable toys.

The merch phenomenon is hardly a US-only thing. Japan married culture, fandom, and commerce early on. In the '80s many anime producers were still operating at a $10,000-per-episode loss after costs of about $100,000. That became manageable through merchandising, which was specifically intended to fill the gap. It's why Sailor Moon has so many friends, why Gundam has so many robots, and how Japan was able to fuel so much animation, a pricey, labor-intensive medium even when done on the cheap.

This made its way into the American market soon enough, with the same companies that made a killing in the '80s by putting My Little Pony and Transformers on televisions to sell toys to kids. They pivoted, and then innovated by once again putting My Little Pony and Transformers on big screens to sell toys to kids.

Hasbro's balance sheet is a testament to the power of pop culture. In the 1990s, they were a conventional toy company, making around $3.2 billion net revenue in 1997, half

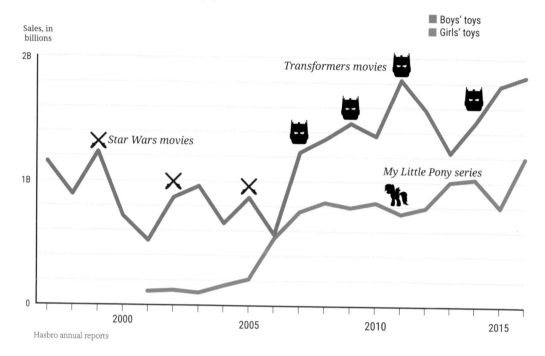

ANNUAL HASBRO SALES
The toy business rides the waves of pop culture

Sales, in billions

■ Boys' toys
■ Girls' toys

Transformers movies

Star Wars movies

My Little Pony series

2B

1B

0

2000   2005   2010   2015

Hasbro annual reports

of it from toys. A little over a billion of that came from boys' toys, another billion or so came from games like Monopoly and Furby, and around $300 million came from the pre-school segment like Tonka, which meant girls' toys were hauling in—just kidding, girls' toys made so little money for Hasbro in the '90s they didn't even bother breaking the number out into its own segment. As late as 2003, the entire girls' toy business was worth only around $100 million to Hasbro, about a tenth of the boys' business.

However, things in their toy business were about to accelerate, and fast, as an enterprising director was about to make a little independent film called *Star Wars: Episode I—The Phantom Menace*. You can see the event on Hasbro's balance sheet the same way a doctor can detect an injection of adrenaline into the heart on an EKG. In 1998, the year before the film, Star Wars still produced 13 percent of toy revenues, but in 1999, upon release of *The Phantom Menace*, the franchise was single-handedly

responsible for 36 percent of Hasbro's entire toy revenue, a $500 million business, which is especially wild when you consider that the film made $427 million at the US domestic box office in its first year of release.

Although the mania surrounding *The Phantom Menace* diminished somewhat when the film actually made its way to audiences, Hasbro lucked out with another winning franchise film the following year in 2000, when Pokémon toys would account for a full 15 percent of their revenue after the late-1999 release of the first Pokémon feature film.

For Hasbro, the old model of producing media to sell toys was alive and well. Their core franchises—things like G.I. Joe, Transformers, My Little Pony, Nerf, and the like—were only around 17 percent of sales in 2001. Seeing the astronomical numbers for Star Wars and Pokémon got gears turning at the company: If new big-screen adventures could rejuvenate a long-dormant sci-fi action franchise of the '80s, or a line of cute characters bolstered by a television show, why not *our* long-dormant sci-fi action franchise of the '80s, or *our* cute collectible animals?

By the time *Revenge of the Sith* came out in 2005—a $494 million business that year, a $285 million one the following year—Hasbro had set into motion their plan to fill the Star Wars–sized hole that was about to appear in their balance sheet. When the *Transformers* movie came out in 2007, the line exploded, becoming nearly 13 percent of the company's revenue that year, to the tune of $480 million. The film itself? Made only $319 million domestically at the box office. That pattern of the toys outearning the movie would continue: *Transformers: Revenge of the Fallen* (toys: $592 million in 2009, movie: $402 million at the domestic box office); *Transformers: Dark of the Moon* (toys: $483 million in 2011, movie: $352 million at the domestic box office). And because the box office had to be split first between the cinemas, then the studio itself, this explosion in sales *was* Hasbro's reward and the end goal all along. It also juiced the whole product line long-term.

The big-screen adaptations of Transformers and, to a less successful extent, G.I. Joe, were far from their only efforts to build in-house pop culture events to pump up toy sales. Remember the anemic sales numbers for girls' toys? In 2003, Hasbro reintroduced the My Little Pony line of products, albeit largely imitating the 1980s format that made the line a sensation. In 2010, they completely redesigned the format, rolling out a television network with *My Little Pony: Friendship Is Magic* as the anchor program. Setting aside the, uh, incidental popularity with the content outside the intended demo, the new show sent Pony sales skyrocketing. By 2013, My Little Pony was doing $650 million in retail sales; by 2014, that number was $1 billion.

By 2016, Hasbro Studios, the division tasked with producing new content based on their owned properties, required about $350 million in cash to produce said content. The company estimated that the division had produced around $2 billion in value. The core brands were responsible for just 17 percent of revenue in 2001. By 2015, that number was up to 52 percent of revenue.

In 2017, which saw the release of both *My Little Pony: The Movie* and *Transformers: The Last Knight*, the franchises were at the peak of their production for Hasbro. Combined, the films made a disappointing $150 million

Hogwarts, now with a gift shop.

domestically at the box office. But that year, the toys related to those two franchises raked in $2.7 billion in retail sales.

Hasbro took the old formula pioneered in Japan—make a show for kids, maybe lose money on it, but then make that money back and then some in toy sales—and updated it for a new generation.

And while this is all a great illustration of how fan culture develops, it's actually missing a critical piece of the puzzle. Hasbro is a toy company. Their purpose is to sell toys to children. The execution of their film and television strategy was a way to increase sales of toys to children, and they succeeded, wildly.

But none of that is directly traceable to the way media and culture have placed consumption and acquisition of merchandise as a central component of identity formation. I own multiple posters of superheroes, and I am thirty-one years old. I have filled out a last will and testament, and yet I also own *more than one* Hawkeye T-shirt. No FCC commissioner did this. No chunk of plastic forged in the late 1970s did this. I haven't touched Hasbro plastic since I was a holiday stockboy at KB Toys during the George W. Bush administration. I am a grown man with over ten years of tax records kept in a banker box—that sits next to a map of Westeros.

Walt Disney did not do this to me. They are not responsible for the way that identity and fandom have become intertwined, how watching something and owning something from that thing you watched are now an integral part of the consumer experience.

What's Up, Doc?

As merchandising became a critical part of the fan experience, for the bulk of the twentieth century those fans were children. The market for toys, merchandising, and apparel capped out at perhaps age fifteen, and the toys themselves were non-choking, often stuffed and depersonalized, and lacked multiple points of articulation. Sizing on the apparel topped out at children's Large.

Compared with the absolute hegemony of fan culture these days, which is fueled by thousands of shipping containers laden with figurines, acres of T-shirts, mountains of key chains, bobbleheads of minor characters, $45 wands, $499 Lego sets, and $40,000 animation cels. Clearly, something changed between the end of the 1980s and the beginning of the 2000s that completely altered the relationship between people, the pop culture they enjoyed, and the products it spawned.

That something was the Warner Bros. Studio Store.

It was the first time that merchandise based on characters was composed of a product line pretty much entirely for adults. And it succeeded beyond the wildest imaginations of every single person involved, while singlehandedly turning a $20 million Warner Bros. licensing business into a multibillion-dollar enterprise in about five years' time. They'd found a brand-new market that nobody had bothered to serve; they'd revolutionized a business that had been the same for decades; they'd changed the way adults consume mass media forever. They also reached too high and overstepped, and then AOL murdered it right before the dot-com bubble.

To understand the present state of pop culture, with its miles of memorabilia and roiling adult online fandoms and its massive ancillary footprint, we have to look at the store that made it this way, the missing link between a handful of fans and collectors and the behemoth franchises that dominate the cultural landscape today. The innovations and business practices they cracked would define not only the next two decades of pop culture merchandise but the very DNA on which franchises are designed, produced, and endlessly exploited. From the Wizarding World to Avengers Tower, from Forks, Washington, to King's Landing, the Warner Bros. Studio Store is the missing link in understanding why pop culture became what it is today. If we want to find out what pop culture is now doing to us, we need to go back to the beginning, to the people who figured out the untapped potential in the adult market, the Warner Bros. Studio Store. We've got to meet patient zero.

In 1987, the Walt Disney Company opened the first Disney store in the Glendale Galleria in California. The store did what Disney as a company had been doing, at that point, for decades: selling toys to kids. The Disney Catalogs of the late 1980s are a time capsule of the prevailing mentality of retail in that era. The apparel was overwhelmingly for kids—there were some adult-sized T-shirts with Mickey, maybe a few Christmas ornaments for Mom, some golf-club covers for Dad, but the bulk of the offerings were for kids. Surveying the holiday catalogs of 1988 and 1989, the product is one-note, and the name of that note is Mickey. He's the only character emblazoned on anything.

For Disney, that was likely enough. The company was built on the Mouse and they knew well how to sell rodents to kids. The business was a success. By 1988, Disney had thirteen locations in California and on the East Coast. By 1989, they had forty shops across the country, mostly in upscale malls and shopping centers. That number grew to 111 locations by 1991. Disney did what Disney does best—sell Disney to the parents of children.

But in 1989, something else happened. Warner Bros., one of the oldest studios in Hollywood, released a film about a dedicated young man who, to get through some stuff, dressed up as a bat and beat up bad guys. For the bulk of Bruce Wayne's existence, Batman was a character for children. Children were the people who bought comic books through the Golden and Silver Ages of comic books; the 1960s television show was a campy, laugh-tracked adventure serial that aired in early prime time; and while Dennis O'Neil and Neal Adams's run on the comic pulled the character back from the brink of camp, even as the comics got grittier and more mature through the '80s the core audience of Batman was still kids. The median reader of comic books was young; sketchy though the data may be, a *Comics Buyer's Guide* survey from 1985 found the *average* respondent's age was just over nineteen, so most readers were teenagers.

In 1989 Warner Bros. released *Batman*, and it was a smashing success. The new Batman was darker, more adult. It became the then-fastest film to make $100 million, selling more than 60 million tickets in the United States. In the end, it made a quarter of a billion dollars and was the top-grossing film of the year by far. Given everything that Warner Bros. knew about Batman, and the history, and the age of the audience, it stood to reason that if you wanted to sell some Batman merch, it'd probably be for kids.

But over at Warner Bros., head of consumer products Dan Romanelli started noticing something very strange. The most fervent buyers of the pins and the key chains with the Batman emblem emblazed on it were men in their thirties and forties.

At the time Warner was the distant second to Disney in merchandise sales, which isn't the worst place to be. The characters' lines didn't really compete, with the Mouse holding the monopoly on their soft, safe, cute characters versus the crafty, rude, and conniving Warner roster. When Disney first rolled out their stores, Warner certainly noticed, but management was skittish about the concept, and nobody really wanted to be the one to gamble their career on the second-best merch store in the mall. So they stuck with the tried-and-true licensing model: Sell the rights to make a product to someone else, let them do all the work, then collect the royalties at the end of the quarter.

But when *Batman* hit theaters, Warner execs noticed unexpected things about their customers.

Romanelli recalled giving his son a pack of Batman pins to give away to friends at school to promote the movie. A few days later, his kid asked for a second pack. The same thing happened just days after that. Romanelli asked him what precisely he was doing with the pins, and then realized his son was making a small killing *selling* them.

"I remember once, after a licensing show in New York, we went into Smith and Wollensky," Romanelli said. "There were eight of us, and the maître d' said, 'I don't have a table for you.'" This was just months before *Batman* would hit theaters. The maître d' quickly clocked the pin on his lapel. "He said, 'If you give me that pin, I'll give you a table now.' I said, 'Well, there are eight of us. How many pins do I have to give you to get a bottle of wine?'

"He said, 'Give me twenty-five pins and I'll buy you dinner.'"

More than just a box office hit, *Batman* was the first home run in the consumer products division under Romanelli. After that, management was increasingly sold on the idea of a store.

The Disney stores were about 3,500 or 4,000 square feet, but Peter Starrett, who was hired to make it all happen, wanted his stores to be 7,000 to 8,000 square feet—and sell primarily to adults. They'd obviously have some sort of kids' assortment as well, but the mix would be the opposite of Disney's, which was 80 percent geared to kids and 20 percent to adults.

The concept was *nothing* like anything in the entertainment market.

"We'll use much more sophisticated building material, much more sophisticated retail fixturing," said Starrett. "It will not look like a kid store. It'll look like a more sophisticated store. They had a little video monitor in their stores showing loops of Disney cartoons? We'll do a giant video wall in the back of our store." The goal was to design a space that felt radically different from a Disney Store.

The Plan

Linda Postell had risen through the department store Bamberger's, then designing Macy's private label, hopping over to Ann Taylor product development in 1988. In early 1990, she got a call from a headhunter in California: Warner Bros. is looking to set up a store. After taking a crash course in Looney Tunes from her stepson, she had her pitch.

The initial plan was four stores with $50 million to get things off the ground within a year. It would be up to Linda to figure out

what precisely they would be selling and who exactly they would be selling to. That year of product design will go down as one of the most consequential in pop culture. What Linda and her team designed and the approach they took would become the blueprint for successful pop culture merch for the next three decades, if not more. She was at least a decade ahead of anyone else.

Postell, with a background in conventional retail, didn't come with any of the biases about what worked in pop culture merch. She saw that the Looney Tunes characters had a renegade streak, that their core customer was the baby boomer who had spent a childhood watching them and had since come into some money. She believed that if they wanted to sell things to adults, the quality had to be legit, and that buyers in that previously unaddressed market were willing to pay for actual quality. She spooled up an entire product design and sourcing unit in-house.

The stores were designed to look like a studio backlot, an expensive but immersive environment that helped justify the higher price point. Just like studio backlots they were totally modular, and the lighting techniques they innovated—and pulled from movie lighting anyway—would become industry standard.

"At the time there was a lot of skepticism about our strategy, even within Warner Brothers," Starrett said. It was a definite risk. "Everybody could see the Disney Store and what they did and asked, 'What are you guys talking about?'"

Game Changer

The first Warner Bros. store opened in 1991 at the Beverly Center in Los Angeles. After a frenzied year of designing a store from the floorboards to the rafters, stocking it from scratch, and conducting reams of market research, it was finally about to open its doors.

"As much research as we'd done and as much thought as we'd put into it," said Postell, "we didn't know how it was going to be received."

There were lines around the block on opening day.

Romanelli recalled then–Disney CEO Michael Eisner swinging by and looking surprised at all the action.

Three more Warner Bros. stores would open, each in a different part of the country, to test if the Los Angeles store was a fluke. Those stores were also hits. Together, the four stores booked $12 million in revenue in four months, shattering internal projections.

They opened a fifth store in Las Vegas and projected $3 million in annual sales. The first *week* it was open, it did $400,000. It went on to do nearly $20 million the first year in business. Company brass was satisfied: They greenlit a massive expansion of the concept. Five stores would become dozens, and then growth went exponential.

Most importantly, Postell was learning from her customers. Learning lessons that the animators and the studio couldn't possibly know.

The initial strategy plan—hone in on quality, target the people who grew up with it—was enough to get the first stores off the ground. But once they were actually selling stuff, Postell figured out one last piece that would prove central to the future of not just the Warner Bros. Studio Store but the very future of entertainment.

"What I realized very, very early on was that when you talk to people who grew up in the '60s and '70s, this group of people totally

WARNER BROS. STUDIO STORE

The store exploded in popularity in the 1990s

REVENUE, IN MILLIONS OF 1990S USD

STORES OPEN AT YEAR'S END

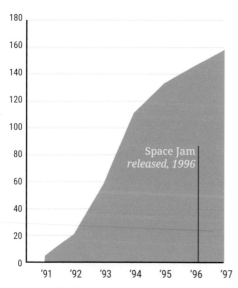

Space Jam *released, 1996*

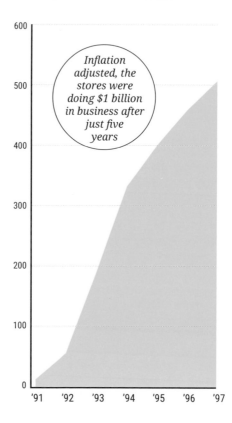

Inflation adjusted, the stores were doing $1 billion in business after just five years

Data provided by Peter Starrett

BE LIKE MIKE

The 1996 premiere of *Space Jam*—the first feature-length film with Looney Tunes characters in a generation, paired with the most popular athlete on the planet, Michael Jordan—was a major moment for the Warner Bros. stores.

Romanelli, then head of consumer products, remembers well the impact that movie had on the retail side of the business, but also that he landed a creative note for the movie. When he saw a rough cut of the movie, he loved it, but he noticed that when they announced the Looney Tunes characters for a game, everyone cheered, even when Daffy Duck emerged. This, he realized, reflected a fundamental misunderstanding of Daffy Duck's relationship with his fan base.

"I said, 'No one cheers. You hear *crickets*.' And they changed it."

Warner Bros made $1.2 billion in licensing from *Space Jam*.

But by the mid-nineties, the stores had already hit their turning point. They went from a $20 million business in 1991 to over a half billion in sales in 1997 across 158 stores around the world. Competitors and peers had long since taken notice, just as a new wave of consumer products—first Pokémon from Japan, then Harry Potter from the UK—were poised to wash up on US shores.

---

identify with one, maybe two characters, period," she said. "If they're a tough guy, and they have a Harley-Davidson, they're a Taz guy. If they're sarcastic and glib, they're a Daffy Duck guy. If they're straight down the fairway, maybe it's Bugs. Everyone has their love of certain characters."

That customers individually identified with a single character gave the designers room to make things specifically *for* different customers. You wouldn't make a biker jacket of Tweety, nor would you design a gardening set featuring a Tasmanian agent of destruction. But the Harley-Davidson jacket with Taz on it sold out in *a week*. A gardening set for the Tweety gang was a bestseller from Macau, China, to London, England.

"The personality of that character really came through into the customer," observed Postell. "There's a group of people that love Foghorn Leghorn—and they all look the same. It's mind-boggling."

As they needed more concepts, she pulled more obscure assets from the canon, emphasized the personality within the characters, and pushed them into the popular consciousness. But even when the characters weren't Bugs or Porky, they were still

fantastically appealing—and lucrative—to subsets of fans who saw those characters as image-defining.

From 1948 to 1990, the character of Marvin the Martian appeared in merely seven cartoons lasting a total of fifty minutes and didn't even have a formal name. But if Looney Tunes wasn't able to make him a star, Postell's team—in need of a product for techie types who wanted to display the feeling that they had little patience for those who did not innately trust them—well, certainly they could!

That's All, Folks

The stores had massive appeal overseas, because there is no language on earth where the attraction of Road Runner thwarting a coyote does not come across loud and clear. Soon, the stores expanded to locations including London, Germany, Singapore, Indonesia, Japan, Spain, and Saudi Arabia.

As the stores took off, the licensing business—signing a deal to put Bugs Bunny on a cookie, or a candy bar, or a Walmart tee— exploded with the stores. Postell put the licensing and consumer products division at maybe $20 million from 1988 to 1990. Within four years, that became a $2 billion or $2.5 billion licensing business.

The stores continued to go on a tear through the late 1990s, but growth soon showed signs of ebbing, and the executives who designed the venture from the beginning began to depart.

The merger of Warner Bros. with AOL would ultimately spell doom. Warner executives thought they were merging with AOL, and AOL executives thought they were buying Warner. AOL presciently believed all retail was going online and didn't want to be in brick-and-mortar assets. They were right, but ten years too early. Although the stores still printed money, they weren't seen as central to the mission of AOL; they were just something nice to include in press releases and for hosting events.

The company went into a tailspin, a casualty of which was the stores, all of which folded in October 2001, a monumental event in the history of retail and merchandising that is not an indelible part of cultural memory, largely because of the September 11 attacks.

But what the Warner Bros. stores pioneered—the selling to adults of merchandise originally made for children that helped those adults define and articulate their identities—lived on.

For starters, the Warner play instantly changed the approach of their crosstown rivals. By 1997, you could see a marked increase in the amount of merch for adults in the Disney Catalog, the pages full of collectibles and tchotchkes from the Disney Renaissance period of films that ran from The Little Mermaid to Tarzan and, point, was winding down to a close.

Disney would spend the next two decades looking not to the future but to the past, scooping up the baby boomers' franchises, throwing fresh coats of paint on the Star Wars and Marvel properties, even on their own animated features. They'd lean into the identity

component that Warner cracked, the idea that you could sell nostalgic adults high-quality products, provided they tapped into some innate sense of identity.

The experiential entertainment style of retail that these shops pioneered soon became the norm. Expensive up-front investment into digital video boards, coordinated sound, design features like modularity and set-piece lighting—these approaches were picked up by retail shops from Fifth Avenue to the local strip mall.

When the Harry Potter franchise entered its post–*Deathly Hallows* phase, it sustained audience interest not by trying to sell Ron Weasley action figures but by offering the adults who grew up on the books the robes, wands, and stationery that *they* would have had if *their* letter to Hogwarts had arrived. It wasn't about playacting as Harry and Hermione or facing off against the dreaded Draco; by the middle of the franchise, the unspoken fan narrative was about which house the reader would belong to. Slytherins were softened from wizard bullies and fascists in *Sorcerer's Stone* to cunning people who incidentally attract a couple fascists by book six. Learning the material of one's wand was made to resemble learning your star sign of the zodiac.

In the decades since Warnes Bros. evolved the art of merchandising, the entire pop culture business has emulated their thinking. Although the 80-20 adult-to-kids ratio is far from standard, the 80-20 kids-to-adults isn't common anymore either. And the proof, as always, is in the numbers: In 1996, the retail side of entertainment licensing was a $16.7 billion business. In 2018, the global industry had $122.7 billion in sales. At the end of the day, adults are the ones with the money.

Marvin the Martian

The Identity Industry

Merchandising evolved to be more than just character-branded items of value. When you bought the Tweety Bird gardening set in the '90s, you were genuinely getting a gardening set, tools of actual value, albeit with a mild price premium versus a standard-issue gardening set because of the iconic bird on it. The clear utility of the items for sale at the time was clear: They were able to keep people entertained and playing without falling apart after a single use.

The merch of the 1990s and early 2000s consisted of either toys or consumer products like kitchen and outdoor supplies, useful things, fashion that you could wear over and over. But even then, a new class of merch was emerging on the margins. Christmas, the seasonal reserve of the ornamental, suddenly had competition. With adults as the new primary customer for aging franchises, the ornamental became year-round. On the high end we're talking figurines, die-cast sculptures, and mass-produced posters. For starters.

Star Wars fans always have some sort of light saber at their disposal, with increasingly sophisticated effects as time goes on. But at best it's a centerpiece on a shelf—it's not like you can trim the hedges with it. Even the most robust plastics won't survive long as a bona fide sparring weapon. Marvel fans have their Infinity Gauntlet, an eye-catching sculpture that could go for anywhere from $50 at the low end to nearly $5,000 at the high end, but as a glove it's useless.

Even Harry Potter stores—a franchise where it's *absolutely central* to the plot that high-quality useful household instruments, brooms, be readily available—don't sell brooms! They sell wands, ornate sticks of molded plastic that allude to a wand prop from the films but are mass produced from the same mold. There is absolutely no real-world utility to owning an officially licensed plastic magic wand from the Harry Potter store. But replicas of Harry's and Hermione's wands are among the top sellers at the official shops.

These items, cheap replicas, defy conventional means of product categorization. They could be easily derided as kitsch, tchotchkes, junk, or whatever—they are items with strictly sartorial, decorative, or imaginative uses, art on their own merits at best. But they mean something to the people who own them. Their value is not outward but inward, and they are

Which piece of intellectual property will temporarily satisfy your fundamental need to belong for approximately $9?

FUNKO LICENSES

How a bobblehead company signed licenses with all of pop culture

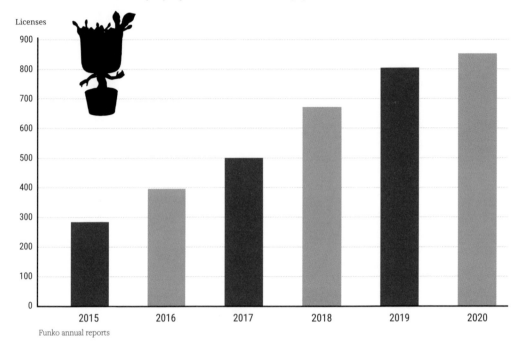

Licenses

Funko annual reports

driving growth in entertainment merchandise.

To understand how quickly this shift is happening, consider the arguably most successful producer of "sculpture" in the world: Funko.

Bobbleheads, once the sole domain of baseball players, have become the lingua franca of popular culture. In 2021, Funko booked $636 million in sales, the overwhelming majority of it in Funko Pop figurines. In case you're unfamiliar with them or are reading this book in a far-flung future in which spiraling resource scarcity has rendered a company that produces millions of polypropylene bobbleheads of ephemeral characters vestigial, I will explain the product.

Funko developed a cutesy in-house style and reliable format where they are able to design and quickly produce bobbleheads (small plastic models of people with heads that "bobble," or wiggle delightfully, when flicked) of characters based on popular movies and shows (and sometimes of characters from unpopular movies and shows). Because they

are pretty much the only company that makes cute bobbleheads of pop culture personalities and as such remain the only game in town, they have been able to assemble what is genuinely the most impressive roster of licensing agreements in the world.

When a studio wants to mint action figures, there are two companies they can enlist to make those figures. When they want a T-shirt, there are countless producers engaged in globe-spanning cutthroat competition to screen-print an image on cotton. When the studios want to make bobbleheads of every named character on a film's call sheet, well, there's only one company they call: Funko.

"People want stuff they emotionally resonate with," said Dolly Ahluwalia, VP of licensing and business development at the company. "What has changed specific to collectibles like Funko is that saying you're a geek and collector used to be kind of a faux pas—no one wanted to admit it—and now it's cool."

What makes Funko revolutionary is that they don't create or own the properties they're making. They don't have stores, and although they have a direct-to-consumer channel, most Funko Pops are sold by other retailers. They don't even have factories; contractors in Vietnam produce the actual bobbleheads. They're a company that takes licensing deals as inputs and has in-house creatives who design the Pops, and the overseas factories handle the rest. Disney, whose products in 2019 accounted for about a third of Funko's sales, effectively receives checks in the mail every quarter and doesn't have to do anything besides keep making movies. Funko, which has to mail that check every quarter and produce new designs based on those movies, never has to melt a single plastic pellet.

Besides the expansion in the number of properties it produces, Funko's balance sheet reveals another trend. In 2016, sales from evergreen properties—things like Batman and Terminator and Avatar, older franchises that aren't pegged to new movies or shows—made up about 43 percent of sales. By 2020, that figure had jumped to 66 percent, fully two-thirds of their production. And although that jump was doubtless caused in part by pandemic-era declines in new content releases, the figure had been rising steadily for years.

People were dying to buy up physical representations of pop culture they liked, they weren't just buying what was new and fresh.

They were mining their own nostalgia.

Spinoff, Sequel, Reboot, Prequel

Reboots are not new. In fact, the concept of reimagining an old story is almost as old as the original stories they steal. *The Aeneid*? A reboot of Homer with a more likable protagonist. *All's Well That Ends Well*? Since this is Shakespeare, most of his material is repurposed from Plutarch as though he apprenticed under him. The US Constitution? A reboot of the Articles of Confederation, albeit an improvement on the original.

Still, the primary motivation for a reboot, a sequel, a prequel is financial. There are plenty of reasons why a director may want to return to a franchise after time away. Maybe they want to revisit the world they built and expand on it. Perhaps the themes they wanted to address could be accomplished only by getting everyone back together except Robert Duvall and then casting their daughter in a starring role. We can probably conclude that a person who spent most of their life boxing in Philly would want to confront their own looming senescence by way of a film about an underdog fighter. Maybe we really need to address exactly where the Minions were between the years 1939 and 1945?

But the real reason there are so many reboots is that they're more reliable moneymakers than original films.

This doesn't mean reboots automatically make more money than original films, though. It's a common misperception that the only things Hollywood executives care about are profits. This is not the case. The top priority of most producers is not to make a lot of money, but rather not to *lose* a lot of money. Nobody ever got fired for making a modest bet on a beloved franchise, but many people have gotten fired for making a modest bet on an unknown script with big potential. The incentive is risk aversion, not profit seeking.

The average original film, the kind of movie that is not built off of a preexisting intellectual property, has made 2.8 times its budget back at the global box office since 1980. That's pretty good, the kind of return on investment that puts a film in the black. It's even a little better than a nonsequel film based on a screenplay adapted from another property—a comic book, a television show, a news story, or a magazine article—which on average made back 2.5 times their budget. Your conclusion might

WHY DOES HOLLYWOOD JUST CRANK OUT SEQUELS, REMAKES, AND ADAPTATIONS?

It's not about making lots of money; it's about never losing any money

KEY:

Less profitable — More profitable

Typically the break-even profitability point

	Percent that made budget back domestically	Percent that made budget back internationally	Percent that doubled budget domestically
ALL ORIGINALS	46%	68%	21%
Based on Comic/Graphic Novel	51%	78%	15%
Based on Factual Book/Article	58%	74%	32%
Based on Fiction Book/Short Story	43%	66%	18%
Based on Folk Tale/Legend/Fairy Tale	48%	85%	24%
Based on Game	26%	63%	4%
Based on Play	52%	65%	31%
Based on Real-Life Events	37%	59%	17%
Based on TV Show	53%	77%	30%
Original Screenplay	47%	68%	21%
Remake	58%	78%	20%
Spin-Off	77%	95%	23%
ALL SEQUELS	66%	92%	29%
Based on Comic/Graphic Novel	65%	94%	15%
Based on Fiction Book/Short Story	59%	92%	24%
Based on TV Show	71%	97%	23%
Original Screenplay	71%	92%	39%

well be that original screenplays outperform adapted material.

But the average sequel has made back 4.2 times its budget at the global box office since 1980. Sequels based on original concepts did even better, earning back 4.7 times their budgets at the global box office.

This makes sense, of course. All the work done to establish the first movie rolls into the second, and as the overall cost of advertisements and reaching an audience rise, so too does the cost of promotion. But sequels give you momentum. There's a reason why the people who get to make the most original films—companies like Pixar or Studio Ghibli, directors like Christopher Nolan, M. Night Shyamalan, or Quentin Tarantino—are able to do so based only on the inherent strength of their corporate or individual brand, and in some cases at substantial personal financial risk.

But if the single best box office performers are sequels to original movies and original movies make a profit on average, why don't studios invest in new originals with an eye toward establishing new franchises more often?

It comes down to shareholders and return on investment. If your spending on an original movie nets you 2.8 times return on your investment, those dollars actually represent what you're *not* spending on a sequel, where you can count on an average 4.2 times return on investment. That's how investors and stockholders think, anyway.

There's also the inherent risk of *not* earning back your budget, which perhaps a director could survive if it happened only every once in a while, but it can and does spell the end for the studio exec who greenlit the project. Just 44 percent of nonsequel films make back their budget domestically, and just 21 percent double

BROADWAY: PIONEER OF THE REBOOT

In many ways, Broadway was built on reboots. It loves them so much, there's a Tony for best reboot (called a "revival," but let's not kid ourselves). And although reboots are welded deeply into the culture of our entertainment business, the financial logic that precedes a Broadway revival is particularly revealing and goes a long way toward explaining why they're more appealing than original productions.

The calculus of reboots on Broadway is exacting. In 2005, an economist at University College London wanted to find out why the percentage of Broadway shows that were revivals was growing each season. The answer was risk aversion. From 1970 to 1979, just 23 percent of new musicals on Broadway were revivals. From 1990 to 1999, 38 percent were revivals, a trend not in danger of fading away anytime soon.

The finding was that although the upper bound of performances—the number of performances a show might run for if it's particularly successful—for original first-run Broadway shows was much higher than the upper bound of performances

for Broadway revivals of original shows, the new shows were far likelier to fail before their fiftieth performance than revivals. In that situation, the theater hosting the show is in trouble, the producers have a dud, and nobody's happy.

For consumers hungry for all things new, the ideal situation would be if Broadway producers and theaters made bold new bets on original material each and every time. But then Broadway wouldn't be an industry capable of supporting forty thousand jobs and make several billions annually. Producers fall back on revivals to balance out their bets, to wager on a few sure things rather than gamble the entire house each season.

In addition, the dominant producers of media and entertainment are large-cap, publicly traded American corporations. A corporation has to satisfy not just the creative needs or the long-term business interests of the company but also short-term shareholder expectations that force it to exist in a continuous state of dire finances. So it's not entirely surprising that the instincts are to stick to the proven hits.

FRANCHISE TAXONOMY

The concept of a modern film franchise has become far more complex than the original intention of a trilogy, perhaps a series of films. As studios continue their quest for ever more sophisticated, interlocking, brand-reinforcing and convoluted franchise structures, we must rise to meet their challenge. Here, we look at a typology of topology, an attempt to understand the various structures of a franchise and their inherent instability.

Type 1:

THE ONE-TWO ● Films in this type include: *Blade Runner, Blues Brothers, Bruce Almighty, Ghost Rider, The Shining, Tron*

Type 2:

THE SEQUENTIAL

● Also *Night of the Living Dead*

Type 3:

THE SEQUENTIAL + SEQUENTIAL SEQUEL TRILOGY

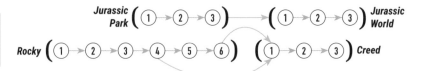

Type 4:

THE SEQUENTIAL WITH REBOOT(S)

● Also *Child's Play* and *The Pink Panther*

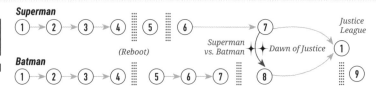

Type 5:

DIRECT TIMELINE, MIXED-UP ORDERING

● Also *The First Purge, Final Destination* and *Insidious*

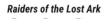

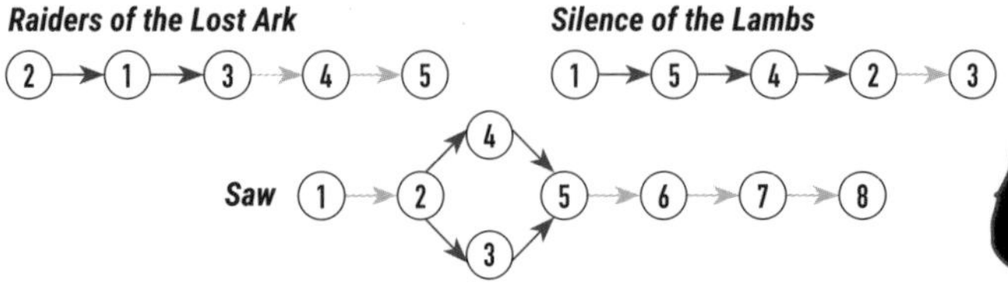

Type 6:

PREQUEL FRANCHISE

● Also *Minions* and *Despicable Me*

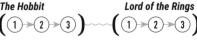

Type 7:

SPIN-INS AND SPIN-OUTS ● Also *Madea* and *Jackass*

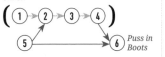

Type 8:

SIMPLE SPIN-INS AND OUTS ● Also *XXX*

Author's analysis of The-Numbers.com

KEY:

First film released ① → Next film follows ②

( ) Trilogy

〰 Time between release

● Similar type of film

✦ Franchise fight

■ Unconnected to main timeline

⋮ Reboot

··· More films to come

Type 9:

PREQUEL/SEQUEL HYBRID

The Godfather ② → (① → ② → ③)

Mamma Mia ② → ① → ②

Type 10:

SEQUENTIAL-PREQUEL-SPINOFF FRANCHISE TO ORIGINAL FRANCHISE

● Also *Alien, Predator, Prometheus*

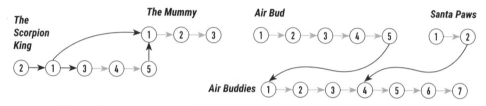

The Scorpion King · **The Mummy** · **Air Bud** · **Santa Paws** · **Air Buddies**

Type 11:

PREQUEL-SEQUEL-SPINOFF FRANCHISE

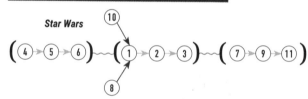

Star Wars

(④ → ⑤ → ⑥) 〰 (① → ② → ③) 〰 (⑦ → ⑨ → ⑪) with ⑩ and ⑧ pointing to ①

Type 12:

MULTIVERSAL TIME TRAVEL SHENANIGANS

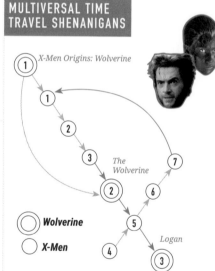

X-Men Origins: Wolverine

The Wolverine

Logan

⬤ **Wolverine**

◯ **X-Men**

Type 13:

TIME TRAVEL SHENANIGANS

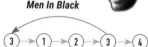

Back to the Future

(① → ② → ③)

Men In Black

③ → ① → ② → ③ → ④

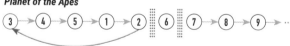

Planet of the Apes

③ → ④ → ⑤ → ① → ② ⋮ ⑥ ⋮ ⑦ → ⑧ → ⑨ → ···

The Terminator

Timeline 1 — ①
Timeline 2 — ②
Timeline 3 — ③ → ④
Timeline 4 — ⑤

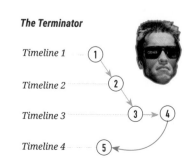

Type 14:

ENDOTHERMIC UNIVERSES

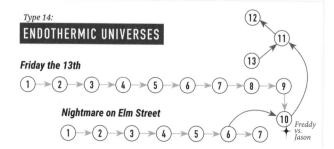

Friday the 13th

① → ② → ③ → ④ → ⑤ → ⑥ → ⑦ → ⑧ → ⑨ → ⑪ → ⑫ with ⑬

Nightmare on Elm Street

① → ② → ③ → ④ → ⑤ → ⑥ → ⑦

⑩ *Freddy vs. Jason*

Type 15:

ECTOTHERMIC UNIVERSES

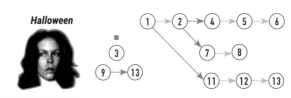

Halloween

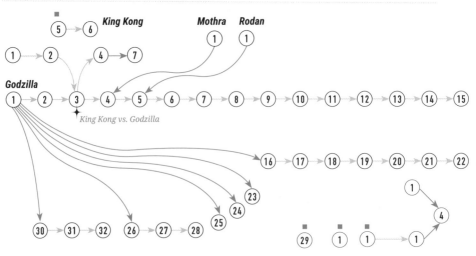

Godzilla

King Kong vs. Godzilla

Type 16:

MULTI-BONDED INTERCONNECTED FRANCHISE

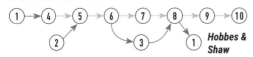

The Fast and the Furious

Hobbes & Shaw

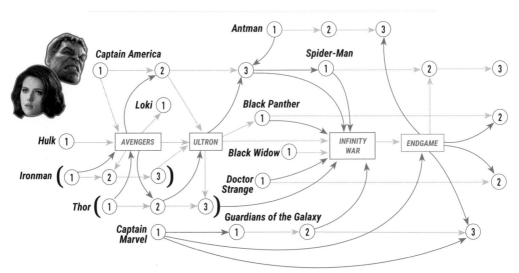

their budgets in profit domestically, which is the rule of thumb for breakeven. Those figures are pretty much the same for both adapted and original screenplays. Meanwhile, 66 percent of sequels make back their budgets and 29 percent double them domestically, with 92 percent of the sequel films earning their budget back globally. So, betting on a sequel has three times the odds of making back the budget Stateside.

Sure, there are some pockets that overperform when it comes to nonsequels, but you'll *never* guess which ones. When it comes to films that aren't sequels, spin-offs make back their budget 77 percent of the time, and remakes earn it back 58 percent of the time. Pretty much everything else is in the red compared with the average film overall.

And when you think about who is *starting* franchises, it's actually rare for the majors to be willing to take that kind of risk. Sure, they'll distribute them, and if you do strike gold, they'll fund the sequels, but peruse any major recent franchise and it's uncommon to find a studio that signed a big check first.

Avatar was released by 20th Century Fox, but it wasn't funded by them, with James Cameron and two private equity firms putting up the funding. The Bond franchise was started by two independent producers and is still tightly controlled by the Broccoli family. Tyler Perry had to build his own Hollywood in Atlanta to get his myriad and consistently successful franchises made. The Marvel Cinematic Universe was started by an independent, self-funded comic book company that only later was bought by Disney. And the Star Wars prequels remain the largest and most successful independent films in history, financed by George Lucas preselling the toy rights. Peter Jackson's *The Lord of the Rings* adaptation was the result of the director waging a vicious war with convicted rapist Harvey Weinstein to get the funding for his movies. *The Hunger Games*' $88 million budget was cobbled together by a studio in desperate need of a hit by preselling the international rights and getting an $8 million tax break from North Carolina.

All those improvised fundraising efforts paid off. And when those concepts are proven, the start-up is bought by a big studio, which invests directly in high-ROI sequels. The budgets for the second films in those franchises were likely assembled with considerably fewer checks. The point being that studios are disincentivized to create new things but encouraged to exploit proven properties. And as Hollywood continued to consolidate and the cost of promotion became too onerous, the inevitable result was fewer and fewer original films.

There's an obvious business incentive to make sequels and reboots, but why is one never enough? Why do audiences appear to *want* reboots? Why are they willing to spend yet more money to return to a place where they have already been and, thanks to digital media, can technically revisit at any time?

High Yearners

The major, connecting way that these financial entities are able to capitalize on our emotions—be it through revivals or toys or a Tasmanian Devil ashtray—is by appealing to nostalgia. It's a complex emotion, but it's one of the most direct ways to explain the business of the vast juggernaut of the pop culture industry.

The precise "why" of nostalgia is murky. But we know that, time and again, nostalgia drives people to spend unfathomable amounts of money on things they liked as a kid. What's the thinking behind spending thousands of dollars on a single animation cel from a show you liked when you were young? Why did an entire generation plow the affluence they came into in the '90s into household goods and apparel of the shows they watched while munching cereal on Saturday mornings? Why, despite a college degree, despite a revulsion for nearly everything the former richest woman in England believes about gender, despite a complete disinterest in further enriching her, despite a good life and career and general satisfaction, why on *earth* does a real part of me still yearn for a personalized letter inviting me to Hogwarts?

The key driver of reboots is nostalgia—and a key driver of nostalgia is loneliness.

One study out of Southampton University published in the *Journal of Personality and Social Psychology* in 2006 sought to understand nostalgia through a series of experiments. In one, drawing on a sample of forty-three students, researchers tried to figure out if there was a link between loneliness and feelings of nostalgia.

The subjects were asked to take a test to calculate their score on the UCLA Loneliness Scale, a quick assessment that asks people how often they feel disconnected from others, such as how often they feel alone, or starved for company, or find it difficult to make friends. Researchers then informed each participant of their score and whether it indicated things like a high or low degree of loneliness.

Next, participants took Batcho's Nostalgia Inventory, a psychological test developed by Krystine Batcho in 1995 to quantify how deeply people feel nostalgia at a given time. It's a questionnaire where respondents select a number between 1 and 9 (1 indicating "not at all," 9 meaning "very much") to describe how much they miss things from when they were younger. The topics are things like "family," "heroes or heroines," "things you did," "toys," "holidays," "the way society was," "your house," and "not knowing sad or evil things."

Finally, the respondents were asked, as a means of confirmation, how lonely they felt on a scale of 1 to 5.

But here's the trick. That first questionnaire, the loneliness one, was faked. The researchers pulled questions from the UCLA test but rigged it by tweaking the questions. Then they didn't actually score it, but randomized whether they told the person they had a high degree of loneliness, (in the sixty-second percentile of loneliness) or a low degree of loneliness (in the twelfth percentile of loneliness).

The goal wasn't actually to determine how lonely they were. It was to prime them, to make them think either that they were more lonely than the typical person or less lonely than average. It worked. That confirmation, asking them how lonely they felt? The group primed to feel less lonely—the people who were told they had low loneliness after the fake first test—reported an average loneliness of 1.3, whereas the group primed to believe they had high loneliness reported an average of 2.9 out of 5.

The results were consistent with a causal relationship between loneliness and nostalgia. They found that the group that was told they were lonelier scored higher on the nostalgia index (an average score of 3.01) than the group who believed they were less lonely (an average of 2.56). The ratings of nostalgia for "my family," "the way people were," "having someone to depend on," and "not having to worry" were significantly higher statistically among those primed for loneliness compared with those who were not. It corroborated the idea that there's a fundamental link between feelings of being alone and the psychological emergence of nostalgia.

And although the rise of nostalgia in media is mostly anecdotal, there's repeated evidence that people—particularly younger people—are more lonely than before, and that things like social media can exacerbate those feelings of loneliness. American health insurer Cigna has conducted a large loneliness survey since 2018, with over ten thousand respondents in the sample annually. In 2020, 61 percent of those surveyed were lonely, up 7 percentage points since the survey was first conducted in 2018.

We know there is a compelling link between loneliness and nostalgia. We also know that nostalgia sells incredibly well, that people want the things that brought them comfort as kids when they feel alone.

That's the demand, and the studios are happy to supply it.

CHAPTER 6

HOW CULTURE FUELS EMPIRES

In 1923, the Prince of Wales addressed the British Film League, exhorting them to improve their work, develop the British film industry with haste, and use it to promote the Empire. In the view of the future King Edward, the United Kingdom was falling dreadfully behind its American counterparts in the field of movies, and it was having a serious effect on Britain's status as a global power. The London *Morning Post*, reporting on the speech, put it in starker terms:

> If the United States abolished its diplomatic and consular services, kept its ships in harbors and its tourists at home, and retired from the world's markets, its citizens, its problems, its towns and countrysides, its roads, motor cars, counting houses and saloons would still be familiar in the utmost corners of the world.
>
> The film is to America what the flag was once to Britain. By its means, Uncle Sam may hope some day, if he be not checked in time, to Americanize this world.

This sentiment—a realization that two hundred years of global hegemony enforced by gunpowder and frigates was wilting next to a bunch of ex-vaudevillians with an exportable party trick—hinted at a larger diplomatic shift underway.

Namely, there was a second way emerging for one country to get another to do what it wants.

The first, then and now, is hard power. If you want a country to, say, open up for trade or render military support, and you have the more powerful military, that often decides the

Win the game, reap a fortune.

matter. But not always. And yet sometimes, just the threat of force is enough to get a desired outcome from another nation.

Culture is the second way, one that's much more popular these days. Partially this is because battleships are horribly unfashionable, not to mention that they reek of masculine puffery. But the other reason is that exporting culture turns out to be far more effective than a ground invasion. Sure, it can take longer, be more expensive, and be vastly harder to do—but once you've won, you've won for a generation or more.

A big country can get the outcome it wants not through intimidation or force, but by getting another nation to *want* the same things that the big country wants. Countries accomplish this by so successfully exchanging cultures that each begins to also exchange the values and desires upon which their cultures are built.

It's a core reason that totalitarian states oppose this sort of cultural transfer. It's also why some countries' cultural exports punch far higher than their diplomatic weight without throwing a punch.

If you rely on battleship tactics long enough, eventually you're going to encounter someone with a bigger battleship—or with smaller, faster, scrappier ships that overwhelm you. However, if you make your society and its stories and desires compelling, interesting, and worthy of exchange, a battleship won't do much, because you've already won the hearts and minds of the *people*. Cultural exports are one thing that made the United States a superpower, often working with the same goals of its considerable hard power. But cultural exports have made plenty of other countries enviable powers as well.

Show Business, the Grow Business

It's not a coincidence that the center of global film production and innovation is in Los Angeles. It's the result of decades of policy decisions and business decisions that cemented Hollywood as the nexus of movie production for the twentieth and beginning of the twenty-first centuries.

Film technology was not created or advanced by any one country in a technological sense. In its first ten years, 1895 to 1905, it was actually more of a gadget than a medium. A film would play in the middle of a vaudeville act as a stunt. The emergence of "cinema" not only as a hobby for rich guys and magicians, but as a cultural force, was caused by a combination of factors that all came together in the late 1800s. Individually, none of them would likely have been enough to create movie culture on their own. The oldest was projection technology, based on ancient ideas like "magic lanterns" from the seventeenth century and Constantijn Huygens's camera obscura. Photography came in the 1830s, a technology that ultimately allowed the making of unlimited copies from a single negative. By 1851 came the invention of the slideshow. Roll film was next, where you could take a hundred pictures at a time without having to replace the film. In 1872, sequential images a fraction of a second long were captured for the first time courtesy of a horse in motion. Finally there was celluloid, originally invented in 1868 for billiard balls but not commercially available until 1898.

Macroeconomics was the other side of the equation: Rising incomes, industrialization, and the growth of disposable income and free time meant there was rising demand for diversion. Piano production jumped from 43 pianos per 100,000 Americans in 1850 to 451 in 1909. In the first industrial revolution, which ended in the 1850s, workers opted for longer hours and more money for goods. But in the second—from around 1870 until World War I—they worked shorter hours to have more time to consume services, like movies.

At first, this was great for theaters putting on plays, traveling showmen, and circuses, but those acts were fighting the clock. A vaudevillian could hit maybe three theaters a night. The Barnum & Bailey Circus racked up $10,000 a day in overhead costs—if they couldn't stage two shows a day, they'd barely break even. A rainy season was enough to put a traveling theater company in the red. But film solved all that: It couldn't get sick, a beloved actor could simultaneously perform in a thousand theaters a night, and the daily overhead cost was almost zero post-production. Studios now spent most of their money on research and development to end up with a negative followed by some minor per-film costs to replicate that negative.

In 1905, fixed cinemas arrived—the famed nickelodeons of yore—to play a looping series of films exclusively. This led to a commensurate explosion in the number of films being made. The total length of negatives produced in 1897 was 38,000 feet, with 100 feet equaling about a minute of film. By 1910, that number rose to 2 million feet of film produced. A decade later, it was 20 million feet. The films got longer, too, from an average length in 1897 of 80 feet—less than a minute—to 700 feet by

1910. The business model of the nickelodeons was basically to run sequences of seven-minute films.

By 1920, the average length of a film had reached 3,000 feet, allowing the time for more sophisticated narratives. The number of individual shots in a given movie jumped from 14 in 1911 to 400 in 1918, and the number of scene setups jumped from an average of 7 to an average of 230. These numbers can also be seen as a proxy for the costs of filmmaking, as features still required—per foot of film—more shots and more film and more money to shoot than the shorter features. In terms of reels, the average film jumped from 0.84 in 1911 to 4.77 in 1918, and the costs more than quintupled.

In the European Theater

If the ability to make movies was becoming a kind of power in the early twentieth century, Europe wasn't going to be in competition for a while—namely because World War I would reduce just about the entire continent to rubble over the course of several years, feeding a generation into a mechanized abattoir while eradicating the industrial output of Europe, let alone its ability to make silly little movies. European films went from as much as 60 percent of the market share in the United States to pretty much nil by 1920. At the same time, their own domestic markets were flooded with American movies.

While Europe burned, the United States was largely untouched by World War I. That, along with the collapse of Thomas Edison's patent company—which tried to claim that a patent on movie cameras gave the company license to dictate what became a film—allowed the studios to start vertically integrating, consolidating the complete production chain of film production and distribution under a single roof. A key breakthrough on the business side was that studios stopped just selling movies to the nickelodeons—where they got money up front but the same amount for a hit or a bomb—and essentially began leasing them to theaters, with the company that made the films getting a portion of the profits. This was a huge paradigm shift, because suddenly American producers had a direct financial incentive to make great movies.

Most importantly, American film producers had ready access to capital. Everyone, including the wealthy, was amazed by this sensational new technology and just itching to throw money at anything with *motion picture* in the title. Lots of production companies in Florida, New York, and other parts of the East Coast picked up and moved to Los Angeles, where a concentration of talent and capable workers was clustered and the costs to shoot were lower.

Meanwhile, even after the war, Europe wasn't brimming with venture capital money ready to invest in movies. As a result, it wasn't just the countries ravaged by the war that saw their domestic markets swell with American movies. Sweden was neutral in the war, yet American movies went from a 5 percent market share in 1913 to an 81 percent market share in 1919. American movies just looked better, in no small part because American capital was investing more in movies than British or French capital, with the two European countries spending 20 to 30 percent less on the creative inputs like sets, camera equipment, personnel, and stars of movies.

Hollywood pressed its advantage in this regard, which brings us to the moment in 1923 when the Prince of Wales was exhorting Britain's moviemakers to buck up and make a good movie. Although "have a prince yell at someone" was an effective way to exact policy goals for much of the monarchy, it did not work in this case. By 1924, there were nearly no films being made in Britain.

Films were also ideal exports. Given the American advantage in finance, quality, and performers, US films flooded overseas markets with high-quality products that easily beat out the local fare in terms of production value. Films were simple and cheap to replicate; you could carry one negative in a briefcase and successfully export a film to an entire continent. Compared with a car, where the expense of shipping it overseas added potentially crippling costs per each unit, movies cost virtually nothing to get onto foreign screens.

The Sound and the Lack of Fury

In 1927, sound was integrated into motion pictures, which meant that the English-speaking American market would still be interested in English movies and stars. It had a devastating and near-instantaneous effect on those who made a living as live musicians playing for screenings of then-silent films. Sound equipment becoming commercially affordable not only prompted serious industrial investment into a core film technology but also essentially wiped out the export potential of European films. Whereas an Italian film could once play anywhere around the globe, the era of talkies severely diminished its export opportunities, because suddenly you had to speak or understand Italian to watch it. Especially as Hollywood's capital and quality outpaced films from other countries, sound—which by definition meant a local film producer that produced films in the local language could have an angle

on the local market the Americans lacked—did manage to guarantee a stronger domestic market for homegrown productions in foreign markets.

In 1927, the UK rolled out a domestic film quota, which managed to sustain its film industry in the short term, only to exacerbate its problems in the long term. This capped the number of American films that could be shown. Limited with what they could export, American studios obviously sent over their highest-quality, best-performing films. Their competition was often what was called a "quota quickie," a cheap domestic feature meant to get a theater up to code. To a British moviegoer, the reality was stark: American films were big, splashy, expensive spectacles, and British films were dreary, cheap, and of vastly inferior quality.

US studios made serious money by exporting their wares in the years leading up to World War II. The Hollywood star system began to develop, where a single well-known performer could help sell a movie in the United States or put their name to a film to gain traction in export markets. For the US film business, this meant anyone who wanted to be a movie star had to relocate to Los Angeles, where the concentration of stars was highest. This of course further cemented US dominance in the global commercial film business.

The net result was that the United States pretty much shattered the European industry. But here's what's remarkable: The European film industry never recovered. A European studio that could realistically compete with an American studio has yet to emerge. European talent consistently flocked to America because that's where the money was, and the subsequent talent drain meant that most European films never had much of a shot in the export market. Around World War II, a number of European governments realized the only way they'd have domestic film production was if they subsidized it. To this day, most European countries have a governmental or quasi-governmental agency that subsidizes film production in their nation.

You can put a movie camera anywhere in the world, so why were most of them in Hollywood?

Part of this is that for all intents and purposes the basic tech of film remained unchanged for decades: You'd send reels of celluloid to cinemas, millions of miles' worth of celluloid per year. Absent a technological disruption, rivals had difficulty muscling into the market that the studios could effectively dominate. There wasn't a killer innovation that rendered the studios obsolete technologically or gave a newcomer an angle to compete; there were just marginal technological improvements that the studios were able to co-opt and integrate anyway.

It didn't take Hollywood long to home in on the export market. Studios obviously understood that every translation they made using the film they originally created carried with it a higher return on investment. They had spent all this money on sets and effects and technology, after all. At first, somewhat hilariously, studios localized movies by shooting films multiple times on the same set, replacing actors who didn't speak languages with ones who did, sometimes with the help of subsidiaries abroad. But they soon realized this process was ridiculous, and they arrived mostly at the subbing and dubbing system that persists to this day. This basically worked by dubbing the whole film in the local language for large markets and going with subtitles for smaller markets.

There's an argument that this arrangement isn't bad for the European film fan, who gets not only a homegrown government-subsidized domestic movie industry to cultivate a distinct national flavor of films in their local language but also access to the very best of the very expensive American movies. By comparison, Americans don't have that—they get Hollywood, and that's it.

National Treasure

World War II was yet another important moment for the film industry and how it worked hand in hand with the government. In the United States, the motion picture business was deemed an essential war industry, like steel or cotton—the Office of War Information would emerge to lease the studio space and steer their output for the benefit of the war. Elmer Davis, the head of the OWI, said, "The motion picture is the most powerful instrument of propaganda in the world, whether it wants to be or not." The US Army ultimately occupied the offices at studios, including Disney, and seized facilities for war-related work, with Disney agreeing to produce training films for the military at cost.

"The federal government was working with the media and cultural industries to craft partial and selective stories and images of the *ideal* of the American way of life," said Tanner Mirrlees, who studies how the US government used media during the Cold War and afterward.

For example, the Office of the Coordinator of Inter-American Affairs (OCIAA) wanted

Mrs. Miniver *was an inspiring story of wartime home front resilience and became the highest-grossing film of 1942.*

to promote positive portrayals of the United States to Latin America and shore up public opinion for Americans instead of Axis powers. The results were Disney's *Three Caballeros* in 1944 and *Saludos Amigos* in 1942, two films where a tour to South American locations for animators and Disney staff was arranged by the OCIAA. And as we know, the Pentagon stayed interested in the goings-on in Hollywood over the back half of the twentieth century.

The modern foreign relations apparatus of the American government is keenly aware of the impact of "soft power," or the controversial idea of cultural influence for manipulative ends. "I remember having an Afghan general tell me that the only thing he thought about Americans is that all the men wrestled and the women walked around in bikinis because the only TV he ever saw was *Baywatch* and *World Wide Wrestling*," said then–Secretary of State Hillary Clinton to Congress.

The ascent of Hollywood was pretty much total. The European Union has a trade deficit on audiovisual products with the United States of $8 billion to $9 billion annually, half of which is television shows. Globally, US production accounts for about half of the total audiovisual trade. Worldwide, 85 percent of television exports from one country to another come from the United States. At the end of the day, the Oscars happen in America. Actors from other countries may win at the Oscars and directors can come from anywhere in the world, but the majority of the members of the Academy of Motion Picture Arts and Sciences reside in the United States.

And global opinion is not mixed. A 2021 Pew Research Center survey of populations around the world found that the cultural exports were some of the most universally admired things about the United States. Surveys in sixteen different countries found that 71 percent of respondents said that the United States had the best or better entertainment compared with other countries, which was just shy of the 72 percent who said it had the best or better technological achievements. That appraisal of US entertainment was higher than the 69 percent who said the American military was better than that of other developed nations, the 59 percent who said the same of universities, and the 33 percent who believed the same of the US standard of living.

Not a single country surveyed recorded more than 10 percent of respondents saying American entertainment was below average. In Japan, 33 percent of survey takers called American entertainment the best in the world; in Italy it's 30 percent, the UK 23 percent. Even 24 percent of French respondents, known to have great pride in their own cultural contributions, said US entertainment was the best in the world.

And the sentiment isn't aging. In every single country surveyed, younger respondents were likelier to say US entertainment was the best or above average far more often than older respondents, sometimes by anywhere from a 20- to a 45-percentage-point margin. And it's not just the people who grew up with American entertainment dominating the twentieth century. Vast majorities of people eighteen to twenty-nine around the world cite US movies and television as, on balance, pretty good. Regardless of how you define "soft power," that's an enormous asset, a priceless cache of long-term and future goodwill that took generations to build and maintain.

It's also an asset that Americans themselves don't always appreciate. When asked to appraise their cultural, educational, and technological accomplishments against those of other developed nations, Americans tended to undervalue their own achievements but overvalue their military, standard of living, and health-care system.

Despite the hegemony of the United States in cultural exports, other countries have managed to use the lessons of soft power to their own national advantage. Some have succeeded so well that they're far better known for their artistic exports than their militaries, and are able to obtain massive foreign policy gains with their movies and television that could never be achieved with guns and steel.

The World Is Not Enough

As the United States ascended in global power, it seemed like someone else would have to recede. For much of the twentieth century that was the United Kingdom. But the rules of zero-sum balances that apply to hard power don't work the same with soft power. While Britain's global hard power diminished, its cultural soft power became a masterclass in how to promote the facets of culture that make countries desirable.

The UK managed to both gradually rehabilitate its post-imperial image and underscore its global power in no small part by making excellent film and television that traveled well. It harnessed state money to facilitate the creation of movies and television and enthusiastically participated in cross-cultural exchange. It also played to its strengths: The UK's oligarchical crucible of elitist private schools and meritocratic publicly subsidized arts programs helped create world-class writers and comedians as quickly as America's constellation of Bible colleges mints *Bachelor* and *Bachelorette* contestants. The British government wisely decided to roll with things like giving state money to Monty Python so they could make a television show. And although British actors and directors would commute or relocate to Los Angeles for work, there's a reason they started to get knighthoods for their service to their country. By cleverly playing *with* American soft power rather than attempting to stymie or resist it as the Prince of Wales had hoped, the former British Empire actually expanded its global cultural footprint well beyond what it could have accomplished on its own.

BRITISH FILMS PER YEAR

Britain's domestic film output has varied substantially over time

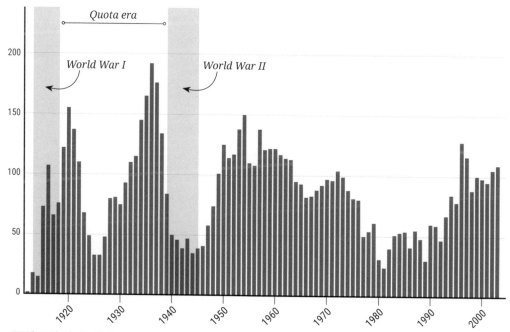

BFI Film & Television Handbook, 2002–2003

Oscars

In a country where domestic production was pretty much limited to "quota quickies," flour salesman J. Arthur Rank saw an opportunity. In 1935, he set up the General Cinema Finance Corporation, which sought to disrupt the movie business, at least domestically, by producing films the same way he produced flour: decent quality, high volume. Rank was hardly a lover of the arts: He saw British film production was cheap and underfunded, and although directly competing with American studios was out of the question, a gigantic pile of money could do a pretty good job of clearing the field. By 1946, Rank employed 31,000 people, owned 650 cinemas, and had revenues of £45 million. That same year he was responsible for producing the biggest hit the UK had had in the United States to that point: Laurence Olivier's *Henry V*, which

would happen upon a great distribution strategy of playing in college towns for one-night-only events, not unlike a traveling Shakespeare production but with none of the overhead. Within a year, *Henry V* had scored Best Picture and Best Actor Oscar nominations and profits of £275,000.

That would tee up the first major triumph of British film on American soil: *Hamlet*. Although the first two decades of the Academy Awards saw the nomination and victory of dozens of actors and directors from the UK, it wasn't until 1948 with Olivier's *Hamlet* that a British-produced film actually won Best Picture. British talent regularly appeared to great acclaim in American features while their domestic industry struggled. *Hamlet*—an adaptation of a very famous British play starring Laurence Olivier, a very famous British actor, and funded by the

BRITISH NOMINEES AT THE OSCARS

Nominations for acting, directing, or best picture categories

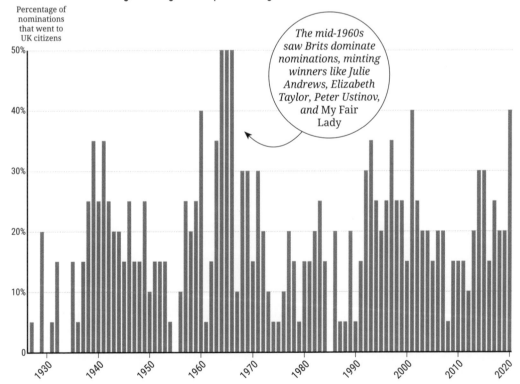

Percentage of nominations that went to UK citizens

The mid-1960s saw Brits dominate nominations, minting winners like Julie Andrews, Elizabeth Taylor, Peter Ustinov, and My Fair Lady

Academy Awards for Acting and Direction

Rank Organisation's British money—proved that despite the sorry state of the domestic film production business, the UK's cultural resources were of interest to international consumers.

This playbook to Oscar glory—a prestige British movie featuring a monarchy story— would net the nation Best Picture Oscars for *Shakespeare in Love*, *The Last Emperor*, and *The King's Speech*—because if it ain't broke, don't fix it.

British actors and directors, whether they're working at home or in the United States, are perennial presences at the highest prizes in the global film industry. Since World War II, there have been just two years—1955 and 1985—when at least one Oscar nominee for acting or directing wasn't from the United Kingdom. It's an incredible track record that no other country besides the United States can claim.

The country's cultural exports next came into acute focus with the advent of rock and

roll, a Black American creation that was adopted by British pop musicians in the late 1950s. The earliest British rock bands would, much like their counterparts in acting, perform with American accents—musicians like Lonnie Donegan, Cliff Richard, and Adam Faith. The cultural assimilation on vinyl seemed to be proceeding much as it had on celluloid.

And then came the Beatles, a Liverpool-area group who would become somewhat popular, changing the peripheral state of British culture and the country as a whole. With Beatlemania, Britain's government finally began to grasp the colossal value of exporting its entertainment.

The Fab Four

By pretty much any metric, the Beatles were the most successful music producers in the history of Britain. They were around for less than ten years and have sold more albums

BRITAIN REALIZED ITS BEST ADVOCATES WERE ITS ACTORS

CBE, OBE, and MBE titles awarded to people known for their work in the arts

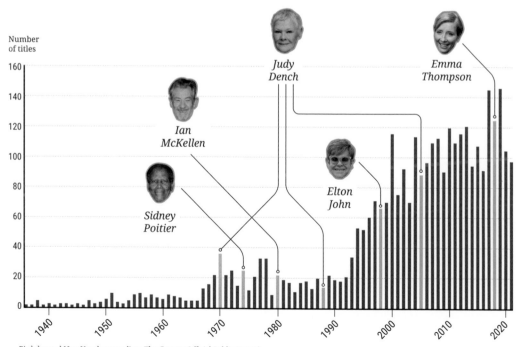

Birthday and New Year honours lists, The Gazette Official Public Record

than anyone else ever has over the course of their entire career, by a *lot*. And there's a good chance nobody will ever catch them by that measure. Even at the time of their global musical hegemony, there was no dispute that they were the most successful musicians on Earth.

What was in dispute was the effect that popularity would have on Great Britain.

The Beatles emerged at a transitional time for the country, which was in an economic stasis at best and a steep decline at worst. Britain's global market share of manufactured goods was down. Economies like Japan, Italy, and West Germany were leapfrogging over them in terms of industrial outputs in automobiles, ships, and overall exports. And while Britain's exports rose 29 percent from 1951 to 1964, West Germany's increased by 247 percent, Italy's by 256 percent, and Japan's by 378 percent at the same time.

In light of that, the emergence of the Beatles was the first bona-fide smash-hit British-grown export that the country had produced in years, and the British political leadership took notice. In 1964, Conservative Prime Minister Sir Alec Douglas-Home called the Beatles a "secret weapon" when dealing with other countries economically, boasting he could just offer up a Beatles visit to get other countries to play nice.

But his successor, Harold Wilson, would be the one to put real honors behind that economic importance. On June 12, 1965, Buckingham Palace announced that the Beatles would be awarded MBEs, or membership in the Most Excellent Order of the British Empire. Paul McCartney was now Sir Paul McCartney. At the time, this was jaw-dropping: Orders of the British Empire were awarded to those who served with esteem in the military, diplomats, politicians, and industrialists. George Harrison himself admitted he didn't think they gave that kind of thing for rock and rollers. Some who had gotten their OBEs for military service expressed shock at the decision, as did both allies and rivals of Wilson.

But it turned out Wilson was on to something. Few people had done more to popularize Britain around the world than the Beatles,

and the recognition would not be the last one for pop musicians and entertainers. The Union Jack, once a detested symbol of military imperialism for millions, had become fashionable once again in quarters of the world previously hostile to it. The Beatles cracked something for the United Kingdom, a pathway to transatlantic stardom that didn't necessitate ejecting a British colonial identity. Thousands of entertainers would follow in the Fab Four's footsteps and be rewarded with Orders of the British Empire for their service to the arts around the world.

While Britain flailed economically, it began to succeed culturally. British musicians became staples on the music charts in the United States. Their comedians and entertainers were popular on the other side of the Atlantic. And their film actors continued to rack up Oscar gold, while their directors—ex-pat Stanley Kubrick among them—developed a local industry that became competitive worldwide.

But one character in particular broadcast a British sensibility that both defined his country's place in the global order and put a positive spin on post-imperial Britain.

On Her Majesty's Secret Service

Despite remaining diplomatically essential and more than capable of acting unilaterally in global affairs, it's fair to say that the British felt anxious about the loss of their empire and the prestige associated with it. However, thanks to its ascending cultural power, the country was able to mollify that anxiety with a figure that typified the ideal version of the UK's role on the global stage.

And that role in the Cold War was of a critical partner of the Americans, a steady participant in the global order, and a sterling intelligence reputation thanks to a decisive espionage victory over Germany in World War II. All these things were embodied by one figure uniquely, someone who nearly perfectly tracked the priorities and anxieties of his country through the turmoil of the Cold War and into the chaos of the twenty-first century: James Bond.

Bond is the best thing to happen to the reputation of the United Kingdom globally since the queen

FREE ART SCHOOL PAYS OFF

The amount of credit governments get for supporting the arts is always a debate, but the UK, like many of its European counterparts, invested directly in making artists through most of the twentieth century. In the late 1950s and 1960s, art students had their tuition paid for by the state. The alumni of this largesse—also counting those who were kicked out—is a who's who of Rock and Roll Hall of Fame acts, including Freddie Mercury, Elton John, John Lennon, Keith Richards, Pete Townshend, Roger Waters, Charlie Watts, Eric Clapton, and more. The British government enabled working-class people, albeit mostly boys, access to arts education that has been repaid in spades.

When the hard industries of the imperial and industrial eras faded, soft power arose in their place. The sons of manual laborers became dancers, and although the shift in philosophy provoked enormous anxiety and derision, those involved are arguably better for it. In 2019, Britain was kept out of a recession largely thanks to its entertainment industry, which had grown 50 percent over the previous four years, vastly outpacing the services industry's 6 percent growth.

---

herself. You could not ask for a better representation of Britain in cinema: Bond is confident, capable, plays well with his American counterpart, and deftly navigates impossible situations with grace and poise. He's a bit old-fashioned, sure, but he's witty and suave.

The Bond as originally written by Ian Fleming in his novels is not the movie Bond, certainly. Fleming worked in Naval Intelligence during World War II and modeled his hero after the people he met. He was publishing Bond when Britain was just beginning to recede from its role as a major imperial power. The Bond of the films remains aspirational, but is nevertheless grounded in geopolitical realities. The punch-up the novels went through en route to the screen greatly expanded their appeal, and, story-wise, it worked out. Rather than relish old colonial victories, on-screen Bond is ahead of the curve when sizing up geopolitics. The movie franchise confronted the post-Soviet threats the Western Alliance would contend with well before the United States did: dealing with rogue states, private citizens who are so wealthy they can inflict large-scale damage, and the nonstate actors of the post-Soviet order driven by radical ideology. Instead of dwelling on the good old days of "owning other countries," Bond on-screen is forward-looking when it comes to how Britain sees itself on the world stage: effective, succinct, respected, independent, in lockstep with allies, and forceful. And the character of Q, the old spymaster and gear geek, is critical to all of this, a brilliant bit of cultural double down on the reputation British intelligence earned during World War II, supplanting the previous reputation the country maintained as an imperialist ghoul.

Still, although the creation of Bond is notoriously British, the Americans are cutting the checks, and the franchise reflects that.

James Bond is actually a reflection of American priorities and aspirations. A group of Korean researchers linguistically analyzed the Bond films, seeking to find the words and intensifiers that were used to describe American things. They discovered that representation of the United States in Bond films is always linked to words like *best*, *safe*, and *world*. When the topic of the United States comes up, it's invariably good: The Americans don't work against Bond—his CIA buddy Felix is ready to help him out if things get weird—and any number of his female collaborators are American women.

Most of all, though, his missions are American. The cities and areas he saves are American: New York, Silicon Valley, or Las Vegas. The technology he recovers are American microchips or satellites. The interests he's defending are distinctly American.

JAMES BOND, INTERNATIONAL MAN OF MYSTERY

Bond movies are a global affair

Year	Film	Bond is...	Female lead is...
1962	DR. NO	🏴󠁧󠁢󠁳󠁣󠁴󠁿	🇨🇭
1963	FROM RUSSIA WITH LOVE	🏴󠁧󠁢󠁳󠁣󠁴󠁿	🇮🇹
1964	GOLDFINGER	🏴󠁧󠁢󠁳󠁣󠁴󠁿	🏴󠁧󠁢󠁥󠁮󠁧󠁿
1965	THUNDERBALL	🏴󠁧󠁢󠁳󠁣󠁴󠁿	🇮🇹
1967	YOU ONLY LIVE TWICE	🏴󠁧󠁢󠁳󠁣󠁴󠁿	🇯🇵
1969	ON HER MAJESTY'S SECRET SERVICE	🇦🇺	🏴󠁧󠁢󠁥󠁮󠁧󠁿
1971	DIAMONDS ARE FOREVER	🏴󠁧󠁢󠁳󠁣󠁴󠁿	🇺🇸
1973	LIVE AND LET DIE	🏴󠁧󠁢󠁥󠁮󠁧󠁿	🏴󠁧󠁢󠁥󠁮󠁧󠁿
1974	THE MAN WITH THE GOLDEN GUN	🏴󠁧󠁢󠁥󠁮󠁧󠁿	🇸🇪
1977	THE SPY WHO LOVED ME	🏴󠁧󠁢󠁥󠁮󠁧󠁿	🇺🇸
1979	MOONRAKER	🏴󠁧󠁢󠁥󠁮󠁧󠁿	🇺🇸
1981	FOR YOUR EYES ONLY	🏴󠁧󠁢󠁥󠁮󠁧󠁿	🇫🇷
1983	OCTOPUSSY	🏴󠁧󠁢󠁥󠁮󠁧󠁿	🇸🇪
1985	A VIEW TO A KILL	🏴󠁧󠁢󠁥󠁮󠁧󠁿	🇺🇸
1987	THE LIVING DAYLIGHTS	🏴󠁧󠁢󠁥󠁮󠁧󠁿	🇳🇱
1989	LICENSE TO KILL	🏴󠁧󠁢󠁥󠁮󠁧󠁿	🇺🇸
1995	GOLDENEYE	🇮🇪	🇳🇱 🇸🇪
1997	TOMORROW NEVER DIES	🇮🇪	🇲🇾
1999	THE WORLD IS NOT ENOUGH	🇮🇪	🇺🇸
2002	DIE ANOTHER DAY	🇮🇪	🇺🇸
2006	CASINO ROYALE	🏴󠁧󠁢󠁥󠁮󠁧󠁿	🇮🇹
2008	QUANTUM OF SOLACE	🏴󠁧󠁢󠁥󠁮󠁧󠁿	🇮🇹
2012	SKYFALL	🏴󠁧󠁢󠁥󠁮󠁧󠁿	🏴󠁧󠁢󠁥󠁮󠁧󠁿
2015	SPECTRE	🏴󠁧󠁢󠁥󠁮󠁧󠁿	🇮🇹
2021	NO TIME TO DIE	🏴󠁧󠁢󠁥󠁮󠁧󠁿	🇮🇹

Author's analysis of IMDb

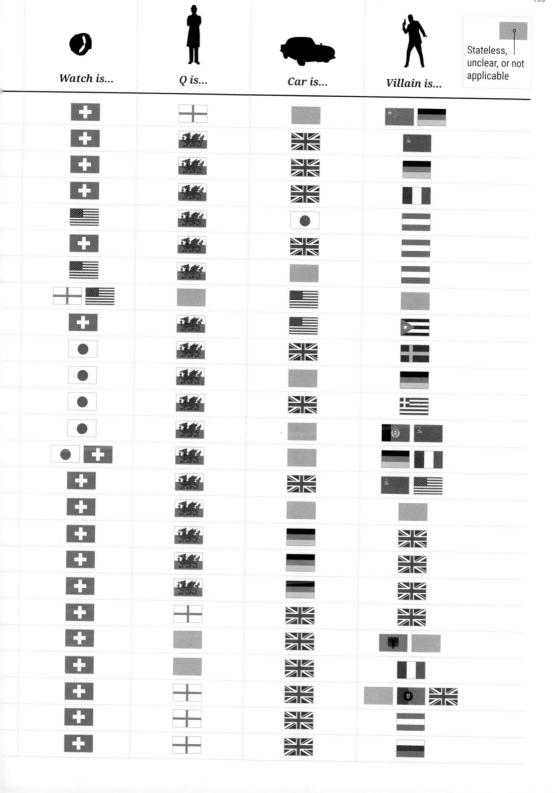

But although the goals are American, they're *also* British. The countries want the same things, desire the same political outcomes, and Bond articulates that partnership to near perfection in cinematic terms. This is the crux of Bond as a soft power tool—he aligns both American and British interests and looks incredibly cool and debonair for all the world to see as he does it.

In James Bond, Britain achieved direct soft power. It made other countries, like America, want what it wanted—respect for British ingenuity.

At the New Years Honours in 2022, Bond actor Daniel Craig got something more consequential than just an OBE. Lots of actors get MBEs, and some get CBEs, but when the queen "raised" Craig, it was to the level of CMG, a Companion of the Order of St. Michael and St. George. It is an honor typically reserved for diplomats, ambassadors, and government officials involved in statecraft at the highest echelon. It is also the same honor Bond himself was raised to in the novels—a fitting recognition for one of Britain's most important diplomats.

The success of Bond set up a replicable system that took root around the world. When Tony Blair's government invoked "Cool Britannia," it was derided. But on the other side of the world, another island nation took note, one with its own economic failures after a dizzying boom, a national reckoning with cultural exports, and let's just say a much more abrupt military wind-down of Imperial hard power assets.

Japan

For Japan, the application of cultural soft power is most of its *entire* power.

And it has dominated global culture on a level unrivaled by any other country since the late 1990s. What's more, it succeeded so spectacularly only after it failed both militarily and economically. Only one country speaks Japanese—Japan—yet in 2009, 3.5 million people around the world were studying the language. That was up from just 130,000 people studying it in 1979, well before Japan got into the cultural export business.

In the years after WWII, Japan was initially reluctant to promote its culture abroad. This was because of the consistently tenuous relationships it held with neighboring countries, which it had invaded, brutally conquered, and then forced its culture upon. Despite how poorly things ended for Japan in its hard power attempts, it nevertheless was the position of the government that they were better off taking a passive role in finding new audiences for their entertainment abroad.

Rayna Denison, a professor of film and digital arts at the University of Bristol, recalled as a kid when ITV aired Hayao Miyazaki's *Castle in the Sky* one Sunday. She and countless other future English anime fans recorded it on VHS and watched it over and over for years. "Even in the predigital day and age, there are these wonderful moments where these exchanges were taking place," Denison said.

Anime began to spread into the United States in the postwar years. The American occupation of Japan from 1945 to 1952 involved a million Allied soldiers, some of whom brought their children and families on assignment. In the 1960s, as American involvement in the Vietnam War escalated, the US military had eight bases and forty-four thousand troops stationed on Okinawa, which would remain an American military colony until 1972. The American military presence on the island remains controversial to this day, but a lot of American families nevertheless spent a great deal of time in Japan during the postwar years, assimilating some local culture before returning home.

Denison points to a number of key moments in Japan's cultural export story. The first was *Astro Boy*, an animated show about a robotic boy who saved Metro City, which cost more money per episode to make than it could earn in Japan. The show was popular, but it needed alternative revenue streams to survive, so the creator began licensing it, both as a character for commercial goods and to air in the United States. The other thing that gave anime a boost Stateside was the advent of Betamax, at the time a new distribution system competing with VHS. One of the large Betamax distributors, in need of content, bought the rights to a bunch of anime, had it dubbed, and sold it to the American market.

This rise of fan culture, fan dubs, plus official distribution through Betamax meant that a small but growing community of anime fans began to emerge in the United States through the 1980s and 1990s.

But anime wasn't an immediate global boom. "We have to remember, Japan is not the best friend of most of its Asian neighbors in the postwar period," Denison said. "It's only as those markets relax in the 1990s that anime starts to really be something that's pushed abroad. Where there's been a grassroots pull from America bringing anime over, the 1990s is the point where the anime industry *itself* starts to really invest in overseas culture."

In response to the 1990s "Cool Britannia," the Japanese noticed and recognized the successful playbook the Brits had run with the Americans, then copied it, literally, in a campaign the government called "Cool Japan."

For years, the Japanese diplomatic operation had been reluctant to export its cultural products around Asia for fear of upsetting former

JAPAN'S ANIME MARKET

The industry projected a decline, but then overseas sales exploded

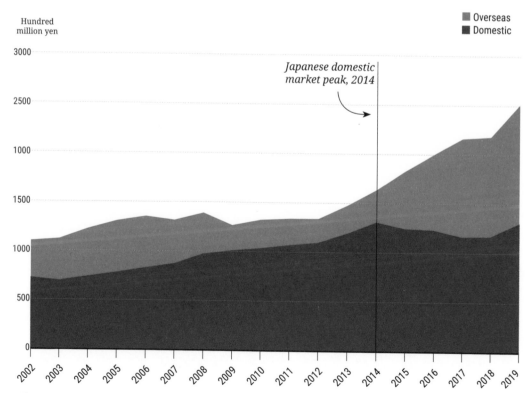

The Association of Japanese Animations

regional enemies. But that policy began to ease in the 1990s and into the 2000s, so much so that larger Japanese media companies began setting up outposts not only in America but across Asia. Soon afterward, anime and manga were being remade in South Korean and Chinese cinema.

Many Japanese animation studios now outsource work to studios in other countries, which in turn builds up animation knowledge and expertise in those countries, who then develop independent homegrown anime studios of their own.

Catch 'Em All

The timing of this cultural surge from Japan could not have been better. The 1997 Asian financial crisis was a bruising period for the country, which suddenly left Japan without the advantages that came with being an international success story after their economic "miracle" in the '80s led in part by their booming automotive industry. But from the ashes of Japan's "Lost Decade" (aka, the '90s) emerged a global phenomenon really unlike anything that had come before: Pokémon.

The inspiration for creating Pokémon came down to two things: Satoshi Tajiri wanted a challenging but accessible game that appealed to kids' imaginations, and he wanted to give kids a way to relieve the anguish of growing up in a postindustrial society.

Tajiri made a social component—trading and battling over a game-link cable—a central conceit of the game, a social step built directly into it and so important that it's impossible to obtain some of the strongest Pokémon in the game without collaboration. Pokémon was also designed to be playable by anyone, to foster inter-player connections years before game developers realized that was their ticket to longevity, and as a result it isolated and exemplified the inherent power of Japan's cultural power in a simple, compact fashion.

The extent to which Pokémon was a success is really hard to overstate.

Pokémon launched in America in August 1998, and nobody was prepared for what would happen. Walmart, Kmart, and Toys R Us passed on the toy lines, so it was an exclusive launch by KB Toys. Hasbro produced 10 to 12 million toys in inventory for the launch; they sold out immediately. Within a year, they had sold twenty times that number.

By 2000, the game was sold in seventy countries, the cartoon broadcast in fifty-one. The movie dropped in thirty-three countries in 1999, and the cards were translated into eleven languages. Put together, this was an enormous footprint for a media product that hadn't existed five years earlier. By February 2000, there was an official Pokémon lecture tour organized not by Game Freak, the developer responsible for Pokémon, but by the Japanese government itself, which seemed to understand what it had on its hands.

Pokémon was primed for export—it was distinctly Japanese, but easy to localize. The names of the Pokémon changed, but the entity stayed the same. The catchphrase "Gotta Catch 'Em All" was so good, it should be illegal. (Seriously: The Federal Communications Commission has regulations against television ads for children that have messages similar to "you must buy this"; that Pokémon's tagline was approved is miraculous.)

Localization was key. With the anime, Pokémon's creators were willing to make changes they could not make in-game to make the franchise more appealing to Americans.

For instance, in Japan the emphasis was on the fantastic, magical world of Pokémon. In America, the focus was on the ten-year-old who had goals of victory, tapping into the competitive urge structured into American stories over the experiential vibe of the Japanese preference.

Ash Ketchum, the ten-year-old who serves as the fan surrogate of the series, was made even more central. The US release of the movie was basically a top-to-bottom remake. *Pokémon: The First Movie—Mewtwo Strikes Back* in Japan involves morally gray areas and ends with Mewtwo just wiping everyone's memory. In the American version there are distinct bad guys, and Mewtwo gives a speech about

IS ASH KETCHUM A GOOD POKÉMON TRAINER?

To find this out, we need to figure out how much value Ash brings to a battle as a trainer over what we'd expect given the Pokémon in that battle.

I simulated 11.6 billion *Pokémon battles—10,000 simulations of what happens when every one of the over 1,000 varieties, forms, and mega evolutions fights every single other Pokemon—to first figure out the probability that a given wild Pokémon would beat another.*

In battle, a Pokémon trainer has two jobs: to pick the Pokémon she'll bring to the fight (like the general manager of a sports team) and to use those Pokémon and tactically win (like a coach of a team).

To figure out how good Ash was at each of these jobs, I pulled every Pokémon League battle, in gyms or in competiton, and the Pokémon that Ash brought against the Pokémon the opponent brought.

This then allowed me to figure out the probability that Ash, in the event he played the battle optimally, would have won this.

Given that a tournament structure on average matches up opponents against peer opponents, and given that gym leaders meet their challengers at their given skill level, we'll assume that each battle has a 50 percent chance of victory heading in.

Then, we'll gauge the impact on victory that "Ash the GM" had by calculating the difference between that initial probability and the calculated probability of victory given his Pokémon selection alone.

Last, we know what in fact happened in each battle, so we know the impact on victory "Ash the Coach" had by determining the difference between that calculated probability and the final probability (1.0 in the event of a win, 0.0 in the event of a loss, and 0.5 in the event of a draw).

Key:

X1: Initial probability of going in to battle

X2: Probability his team beats the other team in simulation

X3: 1 if he wins, 0 if he loses, 0.5 if he draws

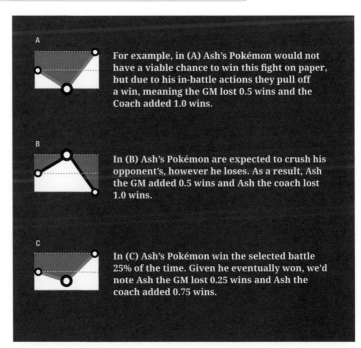

A

For example, in (A) Ash's Pokémon would not have a viable chance to win this fight on paper, but due to his in-battle actions they pull off a win, meaning the GM lost 0.5 wins and the Coach added 1.0 wins.

B

In (B) Ash's Pokémon are expected to crush his opponent's, however he loses. As a result, Ash the GM added 0.5 wins and Ash the coach lost 1.0 wins.

C

In (C) Ash's Pokémon win the selected battle 25% of the time. Given he eventually won, we'd note Ash the GM lost 0.25 wins and Ash the coach added 0.75 wins.

Author's analysis of *Pokémon* television show

POKÉMAN MASTER BATTLES

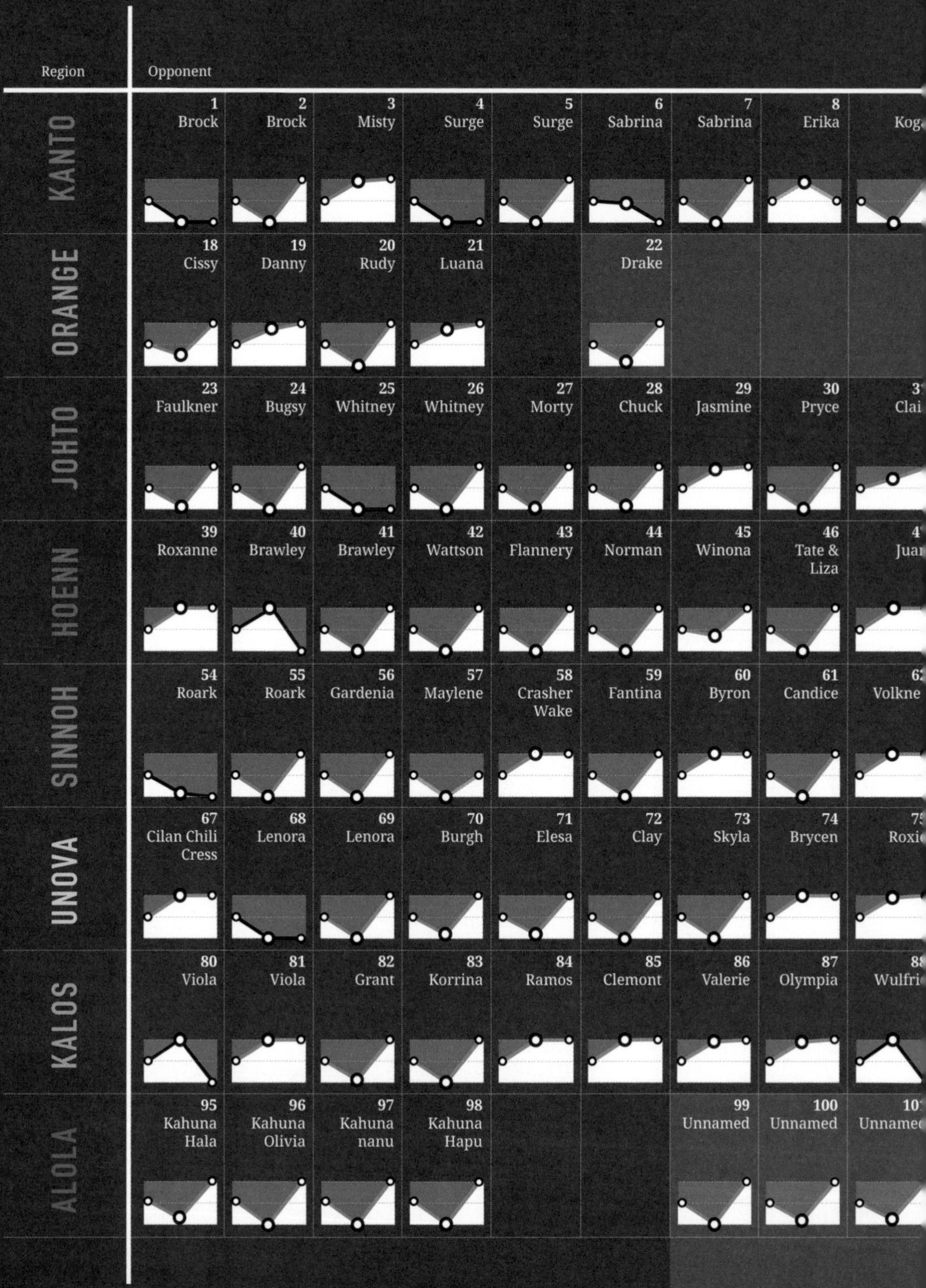

Region	Opponent							

KANTO

| 1 Brock | 2 Brock | 3 Misty | 4 Surge | 5 Surge | 6 Sabrina | 7 Sabrina | 8 Erika | Koga |

ORANGE

| 18 Cissy | 19 Danny | 20 Rudy | 21 Luana | | 22 Drake | | | |

JOHTO

| 23 Faulkner | 24 Bugsy | 25 Whitney | 26 Whitney | 27 Morty | 28 Chuck | 29 Jasmine | 30 Pryce | 3 Clai |

HOENN

| 39 Roxanne | 40 Brawley | 41 Brawley | 42 Wattson | 43 Flannery | 44 Norman | 45 Winona | 46 Tate & Liza | 4 Juan |

SINNOH

| 54 Roark | 55 Roark | 56 Gardenia | 57 Maylene | 58 Crasher Wake | 59 Fantina | 60 Byron | 61 Candice | 62 Volkne |

UNOVA

| 67 Cilan Chili Cress | 68 Lenora | 69 Lenora | 70 Burgh | 71 Elesa | 72 Clay | 73 Skyla | 74 Brycen | 75 Roxie |

KALOS

| 80 Viola | 81 Viola | 82 Grant | 83 Korrina | 84 Ramos | 85 Clemont | 86 Valerie | 87 Olympia | 88 Wulfric |

ALOLA

| 95 Kahuna Hala | 96 Kahuna Olivia | 97 Kahuna nanu | 98 Kahuna Hapu | | | 99 Unnamed | 100 Unnamed | 10 Unnamed |

Author's analysis of *Pokémon* television show

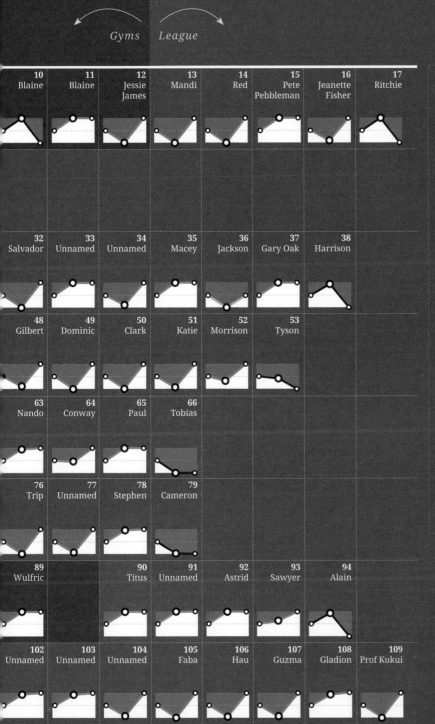

Gyms   League

Key:

X1: Initial probability of going in to battle

X2: Probability his team beats the other team in simulation

X3: 1 if he wins, 0 if he loses, 0.5 if draw

Win

Lose

Draw

Region	AVERAGE WINS ADDED PER BATTLE		ADDED WINS	
	GM	Coach	GM	Coach
KANTO	-0.12	0.30	-2.07	5.07
ORANGE	-0.10	0.60	-0.49	2.99
JOHTO	-0.14	0.51	-2.19	8.19
HOENN	-0.21	0.58	-3.19	8.69
SINNOH	-0.08	0.39	-1.01	5.01
UNOVA	-0.18	0.53	-2.37	6.87
KALOS	0.34	-0.04	5.09	-0.59
ALOLA	-0.28	0.78	-4.23	11.73
CAREER	-0.10	0.44	-10.46	47.96

Author's analysis of *Pokémon* television show

Ash is an incredibly gifted battler—over the course of his career, he added almost

48 wins

owing exclusively to his actions in battle.

However, the numbers indicate that his Pokémon selection is, on paper, sub-optimal: he's willing to buck-type attack bonuses, sometimes he'll fight with under-evolved Pokémon at the highest levels of the game, and he's usually competing with an unevolved electric mouse. On paper, those choices cost him about

10.5 wins

over the course of his career.

That said, you can't argue with results: repeated deep runs into tournaments and a consistently high winning percentage don't lie. His methods may be unconventional, but his record speaks for itself.

tolerance. To an extent, these differences speak to how children in Japan and the United States place themselves within movies and television. Stylistically, anime had reached the point where the characters represented were pan-racial, allowing the viewer to assign their own specifics to the protagonist. For many viewers outside the United States, Ash was less a protagonist than a window into a complex world. Stateside, American Ash was the hero, the character the audience wants to win—and to win, one must defeat something.

"Pokémon had perfect timing, at least in terms of the European and American animation industries," said Denison. "In '97, there was a voice-over industry that had grown up around voicing animation and anime from around the world."

The brilliance of the game is that there really isn't a one-sentence description of Pokémon: Pokémon is not one medium, it's a coalition of interlocking media entities that operate over maybe a dozen different mediums, all of which interact and thus provoke interaction from the consumer, who at times is just a viewer but at other times is an active participant.

Pikachu is different from, say, Mickey Mouse. Yes, both are mice that received a weapons-grade injection of "cute" to play into people's innate anthropomorphic tendencies, but the difference between them primarily comes down to a sense of scale. Mickey is one unified entity who exists across various media, as a character, and maintains a sense of self. There's only one Mickey. But Pikachu is a species, a logo, a character on a television show, half of the ingredients for a Raichu, a mediocre electric type, a terrible card, all sorts of manifestations and all different.

The impact of which is remarkable.

On the quiz site Sporcle, one quiz asks takers to name from rote memory all 151 Generation One Pokémon. When Pokémon were ranked by how often people were able to recall them, the median was 63 percent recall. Fully 11.5 percent of respondents—about one in nine takers—could name all 151. About 20.5 percent could name more than 144, and 54 percent of respondents got at least two-thirds of them correct.

Unsurprisingly, Pokémon has proved to be a remarkably sticky franchise. Whereas many games that spawn franchises peter out, Pokémon still reliably produces a new game every couple of years, often one that serves as the key launch game tied to new Nintendo consoles and handhelds. Pokémon streamers are popular on Twitch, the online trading community remains active, and the trading card game not only persists but experienced a massive renaissance during the pandemic that sent prices soaring for older collectibles. Pokémon Go, a mobile game where adults get to both capture Pokémon through an Augmented Reality mobile app and recapture their youth catching Pokémon, was a hit two decades after the game washed up on American shores. The latter is a manifestation of the designer's original intentions, which was to foster a community within the games and get kids to play with each other. It's a compromise of sorts. We're attempting to fix the digital removal of ourselves from the natural and social world, a process that none of us signed up for, by bringing the digital, the Pokémon we grew up with, to the natural and social worlds.

Localization

One key roadblock Japan faced that Great Britain didn't is the localization barrier. Beyond accents, some slang, and the inexplicable British love of sports where games regularly end in ties, Brits and Americans often can understand each other without needing an intermediary. Not so for Japan, and it's not just about language.

The Japan Foundation was formed in 1972 as a third party to the Japanese government to facilitate cultural transfers, primarily with the United States. The 1970s were productive when it came to countries working with their neighbors, so by the mid-1980s, Japan's government became far less cautious about promoting its culture overseas. They also invested heavily in the necessary infrastructure creative businesses needed to prosper, such as internet and cable access, funding for universities, and making capital available for production. In 1991, the Japanese government formed JAMCO, the Japan Media Communications Center, which translated thousands of shows into English, Spanish, French, and Chinese before sending them out to eighty-eight countries.

Manga

Manga in particular has benefited from its availability in school libraries, according to Denison. Librarians stocking the genre and making it available minted new fans every school year even if it wasn't available for sale nearby, so much so that by the 2000s, manga was hitting the bestseller lists fairly often. Manga and anime also benefited from the Pokémon craze, as well as when movies out of Studio Ghibli began racking up awards and acclaim.

From 1996 to 2006, Japan's total exports—cars, culture, electronics, everything—rose 68 percent, from about $447 billion to $752 billion. But its cultural exports—merchandise, royalties, music, video games, anime—*tripled* over that same period, rising from $8.37 billion to $25.4 billion in 2006.

Today, its cultural economy is a humming, fine-tuned machine: 65 percent of global animation is from Japan, and unlike the corporate behemoths that define American cultural production, the work is spread across thousands of start-ups and small companies. Japan rose from being literally 10 percent of the global market for pop culture in 2002 to 15 percent in 2007. The only creative field where Japan is a net cultural importer is in film, where the domination of Hollywood is just too tough to overcome.

Demand for manga has also continued shooting up.

"Manga was up 46 percent last year," said Kristen McLean of NPD Group of the year

A pile of tickets to Japan.

2020. "It's up somewhere between 90 and 100 percent this year, it is responsible for 75 percent of the growth in adult comics and graphic novels overall in the US right now, and it's all being driven by people discovering anime on streaming platforms and then crossing over and buying the manga."

It's a virtuous cycle. People find a show they like, then they read the manga, then they read manga similar to that, and then they switch back over to the anime to watch those shows.

"These are new readers," added McLean, "not your typical book buyers who are really passionate. What's developing is a very passionate mainstream audience for anime, and that is translating to a very strong market for manga."

This isn't happening only in the United States, either. As a pandemic-era subsidy for ailing arts programs, the government of France created the Culture Pass, which gave €300 to every eighteen-year-old in the country to spend on cultural products like music, tickets, books, and more. By May in the first year of the program, books made up 75 percent of all purchases, and about two-thirds of all those books were manga. That meant about half of the entire French Culture Pass program was funneled into manga purchases.

"Goodwill is one thing, but soft power is really important as well. Japan has been seen as a creative powerhouse because of the success of things like manga and anime, and that's helped all kinds of Japanese creative industry production. I suppose it helps rehabilitate its reputation in some regards," said Denison.

Pokémon—as well as the other anime products that followed up on the cultural beachhead secured by Pokémon—led to two decades of Japanese work being integrated into US cultural consumption. Miyazaki won an Academy Award thanks to an alliance with domestic distributor Disney. This has led to a tourism explosion in Japan that, although interrupted by a global pandemic, is poised to reemerge.

"It's worth noting as well that there's a lot of nationalism in Japanese anime even now, soft cultural nationalism," Denison said.

"As much as there is a positive international kind of feel to a lot of anime, there's also a lot more recently that's been very locally focused. Something like *Your Name* is a really good example of that, where you can go and stand on the steps the characters stand on, you can take the same train they take, because it's so precise about the local culture being represented."

It's also had a remarkable impact on Japan's overall culture business. The country is aging. In 2014, the domestic market for Japanese animation hit ¥131 billion. In the years after, it began to decline, falling to ¥117 billion by 2018. This was a demographic inevitability the domestic studios had been bracing for. But what they didn't expect was the overseas market to bail them out. In 2014, the overseas market for Japanese animation was just ¥32.6 billion. By 2018, that had more than tripled to ¥100.9 billion, the overseas revenues more than making up for the domestic decline. In 2019, domestic revenues rebounded to ¥131 billion, and overseas revenues hit ¥120 billion. For now, the business has never been sounder. Fueled by overseas money bolstering the domestic revenues that shows can rely on, the annual number of anime productions increased from 200 at the bottom of the recession to 350 in 2018.

Monkey D. Luffy, famous pirate.

Japan is cashing a check it wrote to itself decades ago, and the goodwill and admiration it accumulated through peaceful cultural export endeared it to not only a superpower but to its neighbors and the rest of the globe as well. The country faces some remarkable challenges, not the least of which is a major demographic shift overturning decades of social and economic norms. But the global affection it has earned by just making stuff people like, and getting people from drastically different cultures to desire the same values and goals Japan desires, can sustain a nation when its economy fails, or even when its demographic headwinds jeopardize its future.

The Korean Wave

Japan and Britain largely invented the contemporary playbook for investment in soft power through cultural exports, finding ways to cement their cultural wants and desires through those exports. Korea followed, and with considerable success.

South Korea has used soft cultural power deftly for years. When South Korean or American films or television shows made their way into North Korea, they were potent motivators for those who found their stories and the degree of affluence and lifestyle so appealing, it inspired them to escape the country.

After the Asian financial crisis in the late 1990s, South Korean President Kim Dae-jung loosened the bans on cultural imports from Japan. Later, in 1999, the government allocated $148 million to cultural production after the passage of a law to fund it.

As an industry, Korea's pop culture business is dominated by one company, CJ Group, operated by founder and de facto queen of all Korean cultural production, Miky Lee, who basically built the film industry in Korea. An heir of the founder of Samsung, Lee has been the longtime patron and champion of Korean film and culture locally and abroad.

CJ, the vehicle that Lee steered to the top of the heap of culture, is an embodiment of Korean industrialization and globalization. CJ

Miky Lee, on stage at the Academy Awards following Parasite's *win.*

Group started out as a sugar- and flour-milling company. Later it moved into food and beverage production, and then Lee Byung-chul founded Samsung, which went on to compose a very substantial chunk of the South Korean economy.

Lee, a granddaughter of Lee Byung-chul, grew up watching American films. By the time she came into her inheritance, she had decided to invest a little money in a company working in the movie business. Around the same time, other Asian companies were already getting their feet wet in Hollywood: Japan's Sony bought Columbia Pictures, and for a while Matsushita owned Universal, though they eventually sold it to Seagram.

Lee was intrigued by the potential of a company that was being formed by a number of experienced producers attempting something that hadn't been accomplished since the founding era of film—making a movie studio from scratch. The founders had talent and skill, but needed money. That company ended up being called DreamWorks and, along with David Geffen, Steven Spielberg, and Jeffrey Katzenberg, Miky Lee put up $300 million in exchange for 10.8 percent of the company and all distribution rights for DreamWorks films in Asia outside of Japan.

With her resources, access to film distribution and import, Lee was able to build out the Korean market for film. CJ GCV, a subsidiary of the main company, owns 50 percent of the movie theater market in Korea. Partially because when they were built, people came: In 1998, the average Korean saw 0.8 movies per year in a cinema, a figure that now stands at 4.0, one of the highest levels in the world

And although she started as an importer bringing DreamWorks movies into the country, the company has since become a massive producer in its own right, producing films from Korean standouts like directors Bong Joon Ho and Park Chan-wook as well as local blockbusters. As a result, now Korean domestic films are up to half of the market. As Korea's only studio with foreign distribution, CJ is now trying to make two to three English-language films a year.

Lee's accomplishments are inspirational, taking a company from a flour miller to food distributor to film importer to film producer to film exporter, all over the course of mere decades.

Besides the 4,187 screens in 189 countries, CJ also owns sixteen television stations and has released 940 musical albums.

And it's not just CJ: The South Korean national policy of translating and exporting entertainment was logging some bona-fide hits. By 2002, Korea had its first international successes, including domestically popular soap operas like *Winter Sonata*, which had been translated and exported, and were smash hits in Iraq and Egypt.

Korean music was some of the first Korean culture to penetrate internationally, both with regional rivals—EXO, a combined Chinese-Korean pop band—as well as globally, whether with Psy and "Gangnam Style" becoming a YouTube juggernaut or BTS, an unstoppable pop phenomenon. Internally, the global adoption of Korean pop culture—at first in a few other countries in their region, then in countries in the Middle East and Africa, and finally breaking into niches in the United States and other rich, developed Western countries—has been called Hallyu, or the "Korean Wave."

And in recent years, that wave has grown massively, and that success has gone from niche to mainstream. BTS became one of the best-selling acts on the planet, accounting for $4.65 billion of Korea's GDP in 2019.

Korea is influencing American culture in more subtle ways as well. Daniel Dae Kim—an actor best known for roles on *Lost* and *Hawaii Five-0*—operates 3AD, a production company that repackages television concepts that were hits in Korea for export to the United States. South Korea developed and tested—and Kim subsequently imported—concepts like *The Masked Singer*, a competitive singing competition of disguised celebrities, and *The Good Doctor*, a drama about an autistic doctor.

The insatiable appeal of South Korean cultural exports doesn't stop at their northern border, though North Korean leadership tries to do just that. In January 2021, sources

NORTH KOREAN REFUGEE POLL
From a total of 127 defectors from 1998–2017

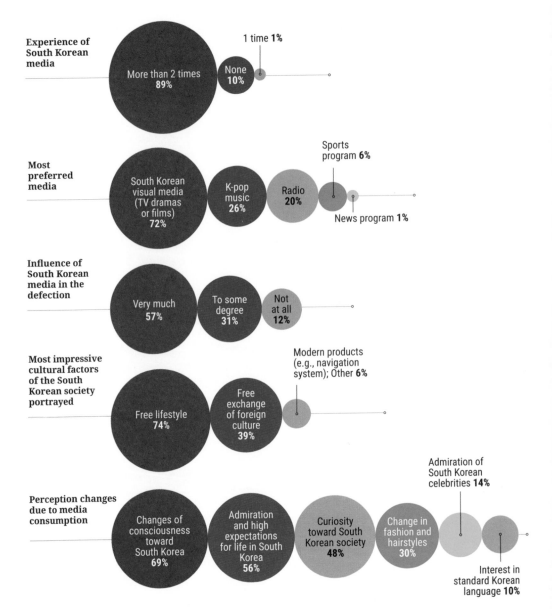

Experience of South Korean media

More than 2 times **89%**

None **10%**

1 time **1%**

Most preferred media

South Korean visual media (TV dramas or films) **72%**

K-pop music **26%**

Radio **20%**

Sports program **6%**

News program **1%**

Influence of South Korean media in the defection

Very much **57%**

To some degree **31%**

Not at all **12%**

Most impressive cultural factors of the South Korean society portrayed

Free lifestyle **74%**

Free exchange of foreign culture **39%**

Modern products (e.g., navigation system); Other **6%**

Perception changes due to media consumption

Changes of consciousness toward South Korea **69%**

Admiration and high expectations for life in South Korea **56%**

Curiosity toward South Korean society **48%**

Change in fashion and hairstyles **30%**

Admiration of South Korean celebrities **14%**

Interest in standard Korean language **10%**

Ka Young Chung, 2018

in South Korea reported a crackdown on people smuggling dramas and music into North Korea, with Kim Jong-un calling it a "vicious cancer" that, if left unchecked, would make the North "crumble like a damp wall." State media regularly rails against South Korean media making its way into the country. One reason appears to be that it's somewhat instrumental in revealing the reality of the conditions in the North compared with the relative luxury in the South.

A 2018 study that interviewed 127 North Korean defectors puts some fine detail to it. Defectors had long sought speedy anonymity after arriving in the South, but when one admitted in 2011 that a motivation for their escape was a K-drama, it got researchers wondering just how much of an impact South Korean pop culture had north of the DMZ.

Of the 127 people interviewed who escaped North Korea, 89 percent had seen South Korean media at least twice, despite only 40 percent of them having secret access to the internet. Seventy-two percent of them said they liked South Korean television dramas and films, with fully 26 percent citing their enjoyment of K-pop. Fifty-seven percent said the influence of South Korean media weighed "very much" in their defection, with only 12 percent saying it had no impact at all. Follow-up questions revealed why: The dramas showed a freer lifestyle, introduced fashion and hairstyles unavailable in the North, and raised expectations about what a life in South Korea was really like versus what they'd been told by the State. Some remarked that South Korean women were able to drive; others noted that the power never randomly went out during a K-drama.

As of the early 2020s, South Korean culture is at the center stage of global pop culture. The success of *Squid Game* on Netflix meant a South Korean program was the most-watched thing on the planet for multiple weeks. Even the white slip-on Vans worn by the characters in the death matches saw sales spike 7,800 percent in the weeks after the show premiered. According to Netflix, the show added $1.9 billion to Korea's economy.

In 2020, Korean content exports hit $10.8 billion, beating out household appliances and creeping up on computer exports, which were $13.4 billion. Entertainment is one of the fastest-growing industries in Korea, with the number of workers employed in creative and artistic services rising 27 percent between 2009 and 2019. In 2021, BTS's song "Dynamite" generated $1.43 billion on its own.

CJ Entertainment & Media in August 2006 said that soon, "Everyone will watch at least two to three Korean movies a year, eat Korean food one to two times per month, watch one to two Korean dramas per week, and listen to one to two Korean songs per day, that Korean culture will be a part of everyday life."

Even in Korea, many thought that was a ridiculous goal. A decade and a half later, it seems altogether reasonable.

After the Best Picture and Best Director wins for Bong Joon Ho's *Parasite* at the 2019 Academy Awards, Korean productions experienced an immediate halo effect. After *Parasite* won the award, Bong and his producing partner spoke, giving thanks and expressing appreciation to Korean film fans and the woman who produced it, who of course was Miky Lee.

In the early twentieth century, studios were tapping into the previously unimaginable power of new film technology to popularize culture globally. That technological leap that fostered the first wave of film globalization? *It's happening again.* The expense and difficulty of distributing a film in 2000 was several orders of magnitude higher than it cost in 2020, thanks to technical advances that are changing what's possible with digital distribution.

The marginal cost of adding another thousand theaters to a film's distribution would number in the millions of dollars in 2000 in terms of the cost of film prints alone. By 2020, making a thousand additional copies for a thousand additional screens costs a couple of bucks a copy. The cost for a nation to export their films is lower than ever: You can add an entire country to your distribution pattern for pennies on the dollar compared with what the film prints would have cost you before digital cinema.

Streaming has made distribution even easier. All those streaming services—Netflix, Discovery, Peacock, Disney+—run on the same Amazon Web Services, or AWS, servers. So do their translators—and so do machine learning models that can actively translate in real time.

"We have over eighty partners just in media supply chain," said Eric Iverson, the head of AWS' entertainment division. Iverson spent seventeen years at Sony Pictures and saw firsthand how massive technological shifts changed how work is produced and distributed. If you want to have a show translated into any number of languages, just having the entire production distributed globally through a centralized production computer makes things far easier than either dragging everyone to Los Angeles or sending copies around the world.

This changed the finances for producers weighing where to release their films. It used to be only the top territories got dubs, and everyone else got subs.

"Just imagine you have to create captions in multiple different languages. You can do it through machine learning," said Usman Shakur, a director at AWS Media and Entertainment

If you can get those costs down, well, why not lower them even more? Why not add subtitles in languages you hadn't even considered worth it? Maybe you're a tiny little independent feature on a slim budget—soon enough you'll be able to get decent subs in a dozen languages. Although lots of AI has proved fickle, the technology behind language models and transcription models is moving quickly and reliably.

"What we used to do a while ago was you release it in one or two or three territories, and then maybe slowly, as you get your editorial teams ramped up, you would release it in another," Iverson said. "Well, now we're trying to release everything more day and date, at the same time, that's good for business. It helps stave off piracy, but it's also good for consumers, because they hear about it, and they just want to watch it."

To get a Ghibli film to the rest of the world in 2000 entailed partnering with a deep-pocketed American company, and their internal translation department would triage the tongues of the world and maybe release it in France, if the marketing worked. Today, a Korean television show can enjoy a simultaneous release on every single national platform of a streaming service, its localization handled by dozens of translators all over the world who are able to ensure that a work can be almost instantly seen and understood on every screen on the planet.

The ability to localize is adding to a pattern now repeating constantly: Nations are able to improve their global cultural footprint by opening up their borders, letting other cultures in, investing money at the governmental level to directly fund the production of art, and then investing in the infrastructure—broadband, universities—to cultivate it. What's clear is that "investment in culture" is not in any way a metaphor: Governments that fund and directly encourage their culture industry, then use their diplomatic weight to spread and promote the assets they cultivate, are the governments able to expand their cultural influence.

The main advantage Hollywood held during its formative era was its superior quality. This was made possible by a concentration of performers, talent, crew, equipment, and investment capital that allowed it to outperform the productions of other countries at the time. Later, as access to tech improved and the cost efficiencies improved, quality was no longer the exclusive property of a single city, or country.

And yet it remains true that whoever designs films that can stand the test of time owns the future.

Which leads to a simple question: What's good?

DIGITAL SCREENS AS A SHARE OF TOTAL SCREENS

Studios had lots of reasons to push cinemas to switch to digital over film projection

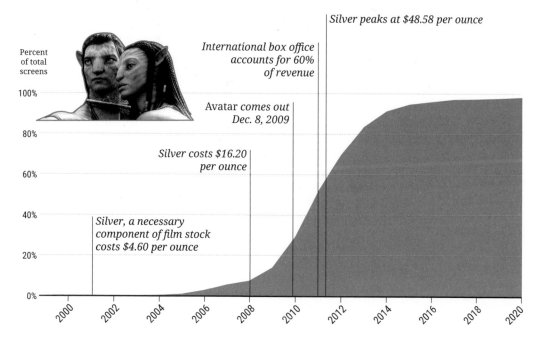

David Hancock, OMDIA; Yahoo Finance

CHAPTER 7

HOW CULTURE SURVIVES

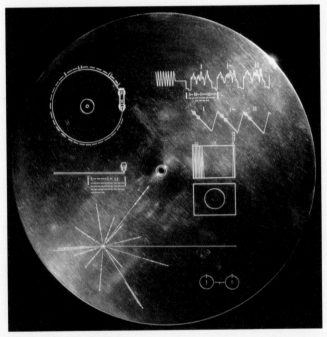

The Voyager *Golden Record.*

In November 1991, the US government assembled two crack teams of scientists to devise the most enduring story ever told, one that was guaranteed to last ten thousand years.

For some perspective, very little of human creation lasts ten thousand years. The oldest pyramids we know about are 4,600 years old. There are some earthworks plausibly older than that, but we don't always understand why they were built, which speaks to the difficulties of durability. The oldest literature we know of is just a hair older than the Egyptian pyramids, but much of it is indecipherable and doesn't hold up as a story. Sure, we have well-known and durable stories, but even though the New Testament is popular and familiar to millions, it's only a fifth

as old as we need, and the Old Testament and the earliest tenets of Hinduism are a third as old as we need. Many stories are passed via oral tradition, and presumably, plenty have endured longer than we can date. Some fairy tales probably have antecedents in the Ice Age, but we'll never be able to confirm a specific date. There are some stories that crop up consistently over time, across too many cultures to be a coincidence, like the one about the big flood, but the list of things that have for certain lasted more than five thousand years is short.

With no evidence of anyone in recorded human history writing a story good enough to last ten thousand years *so far*, you can see the pickle the government found itself in. But it gets harder. Forget a ten-thousand-year story: Could a dedicated group of people come up with a story or a symbol that would be understandable in a thousand years?

Shakespeare, which is probably a bit dense and not particularly readable for many people, is around 430 years old. Chaucer's *Canterbury Tales* is damn near inscrutable, and it's about 600 years old, in English, and opens as follows:

> **Whan that Aprill, with his shoures soote**
>
> **The droghte of March hath perced to the roote**
>
> **And bathed every veyne in swich licour,**
>
> **Of which vertu engendred is the flour;**

Perhaps the nonscholar can make some sense of it, but there are thousands of lines after those four. Languages drift; over the course of every thousand years they retain only about 81 percent of their vocabulary from the prior millennia. By that measure, in twelve thousand years whatever's left of English will have just 12 percent of our current vocabulary.

Back to the government's story problem. It's not normal business for the Department of Energy and the Sandia National Laboratories to organize a storytelling competition among select academics. The reason for wanting to tell the most enduring story ever becomes more clear when you hear the story, which goes something like this:

> Once upon a time, people found some dangerous rocks. They were able to make these rocks more dangerous, and they made them radioactive. Eventually, all the things that ever got near those rocks became poisoned. We decided to bury all of that worthless, poisoned garbage at this site outside of Carlsbad, New Mexico, in a tomb one thousand feet underground. It's incredibly dangerous to be here for the next ten thousand years, and we urge you to leave.

This story has a moral, and the moral is "If you dig here, you and everyone you love will die in agony."

The Waste Isolation Pilot Plant (WIPP) outside of Carlsbad is a preparatory warehouse and factory built atop a shaft drilled deep beneath the desert. In the rock below, caverns were painstakingly dug to serve as a tomb for any equipment, clothes, or discarded materials exposed to nuclear waste during the Atomic Age. Ideally, they would rest there undisturbed for ten thousand years, at which point they'd be as close to "safe" as one could reasonably hope. It was the "undisturbed" part that seemed tricky.

Such a warning story may be simple to communicate and understand now, but far in the future, we don't know how language or behaviors or the world in general will have changed. So fourteen of the finest minds from science, semiotics, geology, and astronomy set to doing the impossible: make the most enduring story ever.

So much of the best culture comes down to a fragment of the aforementioned demand: How do you make something that will truly reach people? How do you make something good, that not only lasts but *deserves* to? What is a classic? What demands a parcel of eternity, or at least makes us, in our short lifespans, think it does? Good stories outlast their peers, great stories outlive their creators, excellent stories outlive everyone who was around when they were first told, but the truly *perfect* stories outlast the civilization that forged them.

How do you ward off people for thousands of years? A spike field.

The Opinion Blender

Humans have always critiqued things. One of the oldest known communications we have is a cuneiform clay tablet sent from Nanni, a customer, to Ea-nasir, a merchant, complaining about the quality of copper ingots Ea-nasir attempted to pawn off on Nanni's servant. So, the oldest known writing we've ever produced as a species is a bad review!

In the 3,750 years since that review was penned, little has changed about our ability to evaluate quality. Except perhaps the medium we use to communicate our complaints. In the interim, there has been no shortage of systems designed to numerically determine precisely how good or bad something is, though arguably nobody's really pulled it off, particularly when it comes to art and culture.

All we ever really get is approximations. Take, for example, an awards show: No human alive will claim that the Best Picture award at the Oscars is batting 100 percent at identifying the best movie of every year, or even the best movie *most* of the time. Online review sites are the aggregation of many reviews from many critics—a flattening of a flattening, a simplification of a critic's nuanced thought further simplified into a single figure claiming to represent the thoughts of hundreds. You can measure how much money a movie makes and argue that people vote with their dollars, but what people financially "vote" on isn't long-term historical quality. They're voting on "how much I would pay to be in this cinema for two hours." They're not buying a ticket to advance a film's case for immortality—they're buying a ticket because their alternative plans were less appealing that night (like drinking liquor and fighting, if you recall).

But neither money nor awards really do a good job of assessing quality.

Let's talk about awards, which, it can be argued *are* a good measuring stick for quality. But movies that win the Oscar for Best Picture tended to be less well received years later compared with the films that were merely nominated. One study compared all the Oscar winners and nominees throughout the history of the award, then looked at which ones ended up on best-ever lists. It turned out, the average nominee typically did better than the average winner. That study determined that the best-quality nominated movie—the one that more consistently showed up on the big retrospective lists years and years later—won just thirty-one out of sixty-six times. And the highest-rated film each year, according to the study's metric, missed winning Best Picture forty-three out of sixty-six times—and went unnominated twenty-five times!

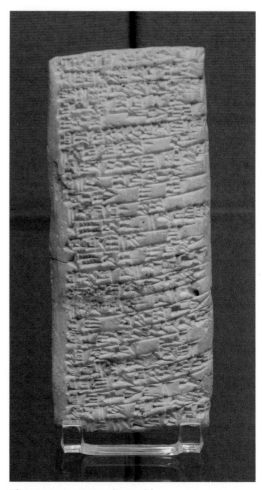

These copper ingots were disgraceful.

Although the study may have overrelied on best-of-all-time lists, I'd say that their highest-rated film of the year winning Best Picture twenty-three of sixty-six times is fairly solid. By comparison, the NFL team with the best record in a regular NFL season has won the Super Bowl about a third of the time across the last three decades. So, maybe the Oscars are fairly accurate in terms of quality.

Or perhaps the secret to longevity is just to get nominated. With the Booker Prize, more or less the British equivalent of the United States' National Book Award, shortlisted books tend to end up with more rereleased editions than winning books. And though authors of winning books tended to be younger than those of nominated books, shortlisted authors went on to write more than winners did. (So, in the extremely rare event that you, reader, are voting on some sort of prize for this book, I beg you to let someone else win the thing.)

Subjectivity is a funky thing: One study found that although prizewinning books tend to attract more readers than those merely shortlisted, they also often receive worse reviews after the fact. Shortlisted books, on the other hand, see a modest bump in readers, but the reviews they receive tend to be more positive. One factor here is that the very expectations we bring to a movie or book can affect how we consume it. Good things that beat expectations are often perceived as superior to equally good things that are extremely hyped and then miss or merely meet our expectations.

If awards are unreliable in terms of long-term perceptions of quality, what about critics? For much of film history, the role of movie critics was clear. Most served a specific geographic area, and although there were national publications, the primary obligation of film critics was to report to their audience the aesthetic merits of a film and where it stood compared with other films past and present. If they had column inches remaining, they might talk more in depth.

With the internet, the idea of a local or regional critic began to lose meaning. All critics were nationalized: You no longer had to subscribe to a local Chicago tabloid to read a given critic, and a critic didn't have to work for a large national publisher to reach a national audience. Suddenly there was an abundance of data from which fans could collect reviews for forthcoming films of interest.

That gathering process would soon professionalize and become a full-fledged business, with sites like Metacritic, Rotten Tomatoes, and IMDb becoming aggregators. Some began calculating a numerical score to describe the overall perception of a film, converting writers into voters. Several of those businesses eventually became industries: Rotten Tomatoes is a subsidiary of Fandango Media, a ticket seller owned by WarnerMedia and Comcast. IMDb is a subsidiary of Amazon, which both sells and creates movies and is one of the largest companies on earth.

And as their work became nationalized, aggregated, and converted into a single number, something happened to critics: They became villainized. Though nothing had changed about the fundamentals of their work in a century—see the movie, write thoughts down—the engines of digital commerce used critics' work as the fuel for their recommendation systems, and suddenly they were on the receiving end of a great deal of ire.

At the same point, moviegoers themselves were being invited to leave reviews and ratings of their own. Before this, the primary feedback people had was making fun of a movie on the walk home, or telling a friend they *had* to see it, or maybe if it was particularly bad, someone would ask an usher for their money back. But with the internet, the power to critique was given to the masses, a major shift.

The next question of course is how this shift to aggregated critic reviews and user-generated feedback affected our understanding of what is good.

The baseline internet review is not especially excellent. Something like 15 to 30 percent of all online reviews are fake, and although that may seem like a relatively small number, the algorithms that use reviews as inputs can significantly amplify the effect. One study out of the Stevens Institute of Technology found that among 2.3 million reviews of 4,709 hotels in seventeen cities, even a small injection of fake reviews—as few as 50, in fact—is enough for someone to drastically alter the ordering of hotels on TripAdvisor.

Because of the algorithmic leaderboard-style ratings employed by internet sites like Rotten Tomatoes, IMDb, Metacritic, and Fandango, a dedicated group of anonymous internet users can disproportionately elevate or tank the score of anything they want. The provenance of where reviews come from, and the motivations of the raters, are invariably suspect on an anonymous and unaccountable internet site. Worse, the rating sites themselves have little incentive to do anything about it, because they don't really have any skin in the game to begin with.

An individual reviewer posting a film review is putting something out there when they post their review, be it reputational, financial, or otherwise. But an aggregator risks nothing. If the reviewer posts a poorly done review, they may have to eat crow, whereas the aggregators can just blame it on errors down the food chain. In fact, there is absolutely no situation in which a ratings or review site can suffer any consequences for the decisions it makes in assembling a numerical score. If they overrate

A machine that turns critics' analyses into fan fury.

a film, the users they failed to serve will blame the studio or the filmmakers for failing to meet their expectations. If they underrate a movie, the users they underserved will blame the critics for smearing a movie they like, or the movie will suffer a financial loss that otherwise it would not have, had the site not posted the arbitrary score to begin with.

One issue shared by both critical and user-generated movie reviews is that the people who write them don't resemble audiences. For critic reviews, the Annenberg Inclusion Initiative launched two studies in 2018 looking at who, precisely, was writing reviews for Rotten Tomatoes. The study looked at reviews of the top three hundred films from 2015 to 2017 and found that 78.7 percent of critics were men and 83.2 percent of them were white. The ratio of white men to underrepresented women was 31 to 1.

Ironically, the entire point of the study was to determine what was having a significant impact on what was and wasn't getting acclaim. The kernel of the idea came at a meeting at Joey Soloway's production company in 2017 with actors Tessa Thompson and Brie Larson. With Sundance coming up, the conversation turned to how independent films were evaluated by critics. The group thought it would be fascinating to run a study of critics; then when Larson was accepting Women in Film's Crystal Award for Excellence in Film, she would tout the study and call for Sundance to ensure that at least 20 percent of top-level press passes went to underrepresented critics.

"Less than a quarter were white women; less than ten percent were underrepresented men. Only 2.5 percent of those top critics were women of color," said Larson in her speech. "What I am saying is if you make a movie that is a love letter to a woman of color, there is an insanely low chance that a woman of color will have a chance to see your movie and review your movie."

The effect of an Oscar winner demanding that the festivals work to include a diverse range of critics had a swift effect: Sundance retooled the accreditation process, and by 2019 fully 63 percent of the press came from underrepresented groups. Years later, Rotten Tomatoes would attempt to tweak its own accreditation process to ameliorate its own imbalances.

That's an important step, because women and people of color make up a disproportionate number of movie audiences. In 2016, the middle year of the Annenberg Inclusion Initiative report, about 52 percent of moviegoers were women. Nonwhite moviegoers bought 49 percent of the tickets sold in the United States that year, despite accounting for only 38 percent of the population. The vast majority of critics were representing a significant minority of actual moviegoers—in fact, the group least likely to see a movie.

That said, it's not like audience-based scores are all that much better.

I monitored the IMDb film ratings for a number of movies released in late 2021 to find out the relative impacts that different demographics of raters had on the final scores of movies over the course of their run. For a sizable fraction of their users, IMDb breaks out sex and age demographic information and goes so far as to break out the IMDb rating of each title for those individual demographic groups.

The shocking thing was that seven of the eight films I monitored launched to less than one quarter of their reviewers being women. Only one of those films, *Sing 2*, ever rose above that, and within two weeks it was back below 25 percent. The exception, *Being the Ricardos*, the Lucille Ball biopic with Nicole Kidman, spent its first ten days steadily declining from around 44 percent women reviewing to 21 percent. At no point did any of the movies have more than half of the reviews categorized by the sex of the reviewer come from women. In the end, three of them had less than 15 percent of their reviews from women, two finished with between 15 and 20 percent, and three finished with 20 to 30 percent.

To be clear, the films encompassed most of the major releases of that December, including the highest-grossing film of the year, *Spider-Man: No Way Home*, as well as the long-awaited *Matrix Resurrections*, star-studded Netflix Oscar contender *Don't Look Up*, Ethan Coen movie *The Tragedy of MacBeth*, Steven Spielberg's musical *West Side Story*, and family flick *Sing 2*. Movies with good reviews, bad reviews, good audience buzz and bad.

Any critic will tell you that the objective of their craft is not to publish a thumbs-up or a thumbs-down in a newspaper but to abet the consumption of a work of art in some way, to discuss the successes or failures of the decisions made in a work, or to place it in the broader canon. What review sites do is grind this sort of nuance into "yes" or "no."

Further, critics don't own a stake in the sites that fuel the ire and conversation against them; Amazon does. They don't get any financial benefits from their insights being stripped down to numerical bones and stuffed into a strawman; Comcast does. Aggregators take on no risk while stoking arguments about movies they didn't make by stripping reviews they didn't write of context they don't respect, and in doing so externalize all the risk to the consumers or the filmmakers.

Lots of people say they provide accurate and reliable information to businesses and consumers, financial analysts, or weather modelers, for example. And if they screw up, they often lose business, or their reputation, or esteem. Online review sites *have* screwed up, doing so at a remarkable clip, but don't face any meaningful consequences for doing so.

But to figure out how to extract ourselves from this cycle—how the conversation about reviews can be changed to serve both the works and the viewers, not corporate aggregators—we first need to understand the neurology of taste, the many reasons we like or dislike works, and then maybe find a system that works with that sophisticated nuance and not against it.

In matters of taste, there can be no disputes.

Your Mind on Music

The neurology of "why we like something" is fuzzy, but some of the most illuminating research has been done around music. Maybe because it's easier to get someone to listen to a song when they're rigged up to, say, an fMRI than it is to have them watch a two-hour film under the same conditions. But appreciating *some* kind of music is so universal, it makes for a good medium to really understand just how complicated it is for your brain to evaluate a creative work, with all the various elements that can play into it.

To start, music can be processed by the same places involved with horror, depending on the content. Think of a song that has random loud noises, which is sonically linked to anxiety, things like the gunshot sounds in "Paper Planes" or when a musician screams during a metal song. You may consciously know you're not in danger, but your brain—specifically the reticular formation in the brain stem and the thalamus—still *notices* those sounds and escalates the experience.

Second, we're not immune to songs that provoke a Pavlovian response. If you've ever set an alarm to wake up to the same song every day, or if your dentist office plays the same Lite FM station for years, you understand the perils of this. We can carry a positive or negative affectation for a song based on nothing related to the content of the song, a process that happens in the amygdala and cerebellum.

You might also experience a song differently depending on where you hear it. In a group setting, your view of the song is changed by social contagion. A slightly controversial idea for why this happens is "mirror neurons." This theory more or less says that when you're empathizing with someone, your brain activity will be similar with that person's on a neurological level if you're doing the same activity. The precise why—and for that matter, if it's really what's going on—is still a little unclear, but people interpret music differently in social situations than they do solo.

Songs also invoke a visual memory. Your brain experiences visual memories related to music in the parts of the occipital cortex and the visual association cortex. It could be imagery from a music video, something triggered in your mind's eye that enhances your affection for the song even years later. Or maybe a great sequence in a movie is paired to a song, one that redefines it in your mind perpetually, like *Fast 7* and Wiz Khalifa's "See You Again" or *Reservoir Dogs* single-handedly ruining Stealers Wheel's "Stuck in the Middle with You."

It could also invoke your episodic memory—registering in the right anterior prefrontal cortex and the medial temporal lobe, *especially* the hippocampus—with some songs specifically linked to a moment in time permanently associated with that event, bad or good. If you've ever shared a song in a relationship, for example, you're not going to be able to evaluate that song objectively in the future. This can also be a more general evocative feeling, like if the song is Bruce Springsteen's "Rosalita" and your memory matches the lyrics to the experience of being seventeen and speeding down Route 17-S in New Jersey, and seeing a skyline in the distance, and feeling for the first time what it truly means to yearn.

And the same song can be interpreted in different ways by multiple people. For me, hearing "No Children" by the Mountain Goats triggers an episodic memory of being an angsty teenager in college, whereas someone who found the song on TikTok could have a visual memory about when it had a dance on the app. Or there's my friend Kim, who might have developed a Pavlovian response because he played it thirty times in a row after the Tampa Bay Bucs lost a playoff game. Same paint, *vastly* different mental canvases, and although that's a testament to the power of art and music, it really presents impediments to determining if something is good.

There's also evidence that music preferences vary from person to person in part based on their personality. A 2020 study from Spotify on 5,808 users who agreed to take the Big Five personality test compared the results of those tests with the 17.6 million songs they listened to across a three-month period. They found that individual personality traits had a pretty strong link to the kind of music someone likes.

People who scored higher on the openness trait listened to more folk, classical, and jazz music. Those with high emotional stability listened to more blues, soul, and country, and those with lower scores listened to more emo, punk, and rock. Extraversion was linked to R&B, country, and hip-hop, and introversion was linked to goth, death metal, alternative, emo, and punk.

When we talk about the things we like or don't like, it's easy to forget that the reasons for it are the result of a nonlinear process, and the people with whom you're engaging are doing the same thing. That people can talk past each other when trying to impartially discuss a movie isn't a bug of cognition, it's a feature.

Despite the repeated attempts of algorithms and aggregators to convince audiences that there's an objective way to evaluate art, they're papering over the fact that assessments of thousands of people are pretty much guaranteed to be unreliable and prone to change—and that our state of mind when we consume something has a lot to do with how we feel about it.

Bruce Springsteen, inspirer of rabid fandom.

The Black List

In 2005, Franklin Leonard was a development executive at Leonardo DiCaprio's production company. He spent his days reading through scripts and trying to find good projects, a step that involved convincing his bosses that it was worth spending money in production expenses on a script he thought was good. Leonard worked for a guy who was, at the time, the biggest star in the world. But he couldn't help but notice that a lot of the scripts coming across his desk—the kind that get shopped to Leonardo DiCaprio—just weren't that good.

The thing Leonard realized is an open secret: Nobody knows anything in Hollywood. The way the industry worked—the risk-averse incentives we know exist—discouraged imaginative scripts with enormous potential because they weren't worth the career risk to a given studio executive. On balance, this meant that dozens of production executives were likely reading great scripts that they would be reluctant to green-light because the professional downside was too great.

So, Leonard did the logical thing: He emailed those dozens of production executives, sending a survey to seventy-five of his peers with a simple question: "What are your ten favorite screenplays this year that haven't yet been made into a movie?" He then tallied the count and sent it back out to the list. With

the confirmation that no, they were *not* alone, and yes, other people *did* love that script, the listed screenplays began to get scooped up left and right. Two of them, *Juno* and *Lars and the Real Girl*, snagged Best Screenplay nominations within three years.

The endeavor has since expanded, with more than five hundred production executives participating in the annual survey. Of the 1,067 films featured on the lists from 2005 to 2016, 322 were made into feature films, movies that racked up 241 Oscar nominations and 48 wins. Through 2022, those movies had grossed over $28 billion at the global box office and won 12 out of the last 24 Best Screenplay Oscars. A Harvard Business School case study found Black List movies made 90 percent more revenue than peer films that weren't on the list.

"We didn't make those movies, so we can't take credit for them individually, but we can take credit for having built a metal detector in an infinite field of haystacks," Leonard said. In short, he was able to find out what was good.

He later struck out on his own and expanded the operation beyond just the annual list. He thought that if the industry was bad at figuring out what was good that was *already* in the system, surely it was also bad at identifying the stuff that *should* be in the system but was not. The options for breaking into screenwriting in Hollywood are limited. One way is to enter the Academy's Nicholl screenwriting fellowship competition. If you place in the top one hundred, someone will probably give you a call. The other option is to move to L.A., get a job waiting tables, and network like hell, which is not exactly an option for most people.

Leonard hired a team of readers to work through submitted scripts and give feedback. But his angle wasn't to find the best script. When he had the readers rate a script from 1 to 10, it wasn't about quality.

"We ask those readers, 'How likely would you be to recommend this script to a superior in the industry?'" he said. "I personally don't believe in the objective standard of art. I think

Franklin Leonard

art is fundamentally subjective and that two people can differ in their opinion on something and both of them can be right, so we're not trying to test the *quality* of the thing," he explained. "The Black List is not a best-of list; it is at best a most-liked list."

What's more, when the scores that Black List readers give to submitted scripts get shared, Leonard makes it a point to never simply release a single number. Their score is not just an average or a mean like you get on Rotten Tomatoes. Instead, they provide the whole distribution of scores for each script. It's important to them that if a film is rated 4 out of 5, it got four perfect scores and one person hated it, versus a script where half the readers thought it was serviceable and the other half thought it was worth a look. There's important nuance in there that gets lost when the output of hundreds of critics are dumped into the maw of Rotten Tomatoes.

"I think part of the problem is just people don't understand what a Rotten Tomatoes number means: 100 percent on Rotten Tomatoes means that, basically, 100 percent

didn't hate it," Leonard said. "It tells you nothing about the volume of enthusiasm for the movie."

A movie with a 50 percent rating on Rotten Tomatoes could have half the critics loving it and half unenthusiastic about it, or it could have everyone feeling middling about it, or it could have a completely even distribution, or it could have half neutral-to-positive and half strongly negative. The single number doesn't actually reveal anything about the movie.

The Black List has been so successful because it first asked the right question: "Would you recommend this to your boss?" Then, they didn't strip out any nuance in the numbers for convenience; they stuck with distributions and not averages. Their goal is nothing short of the Common Application of creative storytelling, and the numbers don't lie—it worked.

"There's always been an uncomfortable relationship between numbers and the arts," said Leonard, "and if we're going to apply numbers to the arts, we have to be really responsible about that and how we communicate those things."

And Now, a Word from Our Sponsors

Since you don't have control over your own subjectivity, how do you find things you like?

One way is to change the way you consume things to improve the chances that you'll enjoy them. It turns out, how you experience something fun and pleasant can change the way you feel about it. There's a classic social science experiment called the marshmallow test. There are all sorts of variations on it, but the gist is this: You put a marshmallow in front of a kid and tell the kid that if they can go fifteen minutes without eating the marshmallow, they'll get a second marshmallow. Then you kick back and see what happens.

The reason it's a classic exercise is that more often than not, the undisciplined child lacks the willpower to survive a brief delay in their happiness, but in doing so will cheat

themselves out of further happiness. And this is precisely what we do with media consumption just about all the time.

Spoiler alert: Despite all preexisting beliefs to the contrary, I came away from researching the effect that ads have on the media they interrupt with an actual respect for commercials. Based on any number of studies about how to watch movies or TV, we know fairly well that binge-viewing is one of the worst ways to consume anything. Despite big dumps of shows becoming the norm and also the way most consumers say they want content, the process really sells the work short in our minds.

Based on multiple surveys over multiple years from pollster Morning Consult, we know the demand comes from consumers, who seem

AND NOW, A WORD FROM OUR SPONSORS

A study found that commercial breaks improved viewers' appreciation of the interrupted show

People who got a commercial break liked the post-break part of the show much more

EXPERIMENT 1

1 *Viewers watched:*

Half watched *Taxi* **without** Commercials Half watched *Taxi* **with** Commercials

2 *On this scale, how did it compare?*

-5 -4 -3 -2 -1 0 1 2 3 4 5

Would totally prefer *Happy Days* — Would totally prefer **over** *Happy Days*

3 *Predicted and actual scores:*

PREDICTED ● ● ● ● ● ● ● ● ● ● PREDICTED

ACTUAL ● ● ● ● ● ● ● ● ● ● ACTUAL

EXPERIMENT 2

1 *Viewers watched:*

Half watched *Duel* **without** ad Half watched *Duel* **with** interstitial ad

2 *On this scale, how did it compare to control clip of clowns fighting?*

1 2 3 4 5 6 7

Bad — Great

3 *Actual scores:*

ACTUAL ← ● ● ● ● ●●● ● ● → ACTUAL

4 *Amount each would pay for DVD:*

$4.18 $5.42

EXPERIMENT 3

1 *Viewers watched:*

Half watched documentary **with preroll and postroll ads** 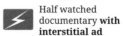 Half watched documentary **with interstitial ad**

2 *How would you rate this film?*

1 2 3 4 5 6 7 8 9

Bad — Great

3 *Predicted and actual scores:*

PREDICTED ← ● ● ●● ● ● ● ● ● → PREDICTED

ACTUAL ← ● ● ●●● ● ● ● → ACTUAL

4 *Ratings:*

First half: ← ● ● ● ●● ● ● ● →

Second half: ← ● ● ● ●● ● ● ● →

Decline in enjoyment of second half: -0.53   -0.2

Leif D. Nelson, Tom Meyvis, and Jeff Galak, 2009

to fail the content marshmallow test with downright enthusiasm.

In 2019, 49 percent of those polled said they preferred that all the episodes in a given show's season be released at once, compared with just 14 percent who preferred the historical release strategy of one episode a week. The respondents who were aged eighteen to forty-four preferred the full-season drops 60 percent of the time, compared with just 10 percent who preferred the conventional release pattern.

Further, when watching the shows, 44 percent preferred watching the whole season at once, with 21 percent saying they liked to watch a few episodes at once and pace them out, and only 15 percent saying they watch about one episode a week.

Unsurprisingly, people despise ads: A 2021 survey asked respondents what they thought about ads on streaming content, and 44 percent said there were too many, whereas just 3 percent said there were too few.

A 2018 survey found that 60 percent of respondents engaged in binge-watching at least once per week, with that number rising to 73 percent among those eighteen to twenty-nine. More than half the respondents said they'd completed a full season of a television show within a week of its release. Fully 29 percent copped to watching an entire season of a show within twenty-four hours of its release, a feat managed by 51 percent, a *majority*, of those eighteen to twenty-nine. For a minority, it's a remarkable habit: 7 percent of television watchers say that the *average* amount of time it takes them to watch a season of a show after its premiere is one to two days.

When asked why they binged, 69 percent said that a somewhat important factor was that it was too suspenseful to wait, and 83 percent said they wanted to see more of the story. Fifty-four percent said they wanted to avoid spoilers, implying that they felt some social pressure to blow through the shows as quickly as possible—a marshmallow test failed because they were worried about someone on social media stealing their marshmallow.

Primarily, binge-watching can have serious effects on both retention and enjoyment of the things we watch. We know for a fact that slowing down the rate at which we consume a likable thing enhances the pleasure we get from it. Adding a healthy variety of things we consume does as well. If you listen to five songs you like five times each, it won't be as pleasant as repeating a five-song playlist five times. Television networks learned this early on and programmed for it: Rather than release four sitcom episodes from the same show in one night, they dole out one episode a week as part of a four-show block across four weeks. Pacing out consumption enhances the evaluation of that consumption.

Perversely, this means that commercials deserve some credit for enhancing the content they interrupt, to my utter dismay. A 2009 study published in the *Journal of Consumer Research* spelled it out. Researchers conducted six studies to see how people evaluated a given work, and how the presence or absence of commercials changed that. Across the various studies, they had people watch shows with and without ads, placed them at different intervals, and even sliced two shows in half and showed the halves in mixed order. Without fail, people liked content that was interrupted in some way more than they liked content that was not.

The thinking is this: The brain is really good at adapting and acclimating to situations the body puts it in. This is a good thing— spend enough time on a construction site and you don't mind the sound; work long enough as a line cook and you get used to the heat. Brains compensate to adapt to their surroundings, which has implications for when we feel *good* as well as when we feel bad. They adapt to pleasant experiences, eventually becoming bored by them. But interrupt a pleasant experience with an ad for, say, McDonald's, and your brain is jolted out of what's called the *progression of affect*.

And it's not uniquely commercials that can do this. What really interrupts the progression of affect is the presence of subplots or "B-plots." It doesn't have to be an ad, it just needs to jolt the brain, offer it something new and interesting to look at before returning it to the previous plot with which it is no longer cozy and in which it is rapidly losing interest.

Functionally, you process commercials as effectively sponsored subplots, and though you may despise them, their ability to reset your head enhances your overall experience at the end of the day. Sad but true.

If moviemakers really wanted to please the people in the seats, they'd bring back the intermission.

And yet seemingly every trend in the entertainment business is moving *away* from encouraging viewers to slow down, to disrupt the progression of affect.

With the best of intentions—giving consumers what they *think* they want versus what their brains appraise as better—everything about delivering entertainment is trending toward removing all the annoyances that we know enhance the experience. We don't watch commercials—we pay another two dollars a month. Theaters did away with intermission to optimize the length of the film and maximize show times. All the tricks showmen built up for decades to tease content, to enhance it, are gone.

This trend extends to the physical realm, too. People don't wait in line anymore; we get movie tickets in an app. Theme parks—where the allocation and optimization of enjoyment is a well-practiced science—know that making people wait for stuff makes them like the stuff more. Yet they're still rolling out FastPasses because people are willing to pay an arm and a leg extra to, in practice, enjoy themselves less.

The culture industry is actively moving away from building in interruption, with many content providers emulating Netflix and dumping all the episodes of a show at once. This helps with a consistent social media rollout, to be sure. And the consumers want it, and the customer is always right.

This all presents a bit of a paradox. If one wants to enjoy a work in a way best suited to appreciate the media product, one has to specifically rebel against the desired package in which the distributor of that work is offering it for consumption and judging its success. The diet metaphor for media consumption doesn't always work, but much like the way plating and pacing can impact how much an eater consumes at a meal, how we watch the shows we want to like can impact how much we enjoy them.

Basically? *Slow down.* Savor it.

Going Global

One way to possibly learn about what's good is by looking at what spreads.

The list of the most-translated works in the world, as you might imagine, is rife with religious texts. Churches naturally have a strong incentive to get the good word out about their respective causes. However, many fictional works also make the list of the most-translated works in the world.

At the top of the list is *The Little Prince*, which has been translated into 488 different languages or dialects. Next is *Pinocchio*, translated into some 260 languages, and *Alice's Adventures in Wonderland*, which has a reported 174 translations. From there it gets choppier,

depending on complete or partial translations. *Don Quixote*, *Andersen's Fairy Tales*, *The Adventures of Asterix*, *The Adventures of Tintin*, and Harry Potter are all near the top of the list.

So what makes these titles so internationally popular?

With the exception of *Don Quixote*—which has a few hundred years' head start on the others—all of them were written for children. *The Little Prince* is a bittersweet storybook that works on a conceptual level and engages with ideas—greed, authority figures, loss—that transcend all cultures and languages.

Pinocchio plays it broadly: Every society in the world has kids, every kid eventually learns that lying can be effective, and every parent will eventually encourage their kid to stop lying. It is as low a common denominator as you can get—and I mean that as a compliment.

Asterix, Tintin, Alice in Wonderland, and Harry Potter are all likable young protagonists who go on adventures. There aren't a lot of Romans around anymore to take offense at the indignities Asterix and his fellow Gauls heaped upon them. Tintin is clean-cut, clearly illustrated, and travels the world. Potter became a global phenomenon. Wonderland can be anywhere. They're all compelling reads, but sufficiently inoffensive that they'll play in most if not all cultures.

These works succeed because you don't need a great deal of knowledge or context to understand them, and they can be shared not just among peers but also intergenerationally, from kids who grow into parents to their own kids. In the same way that children's television programming tries to tell compelling stories for kids who lack the context and are not ready for the sophistication of film (see page 29), all these stories go down in their own self-contained worlds. If the setting is consistent, like a school or a magical world, then readers are in places the author has designed entirely for them, so that they don't need an understanding of the British school system or to have previously set foot in Wonderland or in seventeenth-century Spain.

Although the idea of "lowest common denominator" entertainment can be easily derided, there is power in appealing to sensibilities and touchstones shared by a lot of people. These stories, with their often rudimentary lessons or morals or one-note archetypal characters, are able to succeed on a global, transcultural level because they're homing in on what we all have in common, not what we all lack.

By the same token, even the oldest narrative cave art we're aware of—art that tells a fictional story—has hits that we still play today. Found in a limestone cave in Sulawesi, Indonesia, and described in a paper published in *Nature* in 2019, the work is forty thousand

years old. It shows a hunt, but not *only* a hunt: Joining the hunt are half-man, half-beast creatures. Although portrayals of animals and people are pretty common in prehistoric art, human-animal figures are uncommon. It's also an important indicator of human development—the ability to invent fictional stories is thought to be one of the last stages of forming modern cognition. That idea—the description of an event, but with an added Batman, for example, to kick it into gear—has obviously remained popular to this day.

The Mad Hatter through the years.

From Here to Eternity

Let's go back briefly to the beginning of this chapter, where we left our dozen-odd scientists with an impossible task to design media that can last ten thousand years.

The Environmental Protection Agency had somewhat arbitrarily concluded that to fulfill the "duty to warn" legal requirement for radioactive waste, a site needed to have markers designating it as dangerous that would be effective for ten thousand years. After an obsessive search, they assembled an eclectic crew of astronomers, linguists, materials scientists, and more, a crack team of diverse specialties to solve this impossible problem.

One of them was Jon Lomberg, an aide-de-camp to Carl Sagan who had worked on Sagan's part of the *Voyager* Golden Record, the artifact encompassing a broad swath of human culture that was included along with the *Voyager* space probes that were hurled in the direction of the exits of the solar system.

"We were thinking of communicating with a human audience, but one that was so far removed that they would be aliens in the sense that we don't know anything about them," said Lomberg.

If you're going to build a message that needs to last ten thousand years, you need to write it down on something that will withstand the worst that ten thousand years could throw at it. That's where Victor Baker, a geologist, came in. His doctoral research was about one of the largest catastrophic floods ever documented on Earth, sixteen thousand years ago in Montana. Then, after *Mariner 9* images of Mars came back, NASA came calling, because they needed a guy who knew about flooding. That work made him a fit for the challenge at the Waste Isolation Pilot Plant.

"The main aspect that put me on the panel was that the marker had to persist on longer geological timescales," Baker said. "They were wanting the message to be able to be conveyed for ten thousand years, so that meant that one had to think about the kinds of surface geological processes that could operate on that timescale." Like, for instance, floods.

They also brought in Woody Sullivan, an astronomer who as a grad student in the late 1960s broke into the emerging, leading-edge field of radio astronomy. An astronomer named Frank Drake, the first person to ever attempt to detect an interstellar radio transmission at the National Radio Astronomy Observatory in Green Bank, West Virginia, also was on the project. Sullivan's first key contribution came in 1978 when he was among the first to consider what kind of radio radiation the Earth was accidentally leaking.

"I worked it out in great detail that we were emitting lots of radio radiation that could be picked up, and maybe what we should be looking for, therefore, is not a purposeful beacon, but the leakage from another society," said Sullivan. "And by leakage I mean televisions, FM radio stations, radar, communications of all kinds."

The panel was split into two groups that would come to a number of unifying ideas about how they would attack a problem of this magnitude. Team A's was that "A picture may be worth a thousand words, but it can be difficult to discern which thousand."

Messages are hard. In hieroglyphics around tombs you're constantly seeing carvings of beetles next to illustrations of the buried kings. Now, because I'm a resident of New York City, my interpretation of this is "Ramses had a really bad roach problem." But that's based on *my* experience. If I saw a picture of an Egyptian man surrounded by roaches on the cover of the *New York Post*, I'd just assume it was the story of some sort of landlord-tenant dispute. In ancient Egypt, beetles mean *rebirth*, which is kind of a stretch until you've seen rolled-up balls of dung suddenly teeming with baby beetles, hatching and feasting and rising anew.

This is germane to "nuclear waste in the desert" for a few reasons. The biohazard symbol can be interpreted as something digging downward, which is *the exact opposite of what we want.* The radiation trefoil is not going to work, because nothing about its design pictorially alludes to radiation. A skull and crossbones is not going to cut it. It's younger than you think, designed by medieval alchemists. The skull is Adam's, and the crossed bones represent the promise of resurrection. See the big issue with symbols? Show it to a kid and they're going to wonder how pirates got to Carlsbad, New Mexico.

Marking this site with a monolith is a problem, too, because monoliths have for the entire duration of human history been intended to connect a place on Earth with the heavens above, and most of the time when you dig underneath a monolith, you get "bones of a beloved or rich guy." Wrong message: There is nothing hopeful or aspirational about nuclear waste.

"The key point that I think our group got right is that it isn't just one message; it's a layered process," said Baker. If you came to visit the site years down the line, you would get one continuous message that would progressively raise concern, communicating the same idea in lots of different ways big and small. If one failed, there would be several other ways to get the message through.

"For me, the model was the signage in parks," Lomberg said. "You stop at a scenic overlook and there's a plaque telling you the height of the mountains. You don't think they're lying to you." They came to the conclusion that using

stick figure comics illustrating the danger was best. The human form hasn't changed in tens of thousands of years. Combine a deeply unsettling setting and simple pictographs describing the physical effects on simple human figures should they dig and become contaminated with radiation, translate it into multiple languages, call it a day. Given that America's finest scientists determined that a crudely drawn comic in surroundings that make the visitor feel unwell is the ticket to immortality, I can safely say that *Garfield* will last ten thousand years.

Lots of the researchers never really managed to shake the question of how to make messages last for the ages.

Sullivan is still interested in what precisely Earth is casting off. Seventy light-years out, you can catch *I Love Lucy* if you nail the right range of radio. Today, though, digital's cleaned things up. But we haven't piped down.

Lomberg's work on the Golden Record will live on. "We had six weeks to do the whole thing, from the time I got the phone call from Carl saying, 'I need you to help me on this project' to the time we had to have the finished design. *Six weeks,*" he said. Upon launch it was originally projected to last billions of years. That's now considered a lowball.

"The latest estimates of how long the protected half of the Golden Record will last is it has a fifty-fifty chance of lasting something like ten trillion years," said Lomberg.

The Flood

Among the many future thinkers who set about to inscribe the story into stone that would last millennia, the geologist may be the one who offers the most intriguing idea of what can make a story endure.

Baker started his career by investigating the collapse of Glacial Lake Missoula sixteen thousand years ago. This was a giant lake in western Montana that was a melting holdover from the Ice Age, a two-thousand-foot-deep reservoir held in place by an ice dam. One day

that ice dam failed, and five hundred cubic miles of water gushed across what's now eastern Washington, a geological catastrophe that scarred the Earth itself.

But here's the thing: According to Baker, that wasn't the only time that happened. Far from it.

"There were many other places on Earth where this occurred," he said. "It was at the end of the last ice age. You had these huge ice sheets, and they were surrounded by giant lakes, and there was all kinds of water on the landscape. And these lakes failed and produced floods that went across parts of Eurasia and other areas."

We know the English Channel was carved out by catastrophic flooding in a similar way. A huge lake in what's now the southern part of the North Sea failed, leading to the formation of the channel. It wasn't publicly known for decades because the sonar topography of the sea floor was top-secret military intelligence.

There are multiple places on Earth where you can see the same thing. But here's what's especially interesting about the history of massive flooding.

"There were people around," said Baker. "When these giant floods occurred on the Earth sixteen thousand years ago, there certainly were people. *All over Eurasia.*"

Can you think of a particularly durable story this reminds you of?

"If people saw evidence of these floods, there's no question they would think the whole world was flooded, because the whole

The Voyager space probe's golden record could last billions of years.

world that they knew and understood would be flooded."

As far as stories go, you'd be hard-pressed to find a story more ancient and distressingly ubiquitous than "The Flood." The Egyptian one involves Ra stopping Sekhmet, there's also a Mesoamerican flood myth, and multiple North American cultures have flood myths as well. The list goes on and on: The Gilgamesh flood myth, the Sumerian creation myth, China's story of Nuwa patching the holes in heaven, the legend of Manu and Matsya in India, Korea's Namu doryeong, the ancient Greek flood myths, the biblical story of Noah in Genesis. The folklore of the world doesn't agree on much, but "once there was a flood that was so bad, it destroyed the world, and yet somehow by the grace of God we endured" is a suspiciously common touchstone of humanity's oral history.

"They weren't writing it down sixteen thousand years ago, but they had oral traditions, and they were communicating," said Baker. "If they were experiencing it, it certainly would have been the greatest thing that ever happened within their own lifetimes, and something to be conveyed to others as well."

That gives us a couple of playbooks for ensuring that a story endures. They're blunt, but they work.

So, if you want to write a story that will last forever, here are a few pointers.

Make sure it includes the single most important environmental cataclysm in the history of the species, a scar on the genetic memory of an entire global generation.

Don't have enough ice for that? You can always sear it onto a golden record and hurl it as far as you can into the abyss of space. Or blare it as loudly as you can from a radio antenna. Or you could take the lessons from those charged with creating a message that will survive ten thousand years.

One result of the WIPP project (see page 171) was that the scientists agreed on ten things necessary to get the correct answer. The list was written to help warn people away from buried nuclear waste, but the framework of the things they could unanimously agree on was absolutely necessary to ensure that a message could survive ten thousand years.

And I'm struck by how well those report recommendations can be adapted to culture with just a few tweaks, and can make a blueprint for what makes the most enduring, beloved, excellent work of culture.

1. The work's creators have something to say, and do not hide it. Work that endures has a message, a goal, and necessity.

2. Work that lasts does so because it's multilayered, working on a surface level but also containing enough depth that people can keep coming home and seeing more work underneath the surface.

3. Good work is real, from a place of real love or struggle or anger. Work that lasts has a verisimilitude that is unquestionable and doesn't play with emotion for the sake of it.

4. Once you get to that heart of the work, looking back at the beginning and the surface-level stuff, you see it's been leading there the whole time.

5. The work is about something. It's clear what the heart of the work is, even if you don't necessarily understand the details.

6. The message stays the same, but is delivered in a number of different ways, so even if one stops making sense, the soul of it remains.

7. That which drove a creator to make a piece of culture should be part of the work—central, even—and not buried or obscured.

8. Not every bit of the story needs to be in the work. You can leave some stuff out, and the interested people can find it on their own later.

9. The work can be placed among its peers and is part of a broader conversation with the society that made it and the work that came before it.

10. The work is the product of more than one set of hands, made through a collaborative process and allowing itself to be improved as needed.

By any metric, the "Greatest of All Time" tend to nail these, whether it's *Casablanca* or *Hamlet* or *Pet Sounds*, the Gospels, *The Lord of the Rings*, or whatever is held to be superlative.

Or, again, *Garfield*. Could just be that.

CHAPTER 8

WHAT STORIES DO TO THEIR CREATORS

Cate Blanchett in Tár *(2022).*

It's not just the consumption of culture that can leave an indelible mark on us, but the act of creation itself. It's no wonder, then, that plenty of those who are defined by the entertainment they love feel drawn, compelled—even ideologically or monomaniacally forced—to create it. And to do so regardless of the many personal and financial calamities that can befall them.

We know the dynamic effect culture has on its consumers, but we don't typically spend much time thinking about or studying the creators—or more specifically the process of creation, how it works best, and whom it benefits. But of course we now have more research and data to argue that there are definite advantages to creating art a certain way. That's largely by collaboration—if not directly, then as part of a community. How that community operates is often directly reflected in the quality of the art it produces, which of course affects us, the consumers.

Flow State

How we create stuff and where creativity comes from is a considerable point of contention for writers and creators of all stripes. "Creativity" itself is a subject of serious study. Evolutionarily, the conceit of creativity is a weird one, because although species must be adaptable—as in, genetically it's a plus for a whole species if it's able to survive under a range of conditions—individual animals don't require a lot of creativity in the personal sense. Sharks don't need to be creative—they're fast, strong, and possess many teeth—and they've survived hundreds of millions of years effectively unchanged. Most herbivorous animals don't need a massive capacity for problem solving, because the most common task on the average grazer's to-do list is "consume grass." And since grass is not really elusive, it doesn't take much expertise or innovation to outsmart it.

Predators tend to be more crafty and have larger brains. The brutal economics of the jungle mean that, although there are often many prey for each predator, only the predators capable of regularly catching the meat can survive. In a way, this requires some creativity.

For us, the large brain-to-body ratio is pretty much the whole deal. Creative thinking is far from exclusive to humans, but it is *the* thing that defines us in comparison to other species.

For this and other reasons, the origins of creativity in the brain have been the subject of considerable study. Of particular interest to neuroscientists is musical improvisation. It's not just a convenient way to get at the origins of creativity; it also offers insight into how the most accomplished creatives differ from the rest of us. On the practical side, it's also easier to peek inside the brain of someone who's standing still while playing an instrument than, say, a comedian doing improv. And the quality of an improvised musical composition is easier to evaluate than, say, the results of a brainstorming session.

The most influential model of musical improvisation was developed in the late 1980s by a researcher named Jeff Pressing, who got his PhD in chemistry but chose to run a university music department in Australia. A polymath, Pressing dabbled in musical experimentation and early computer science work in transcription. In the '90s, his research turned to a passion of his, musical improvisation. His own music experience led him to believe that the creative elements of musical performance are built on a foundation of memory. He believed that creativity, the relative ability to improvise in music, is not a circumstance of birth but a cultivated, learned skill. For Pressing, a musician's ability to improvise is achieved through training and deliberate practice.

Only through practice can they build a mental database of movement to draw from when they improvise. Accomplished musicians can absorb feedback in real time and adjust on the spot. Processing that level of information demands a lot of the brain, and then making decisions about what to do (or play) next is equally demanding. The conscious mind can do only so much. To be successful at processing that level of information and making decisions, an improvising musician must draw from their mental database *subconsciously*. The only way they're able to do that, and to trust that the database won't let them down, is through years of practice building that database of mental and physical skills.

Later studies were able to put that theory to the test in terms of monitoring people's brains during actual performances with fMRIs. Two studies—one on professional jazz musicians, one on professional freestyle rap musicians—found decreased activity in the dorsolateral prefrontal cortex, which is used for things like planning and reasoning, decision making, and working memory, with increased activity in the medial prefrontal cortex. The latter is active when a person is daydreaming or when they're not focused outside the mind but are thinking about themselves or recalling the past.

Other studies point to the activation of other areas, such as the inferior frontal gyrus

(IFG), which has been shown to light up when doing tasks that require drawing on long-term memory and during idea generation. Another area that engages is the anterior cingulate cortex, which is associated with conflict monitoring, emotion, and the kind of snap decision making involved in impulse control. But it's the IFG that's of particular interest: A review of several dozen fMRI studies finds that it's reliably linked to divergent thinking, a key component of creativity. In a lab setting it can be measured, for instance, by asking someone to devise new uses for everyday items, then evaluating how many they come up with and how creative they are.

All of this backs up the theory that, when improvising, the brain isn't actually thinking hard or making active decisions, but rather is being allowed to wander. The most successful musical improvisers are adept at suppressing the part of their brain that wants to actively manage and plan in favor of engaging the parts that let the mind do its own thing. At the same time, the brain is drawing on a lifetime of experience.

Studying differences between professional musical improvisers and nonprofessionals just playing around on an instrument is also revealing. Neurologists found that the main difference between improvising musicians and improvising nonmusicians was that musicians deactivated a part of the brain called the temporoparietal junction, whereas nonmusicians kept it engaged. The temporoparietal junction, or TMJ, is a part of the brain that takes in information from the senses—sight, sound, your brain's conception of the world around it—and processes it. So, when we compare musicians with nonmusicians, what we're seeing is that musicians have an ability to suppress their sensory experience of the world around them, to zone out and reduce the noise of the world outside their minds. Nonmusicians, on the other hand, tend to not let go, to remain keenly aware of the world around them.

Rather than creative thought being an active task that you turn on, neurologically speaking it's the opposite: It's about letting go, turning off, suppressing. It actually recalls what we know about visual attention. While a spotlight is turning up the focus on a subject, it's also turning down and tuning out the things that aren't the subject. Except with improvisation, the things we're tuning out are the world at large and our urge to plan. It's not enough to turn up the creative juices; you also need to let go of the parts of the brain that want to consciously steer that flow and to think about how other people are reacting to that flow.

Indeed "flow" isn't just a convenient shorthand for how it feels when creativity exits the body. A "flow state" occurs when a person is completely engrossed in a task that commands their full mental attention. This is often pretty thrilling: A flow state happens when the challenges of a task meet a person's high skill, something that leads to a sense of self-satisfaction. Conversely, when a challenge exceeds a person's low skill, they feel anxiety; when something unchallenging is beneath a person's high skills, they feel boredom, and when someone unskilled does something not challenging, they feel apathy. But when a person's high skills meet a challenge, studies show, they'll often get a boost in mood compared with their counterparts.

Improvisation requires letting go.

Doing creative things has been shown to be good for those who do them. Although the idea of the tortured artist is popular, incorporating some kind of creative activity into day-to-day activities has been shown to have a positive impact on mood. We also have evidence that people tend to be more creative when they're in a good mood. Multiple studies have shown that a positive emotional state is linked to more creative problem solving. This isn't exactly revelatory: It's easier to do most things when the vibes are good.

But we also need to remember that creativity rarely takes place in a vacuum. It is rarely a solitary process. And if we want to understand the bigger picture—how individual creativity is fostered or stymied in broader fields—we need to understand how the environments we build around creative people can affect them.

With few exceptions, no great work is made alone. Behind the scenes there is usually a collaborative component—working with trusted contributors, as well as forging unsteady relationships with brand-new ones—that is found to improve the work. One study of 6,446 movies from the early days of Hollywood found a distinct link between new collaborations between veteran creatives and then the resulting films having a higher rate of unseen combinations of genre ending up on screen, evidence for new innovations in storytelling.

Indeed, to foster creativity it's essential to cultivate an environment that fosters and encourages experimentation, development, recovery from errors, and growth, and although many companies aspire to that, few actually deliver. Genres and storytelling communities don't thrive or fail by accident: Specific choices are made by the community or the company or the broader market that lead to a flourishing or a calamity for those involved.

To understand just how important creative environments can be, we're going to look at how rewarding bottom-up experimentation and growth can be in two very different artistic worlds. Each was born in the lawless frontier of culture, looked down upon by more assured and established pursuits, but nevertheless became extremely popular. Both have histories, both undercompensate their labor considerably, and both have maintained frenetic, committed fan bases through tumultuous times over the course of decades.

The Screwjob

I am at the Barclays Center in Brooklyn, in a seventy-dollar seat that can charitably be described as lower nosebleed. Hundreds of feet below, in a ring rendered in high definition on an enormous screen at roughly eye level, is a wrestling ring, the site of *Survivor Series*, one of the four big pay-per-view events offered by the global sports entertainment hegemon WWE, or World Wrestling Entertainment.

The event will settle an annual score: Which of the two flagship programs—*Smack Down* or *Raw*—offered by WWE is superior? Beyond the intra-corporate spectacle, wrestling's equivalent of baseball's inter-league play, the buzz in the arena is that Dwayne Johnson, the most famous actor on the planet, may be in the building and may even take the mic at some point, or maybe even get in the ring. And more, that he could emerge at some point at the wrestling promotion of which he was the star a lifetime ago, as The Rock.

From my nosebleeds, I saw a half-dozen matches. The Brooklyn crowd was rambunctious, to say the least. The first was between Charlotte Flair and Becky Lynch, by far the best match of the night, one that drew chants of "This is awesome!" Naturally, it ended with a simple, boring roll-up, a rudimentary maneuver where the victor pins the loser by simply smothering them to the mat, how too many matches seem to end these days.

This was followed by a men's five-on-five, then a twenty-five-man battle royale, a contest of more than two dozen combatants in a quest to—no joke—win a prize of three pizzas furnished by the Pizza Hut corporation. In the women's five-on-five, to the exasperation of several people around me, multiple high-flying altercations concluded with a boring roll-up. A twenty-two-minute finale between Big E and Roman Reigns, the largest star on the entire roster and an up-and-coming new champion, respectively, was serviceably compelling to watch if just a bit predictable: Reigns had been undefeated in pay-per-views for years, so the tension was low. A sense of disappointment pervaded the crowd: The rumors of The Rock, no doubt goosed by repeated highlights of Johnson airing between matches, as well as an inexplicable subplot about a golden egg that was linked to a recent Johnson Netflix outing, never came to fruition. In the end the whole thing felt overpromised and underdelivered.

The matches were perfunctory, and there was no beef, no long-held animosity that leads good men to come to blows, no invariable set of differences that forced Charlotte Flair and Becky Lynch to end negotiations and reluctantly settle their irreconcilable differences in the ring. Not a single folding chair was swung. More than one match entailed high-flying acrobatics but ultimately ended in a boring hold. The corporate sponsors—Yum! Brands and Netflix chief among them—were likely pleased. Reviews were largely negative. WWE made a fortune.

And what of the wrestlers themselves?

A few days before *Survivor Series*, WWE fired eight wrestlers. That followed a previous round of layoffs a few weeks before that when they released eighteen wrestlers, bringing the total number of wrestlers they'd cut since the beginning of the year to eighty-three. On the day of the event, WWE had 255 wrestlers on their roster, down 7 percent from just a month earlier. Wrestlers cut from the top of the sport so a septuagenarian billionaire could seemingly find more time for skits about a golden egg.

But it wasn't always that way.

A Brief History of Flying Elbows

Professional wrestling as a performing art originated in the 1930s, before which it was a legitimate sport performed for spectators—not unlike boxing or any other combat—and then later became something more theatrical. Which isn't to say it was entirely scripted, but the objective wasn't to simply cause an adversary pain to the point of submission; rather, it was to put on a good, improvisational fighting show for a gathered group.

Through the '40s, these individual wrestling bouts coalesced into multiple regional promotions, where the wrestling within a specific region was controlled by one company or group. Until the early '80s, this was how professional wrestling worked in the United States: The wrestling in your region was organized and operated by a particular outfit, but big-time wrestlers could move from one region to another. Connected by a loose-knit confederation, this was known as the National Wrestling Alliance (NWA). The modern WWE was an early member, albeit then known as the New York–based World Wide Wrestling Federation, or WWWF, which would then become the WWF, eventually molting one more time before emerging as the WWE.

In their formative years, the regions were in fierce competition for talented, adaptable performers—the kind of wrestlers who could work well with other wrestlers to put on an excellent show and sell some tickets. Eventually, the twenty-five-odd regional outfits realized that going to war with one another over turf and talent was unsustainable, so they assembled a loose confederacy that honored the regional control. Wrestlers could still come and go as they pleased: When a worker got burned out in one region, they could go to another region, to benefit from a new environment, to ply their trade elsewhere so both territories benefited from the novelty. Outfits competed for top performers, but none of the promoters were trying to destroy the competition in the next state over, so they were able to get a steady supply of fresh talent circulating the country.

During the territorial era, breaking into wrestling meant getting roughed up in a gym by a seasoned wrestler. At the time, wrestling still purported to be real to fans, so if the wannabe wrestler

The Great Goliath vs. Chavo Guerrero, 1975.

returned to the gym, a few weeks or months of training would follow. Then the young wrestler would be sent on the road to wrestle regularly, learning by doing, typically with one or more experienced wrestlers. They'd do a match, then talk over the match during the drive to the next town.

Laurence DeGaris, a sports marketing professor, has written extensively about wrestling. Within the industry, he writes, professionals are known as "workers," and older wrestlers speak about the industry in distinct worker-first language.

"'Work' as a proletarian term also reinforces awareness of labor relations between promoter and employee and reflects professional wrestling's blue-collar roots," he writes. "Full-time professional wrestlers—though vastly diminished in numbers during the past fifteen years or so—must still focus on basic elements of the *job*."

That began to change in the 1980s, when the territories began collapsing.

Enter the Behemoth

Vince McMahon bought the World Wrestling Federation from his father and three business partners in 1982 for $1 million. At the time, the WWF was the New York–based outfit that controlled professional wrestling from Maine to Maryland. Within a decade, the younger McMahon managed to buy out or force out nearly all the other territory owners.

As a matter of practice, lots of promoters would buy time on local television to air matches as a way to juice enthusiasm (read ticket sales) for live events, a practice McMahon perfected. But McMahon would also mount media market incursions into rival regions to push WWF and crowd out the local competitors. Without the access to television airtime McMahon bought out from under them, the regional outfits folded like chairs slamming into the heads of unsuspecting wrestlers.

McMahon also recruited the best wrestlers from competing regions as his ability to dominate the airwaves increased, thereby sucking out the stars and further consolidating

PRO WRESTLING EVENTS PER YEAR BY TERRITORY

WWE killed or consumed the rival territories

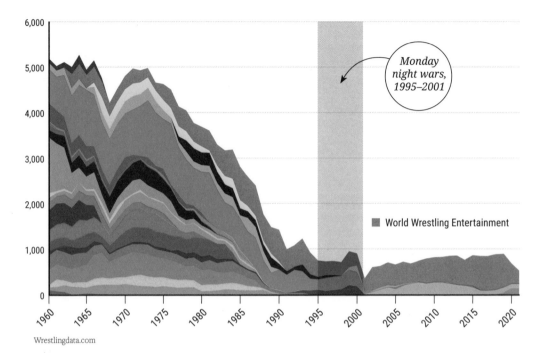

Monday night wars, 1995–2001

World Wrestling Entertainment

Wrestlingdata.com

attention and viewership to the WWF. The National Wrestling Alliance and the southern promotions preferred wrestlers who were able to impress fans with their prowess and charisma; McMahon's approach was to poach big guys and put them in elaborate costumes with specific gimmicks. Hiring away the biggest talent, the headliners, from the other territories ensured something flashy and interesting was on TV when people were idly flipping through the channels.

Once on the WWF roster, poached stars would often get a rebrand. At first, that was rather good for the workers. With National Wrestling Alliance wrestlers able to go to the ascendant WWF, any ability for the powers that be to blacklist a talent nationally was gone, replaced by a motivation to keep top talent happy and well compensated. In 1984, McMahon lured Hulk Hogan from the Minneapolis-based American Wrestling Association territory, then Roddy Piper and Greg Valentine from Jim Crockett's region in

Charlotte—all top talent whose departures dealt serious blows to their former employers.

Through 1986, McMahon cut arrangements with large arenas throughout the country, securing exclusive deals that prevented any non-WWE promotion from putting on shows for thirty days before and after their events. McMahon would then run at least one show in those venues every ninety days, making the window for his competition to score the big venues impossibly small. Battleground regions such as St. Louis, Missouri, would be treated to massive shows to win over the local base of wrestling fans. In 1984, the WWF's director of promotions said the company was staging fourteen shows a week, up from five before the McMahon regime.

When rival outfits would run local live pay-per-view events—the lifeblood of the media side of the biz—McMahon would buy competing local airtime and put on matches for free. The strategy started to work. The tiniest rivals began to fold, with the largest territories withering amid the onslaught of a talent drain, getting outmaneuvered in promotions, and the unrelenting air war on television.

Only the largest WWF rivals could compete at the national level. In 1985, the head of San Antonio's southwest promotion told the *Los Angeles Times*, "You've either got to be big or little, you can't be in the middle. And we can't compete with the big three who have that kind of money to provide first-class shows." He'd sell his stake in the promotion by April.

By 1987, the once-mighty NWA was functionally controlled by Jim Crockett Promotions. A sale to Ted Turner in November 1988 would reduce the number of national wrestling promotions to two, a status quo that would stand until WWE bought them in 2001. Vince McMahon had won: Twenty-five territories were now just one.

Wrestling Post-Vince

After the consolidation, the pro wrestling story becomes about what happened to the creatives who were left behind. The country was awash in veteran wrestlers who spent the previous decades working, but now with just World Championship Wrestling (WCW)—the strongest of the remaining regional promotions, which also maneuvered into a national brand—and WWF hiring there weren't many jobs, so many of them set up schools to teach the trade. Around then, at the tail end of the territory era in 1988, a young man walked into Johnny Rodz' wrestling gym in Brooklyn with an eye on making it. It was a liminal time for wrestling, just after the end of something big yet just before something bigger.

"That's when things have changed, that's the big shift," said Larry Brisco, a wrestler who performed around the world throughout the 1990s. "Because the guys who came up in that system, the culture and especially their work is completely different than the guys who came after. It's just, it's night and day. And for my money, the old-timers, they're better."

Babyfaces, who were often younger and more heroic wrestlers, fight heels, nefarious and villainous wrestlers, most often those who've spent a while in the business. When such things weren't scripted, the heel would call the match: If it was a dance, the heel would lead, literally showing the younger wrestler the ropes. This wasn't a talked-out process; rather, there was a spontaneity to it. A good heel could make a meatball parmesan sandwich look like a superstar. In fact, that happened at a 1983 match, where Lou Albano did that very thing.

"Here's fucking Lou Albano," Brisco said. "He'll do a job for a fucking meatball sandwich. This is why the guys in the locker room loved him. He'll do anything to get you in. He did that for a meatball sandwich, look what he'll do for you."

In the true spirit of wrestling, it's time for an unmasking: Larry Brisco is, in fact, Professor Laurence DeGaris.

After wrestling professionally after college, he went to grad school at the University of Connecticut and set out to make a living as an academic with a keen eye toward pro wrestling, becoming a professor at the University of Indianapolis and the man who literally wrote the textbook about sports marketing.

Still, his firsthand experience with grappling as Brisco gives DeGaris a fundamental appreciation for the form. His first match as Larry Brisco was in 1988 against Charlie Fulton at a high school in Connecticut.

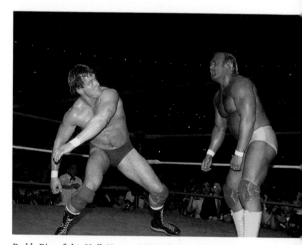

Roddy Piper fights Hulk Hogan at WrestleMania I *in 1985.*

"Charlie was a veteran heel, and I was a young, green, clueless babyface," said DeGaris. "You just follow. Charlie was a good dude. He was very patient and helpful. After the match, he spent like a half an hour talking to me. . . . Now if I work, I swear I say to young guys, 'You just got to calm down, and just got to relax, wait, because you're so eager to do the stuff that you learned.'"

The two dozen regional circuits were an ideal way to recruit young talent into the trade, providing a training program for interested wrestlers and opportunities for inexperienced talent to develop a rapport with steadier hands. Great wrestlers were always on the move from promotion to promotion, so ideas and techniques could be transmitted around the country and across generations through mentorship and temporary collaborations with new and compelling colleagues.

A booker would approach two wrestlers who they thought might have good matches together, sit down with them, and chart out a six-month program. The performers would weigh in, throw their ideas around. Wrestlers new to working together would talk to each other, figure out which kinds of bumps—the way they could hit the mat—the other took. Maybe one had a bad shoulder or a bum knee, so wrestlers would call their own bumps. The booker would propose a twenty-minute time limit draw with no resolution, and then the wrestlers would figure out how to keep things interesting for twenty minutes. They'd return the next week, only this time they'd have thirty minutes because of the *outrage* that they had been unable to settle the score the first time. They'd work that angle, increasing the animus between the wrestlers, and build up sales. Soon enough they'd be going for a sixty-minute bout—again, filling the hour however they chose—but at fifty-nine minutes one of them would get disqualified, yet another outrage. Of course then you'd have to stage a no-disqualification match, on which you'd build, and build, and build.

"And eventually we end up in a cage, and that's it," DeGaris said. "There's no ref, and this is the end, this is the final resolution: Somebody is walking out and somebody isn't."

Since there were no longer twenty-five different employers, but just one, the negotiating power of an individual wrestler evaporated; the WWF is alleged to have sacked and blackballed (a permanent ban) Sergeant Slaughter in 1984 because he brought up the idea of unionizing. But the lack of mentorship, development, and opportunity to leave for better work in other regions left the older guys between a rock and a hard place. Why bother sharing their skills with possible rivals? The result was a new generation of younger guys who didn't understand the fundamentals of the improvisational art of wrestling.

The very structure of the regional territory system meant that when someone was getting ready to leave one promotion, it was just what you did on the way out—you helped put someone over, because what difference would it make? Perhaps you'd return in a few months or years, but that was an eon in wrestling time. A well-established heel going down to an up-and-coming star is a hallmark. Andre the Giant was beloved by other wrestlers for this, as someone who would work to sell young talents as serious threats, someone able to go toe-to-toe with a giant.

But when only one company exists where you can make a living, that calculus changes. "Stone Cold" Steve Austin was popular, but he became a star only after he wiped out Jake "the Snake" Roberts, and became a superstar only after defeating Bret Hart.

"I mean, Jake gets guys over," said DeGaris. "He'll sell for you, you know, he'll sell for you. And then who got *him* over as a babyface? Bret Hart. Who's going to do that for you now?"

Brisco points to Ric Flair, the Nature Boy, father of Charlotte Flair. There was a Nature Boy before Flair, Buddy Rogers, who was semi-retired and fifty-seven and came back to the ring to lose to Flair and pass the torch. But Flair's a septuagenarian, and he's still the Nature Boy.

Today, WWE develops its own talent, which all comes from the same training camp. The matches and the banter are scripted by a team of writers often pulled from a soap opera background.

"Your matches are scripted, your character, your gimmick is dictated, your promos are scripted. I mean, it's really legit paint by numbers," said DeGaris. Do this move. Then do that move. Make sure to get some acrobatics in there. Set up a big jump while the other guy inexplicably lies down to catch his breath. Fifteen minutes of talking followed by ten minutes of slow wrestling. A few elaborate flips. Nailed the choreo? Need to end it? Eh, just finish it with a roll-up.

In the territory days, promoters were often former wrestlers themselves. They would come up with an overall plan for the match while delegating the tactics and blow-by-blow to the wrestlers, explained Brisco. That's inconceivable today.

"There's a lot of creativity, a give and take with the crowd," said DeGaris. "I mean, we're not being dictated by the crowd. We're cultivating them, but there is give and take. When we say timing, that's what we mean by timing."

The wrestling world has greatly diminished in variety and depth of talent as a result

PRO WRESTLERS WHO WORKED A GIVEN NUMBER OF SHOWS PER YEAR

When the WWE became the only show in town in the 1980s and '90s, workers were affected

Popular wrestlers and their first WWE championship year

Bruno Sammartino 1963 · Ric Flair 1981 · Hulk Hogan 1984 · The Rock 1998 · John Cena 2005

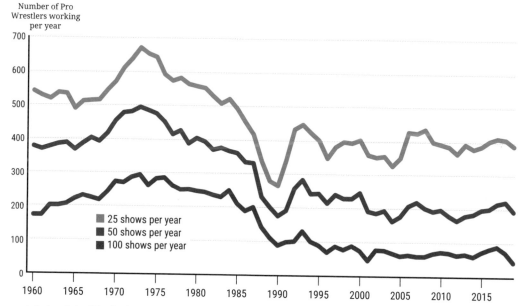

Author's analysis of Wrestlingdata.com

of the consolidation. Many of the twenty-five regional concerns had a twist on the formula or a house style that differed from their peers, but no longer. And the enormous wealth accrued by investors and bosses has not trickled down; pro wrestlers don't have a pension, a health insurance plan, an escalating wage based on experience. They're independent contractors, mostly on their own, left to work their physical art in someone else's style, paid to play only, and abandoned when they are no longer optimal. It's a creatively stifling environment.

"Now, it's they give you a script," DeGaris said. "'Here's when you're doing your comeback, regardless of what the crowd is doing, here's what the match is.' There's no give and take with the crowd. There's no give and take with your partner, you know, your opponent. There's no creativity. And to me, people see that. You feel a sense of they all clap like *That's a fancy move*, but they don't *cheer*."

Amid the consolidation under WWE, wrestlers went from independent craftsmen able to improve and ply their trade wherever there was work to interchangeable cogs in a roster, one of three big guys who had to take what was offered lest they lose their place to the fourth-placed big guy.

WWE's roster is only around 250 people. There's room for a couple of wrestlers of each type—a few big guys, a few acrobats—but outside the top draws you're looking at people who can step in and fill a role as a specific type of threat. But what if you're not one of the eight large guys who can stay on the roster? Why would you pass the torch to the new kid, and thereby undermine your chances to keep a job?

"Without a compelling story, pro wrestlers today must resort to the spectacular to get noticed," DeGaris wrote in a paper on the topic. "The bar continues to be raised with respect to acrobatics. The end result is a rate of injury I believe is unprecedented in the history of the business."

Maybe you start agreeing to stunts you wouldn't try if you were calling your own bumps. Perhaps you take on gimmicks you would have avoided if there were another territory next door. Instead, you follow the script, do the match, and leave the feedback to the microphones. It gets impersonal: You are just a 1099 to the boss, an action figure to the writers, a WWE-owned brand name to the fans, this week's assignment to your opponent, a career threat to the more famous guys on the roster, and the obstacle hogging the next rung on the ladder to the less-famous guys.

Besides that, there's a distinct lack of logic in the fights themselves.

"Now, I mean, I just don't do it, you know?" DeGaris said. "I'd say I'm not retired, but I don't get booked. Last time I was in a gym, this kid is like, *I want to do this spot*. I'm supposed to sit in the middle of the ring, like, just sit in the middle of the ring, and he's gonna run to the rope, and then run back and kick me. And I'm kind of like, *Well, what the fuck am I supposed to be doing while I'm watching you run across the ring? I'm just gonna sit here? Explain this to me*."

By, and For, the Fans

Fan fiction might be the exact opposite of professional wrestling because the community of artists working in the space has relentlessly rejected the kind of consolidation that could make them into employees.

As WWE resulted in more sanctioned matches, more oversight, and top-down consolidation, fan fiction went in the other direction: It got freer, more unsanctioned, and flirted ever harder with intellectual property peril. For those unfamiliar with the term, fan fiction takes the characters, settings, and themes of established stories and puts them into unsanctioned original works. The idea is to expand on the stories within a canon or explore new genres or relationships between characters established by other authors. Fan fiction lives fast and loose, and though it's free rolling and tumultuous, it's not going anywhere, and the price of entry is low—only your effort is required.

Fan work is a very, very difficult medium in which to make money. Ironically, this has at least protected it from the depredations of corporate ownership, if not a cut-and-dried target of corporate legal ire if someone tried to make a fortune from trespassing in someone else's IP.

Similar to wrestling, the publication of fan work before the 1990s was highly territorial. Private forums, newsletters, zines, electronic mailing lists—the way fan works were consumed was informal and clustered in a way that really doesn't exist on the internet anymore. Harry Potter—a rare, largely unprecedented literary event that entranced a generation of internet-connected adolescents all at once—changed pretty much everything related to the concept of fandom, and continues even now. That's a larger story, but for our purposes that Harry Potter, plus the passage of the Digital Millennium Copyright Act, complicated the legality of fan work at the precise time that interest in it had never been higher. That scattered archipelago of fan-fiction writers was unable to feed the demand onslaught or navigate the legal issues, pushing communities to services like FanFiction.net.

However, a consolidated location that was owned meant management could create policy by fiat—and that's exactly what happened when FanFiction.net shut down entire author sections and predictably banned pornographic material, which was a key part of the appeal for many people. LiveJournal then emerged as a fan-fiction host, but the site was not designed to be a writing repository and bristled under the operational pressure of being a social blogging network that got hijacked into being a library. Eventually, they realized that the DMCA didn't protect them if the work they stored was indecent, leading to mass deletions and a subsequent outflow of users from the service.

These false starts would become a pattern, as larger concerns aggressively, consistently, and deliberately worked as hard as possible to ensure that fan-created works were unable to exist in their ecosystem. Whereas the wrestling promotions were vacuumed up by moneyed interests in less than a decade, fan-fiction creators were ejected by moneyed interests the minute they discovered what "slash" was.

In the end, a separate open-source site—Archive of Our Own (AO3)—was formed under a not-for-profit group called the Organization for Transformative Works, with a terms of service that guaranteed a place for any fan-fiction material as long as it was adequately and accurately tagged for content. It became a Hugo Award–winning site that contained 3 million works as of 2017 and was growing: 1.5 million users, 25,000 fandoms, and a legal team that voraciously fights on behalf of the form. FanFiction.net, another platform, included 7 million stories with 61.5 billion words, plus 176 million reviews in that same year. Fanfiction authors produce tens of thousands of chapters of material per month, and in no small part that's because the community surrounding fan fiction is decentralized, encouraging, and thriving.

All this is to say that the ability of talented creators to make things is defined by the health of the ecosystem they inhabit, and that the ability to be creative and do your best work is extremely dependent on the context in which you're trying to do that work. Part of that comes down to the availability of training, mentorship, and the opportunities to experiment and play at a low level for a little while until you improve. To be creative, this is absolutely necessary. We saw that wither on the vine in the wrestling scene, but a number of studies of fan fiction demonstrate how writers are directly served by its existence and grow in their craft over time.

WITH FAN FICTION, FEEDBACK EQUALS PROGRESS

Average writing comprehension score of work based on how many reviews a fan fiction author had received. The size of each dot is scaled to the number of authors who reached that level of feedback.

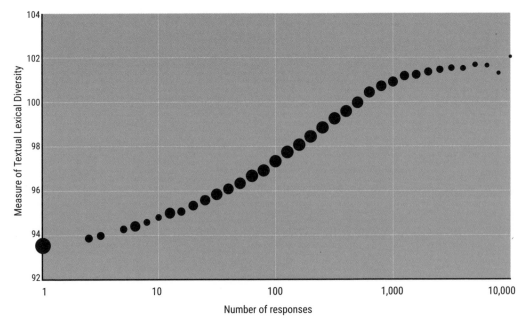

Jenna Frens, Fanfiction.net data

Slashing through Gatekeepers

Cecilia Aragon's experience with fan fiction goes back to her childhood, before she even knew what it was. As a young girl she was a big fan of Tolkien's *The Lord of the Rings* but distressed at the complete lack of women in the books.

"So I rewrote the story," she said, "regenerating a number of the main characters and putting in some new scenes that I thought Tolkien had missed, you know, having these female characters actually doing adventures rather than just being beautiful. Of course, I never showed it to anybody. I didn't even really think it was a story because it was just kind of a copy."

Though fan fiction did exist at the time, it wasn't available to Aragon. Only with the advent of the web did the field truly aggregate, so when Aragon's daughter first took an interest

in it and introduced her mother to it in the late 2000s, there was a sense of recognition.

Since her Tolkien "punch-ups," Aragon has become a computer scientist, for a time working on massive data sets about supernovae, the largest explosions in the universe, research that would ultimately contribute to a Nobel Prize for the principal investigator for whom she worked. Her specialty is now human-centered data science, studying visual analytics and how people interact with them.

Katie Davis stumbled into the world of fan fiction through a series of interviews she did with girls using LiveJournal. Her research focused on the passions involved with specific fandoms and how those fans engaged with other journalers to form the basis for a big portion of their online identities. She and Aragon were colleagues, and would often eat together.

Chapters uploaded to Archive of Our Own over time

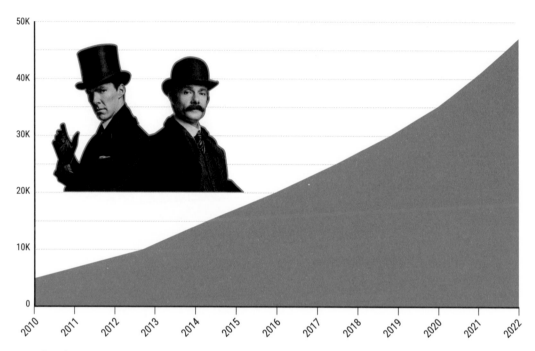

Archive of Our Own

One time over lunch, Aragon and Davis were talking about an article that derided young people as the dumbest generation, which they found not only condescending but also obviously wrong based on what they knew was happening on the web.

They came up with a project designed to understand what was driving young people to write so much online, and what they were getting out of it.

"It's not just a passion, it's part of their identity in a deep way," said Davis. "It's a way to work through their identity. It feels really pressing and important, because it's not just like, *Oh, I love doing this*, which they do, but it's like, *I actually need to do this to figure out who I am*."

Using self-determination theory—the idea that humans have three basic psychological needs: relatedness, competence, and autonomy—they realized that online fan-fiction communities absolutely hit that trifecta. They make it incredibly easy to find people interested in precisely the same things, the lack of barriers to engagement helps build autonomy, and the positive feedback you receive from participating typically engenders a strong sense of competence.

Weigh, for a moment, how the average interaction on social media holds up against this standard. Do people usually leave Instagram with a stronger sense of their own abilities? Besides retweets, does Twitter build autonomy for its typical users? And who ever genuinely felt more related to their fellow humans after twenty minutes on Facebook?

"Identity construction is such a social process," said Davis. "We use parts of the culture, we use parts of our relationships with other people, to define ourselves."

Davis and Aragon's conversations with fan-fiction writers were particularly illuminating because the way they were learning the craft of writing and how they improved was so unlike the traditional way we train writers in school. The people they spoke with didn't have teachers, they didn't have mentors, they just had comments.

"And through those conversations, we came up with the concept of distributed mentorship," Davis said. As the name implies, distributed mentorship expands on that to the idea of mentorship, but rather than learn from one personal mentor, small moments of mentorship can come from a distributed community.

But what kind of writers were being made this way? Is fan fiction already a training ground for the best writers of the future?

Davis and Aragon focused on FanFiction .net because it tended to attract a younger demographic than AO3 and was often the first platform visited by adolescents interested in fan fiction.

In February 2017, they received 672.8 gigabytes of data from FanFiction.net, including 6,828,943 stories—61.5 billion words—and 176,715,206 reviews of those stories, a sample set that was 6 billion words. For perspective, Project Gutenberg is the largest e-book collection on the internet, with about 53,000 works. FanFiction.net's 6.8 million stories—28.4 million chapters—covering ten thousand fandoms makes the official canon look rinky-dink by comparison.

Typically, we have no statistical insight into how people develop as fiction writers. You could go to Oxford and check J.R.R. Tolkien's papers, but it's not the same as tracking down the entire oeuvre of a *Sherlock* fan-fiction author who's developed from a tyro into a compelling, gripping read over ten years of posts. Within their enormous download of information, Davis and Aragon were able to get a glimpse of authors as they developed into budding talents in real time, with no authority to stifle them and no gate to keep them in.

They could actually see what creating stuff did to the people who made it.

Because the volume of text they received was simply unreadable by human beings, the only way to understand it was through computer analysis. Over time, lexical diversity—essentially, what the words you use says about the number of words you know—has become a well-understood and fairly objective way to measure general writing ability. Studies show that Measure of Textual Lexical Diversity, or MTLD, is a good proxy for a person's overall writing proficiency. A mediocre undergraduate essay can have an MTLD in the low 70s, and a proficient one could be in the high 70s.

From the 284,448 user biographies that had self-reported ages, Aragon and Davis had enough information to help them determine that 72.5 percent of those profiles—and likely users of the site overall—were adolescents between the ages of ten and twenty.

First, they plotted the MTLD of given chapters against the purported age of the user when they wrote that chapter. They found something that was pretty much expected: People get considerably better at writing between the ages of fourteen and twenty, at which points the gains slow down and eventually level off as the writer enters adulthood. But what they did next, plotting writing skills against the amount of *feedback* a writer received, was revealing. As a rule on sites like FanFiction.net, more work means more feedback, and more feedback—provided it's not stifling—can encourage more work. So what effect does that cycle have on a writer's skills?

An *enormous* one.

"We found out that just the sheer volume—what we call the abundance—of even very shallow positive reviews makes a difference in people's writing quality," said Aragon.

The average MTLD of a chapter written by someone with zero prior reviews—the first chapter that someone posts, for instance—is 93.4. But the mean MTLD of the 719,000 chapters written by someone who had received ten reviews is over a point higher, at 94.8. The rise is steady as feedback pours in: For chapters written by users with 40 to 50 reviews, the MTLD averages 96.4; once they get to 100 reviews, the mean is 97.4; once they've got 400 to 500 reviews under their belt, the MTLD is 100.0. Again, those reviews needn't be—and aren't often—in-depth feedback with specific writing tips. Their analysis of comments found 35 percent were just positive and shallow like "good job," and 28 percent just encouraged updates. Less than half the time, 46 percent, the feedback actually targeted an aspect of the text and engaged with it constructively.

"It's so different from what you might see as the average English classroom in a high school in the US," said Davis. "I started off as an elementary school teacher. . . . And to watch young people be self-motivated, and learning from each other, on their own time, is something that every educator wishes they could replicate in a classroom environment."

The distributed mentoring isn't organized, planned, or directed. It's just what happens when a writer engages with a fandom, and members of that fandom who like to read fan fiction leave feedback and comments. Just like in the days of the wrestling territories, it was peers who discussed what they had accomplished and what needed work and how they felt while engaging with others' work.

The absence of a financial incentive—the very thing that prevents large media corporations from setting their lawyers upon fan-fiction sites like vengeful ghosts in the night—is also a potential contributing factor for people experimenting in ways they otherwise wouldn't.

Perhaps the proof of this concept is that a whole lot of professional authors—E. L. James, Lev Grossman, S. E. Hinton, Rainbow Rowell, Andy Weir, and countless more—honed their craft on fan-fiction sites.

"But what I think is interesting and less publicly known is that many authors said, 'I got my start in fan fiction, and I still write fan fiction because I enjoy it,'" Aragon said. "'Even though I don't receive money, I get more feedback in a week than I get on my traditional covers in two years.' That says something about the value of distributed mentoring, that power of having somebody read your story and tell you they love it."

Aragon and Davis think there's a lot more to fan fiction, including using it as a tool to teach creative writing in high school, which could help groups that are often underserved by standard writing education strategies into writing. But the complicated, dramatic community around fan fiction offers much more beyond educational strategies: It's some of the best proof we have that community is what drives creativity. It's not enough to have a clever angle or a muse; only by forging a community of fans and peers will creators be encouraged to truly produce their best work.

Heel Turn

It would be convenient to say that wrestling is an example of what happens to individual creators under consolidation and fan fiction shows what independence and nonhierarchical structure can encourage. But of course the truth is not quite that simple. For starters, fan fiction has not remained entirely nonprofit. The maw of the industrialized pop culture pipeline has turned its attention to the billions of words being cranked out by the very same young people the network is trying to hook.

Wattpad, launched in 2006 as a for-profit repository for fan fiction and original serialized works, had accumulated over 90 million monthly users and 1 billion stories, and was drawing 22 billion minutes a month in reading time by 2020. Sitting atop this mountain of user-generated and user-owned content, Wattpad executives realized that not only did they have incredible insight into what was popular and trending, but they were also the only corporation with a direct conduit to the pseudonymous users.

And with companies like Netflix and Hulu constantly scrounging for popular and trending stories for a youth audience, the company decided to set up an internal talent team to identify writers who produce up-and-coming stories, offer them representation, and package their stories for large studios. Their first huge hit was *The Kissing Booth*, which led to a Netflix film that chief content officer Ted Sarandos described, upon release, as one of the most-watched movies in the country, with some 66 million viewers in its first four weeks. Two sequels would follow.

That model is expected to be enormously profitable. In January 2021, Wattpad was bought by South Korean conglomerate Naver for $600 million. And while AO3 and FanFiction.net remain independent—the first a nonprofit, the second a closely held business owned by a single programmer—there are certainly a few former regional wrestling promotions that can tell you what happens when one wealthy company tries to corner the market on talent. Add to that the incredible market intelligence Wattpad has that its rivals do not, like the ability to spot developing trends and sell that information to studio partners, and it's clear that fan fiction is hardly immune to market forces of consolidation.

But even consolidation is not impervious to competition. The emergence of the web and the insatiability of large content providers has opened up opportunities for would-be rivals to the hegemony of WWE. And it is doing so in the same way that the advent of televised wrestling helped McMahon wipe out opportunities for then-established rivals. The emergence of All-Elite Wrestling, a viable second promotion with the distinct advantage of being owned by a different billionaire, has provided a safe harbor for wrestlers upset with the working conditions at WWE. Wrestling's inherent direct-to-consumer model, where the productions are live events first and foremost, has also allowed a number of smaller, independent promotions to make decent money.

And *that's* how I ended up at a barbed-wire wrestling match on the outskirts of Philly.

The Hardcore Hustle Organization wrestling promotion—H2O, for short—is about as indie as indie wrestling gets. They're based out of a wrestling gym in Williamstown, New Jersey, that was once the home of Extreme Championship Wrestling, a hard-core promotion that suited the tastes of the Philadelphians who sustained it. And although ECW sold out to WWE years before, the fans never went anywhere.

As I walk into the gym, two determined men are dressing a door in barbed wire. Entrance costs twenty-five dollars, and I settle into a second-row seat in a folding chair not ten feet away from the ring. Once the locals and the rest of the fans file in, perhaps fifty people are in attendance. The walls are covered in memorabilia from the territory era, old posters heralding giants who found themselves in Philadelphia and came to blows.

When the matches begin, I experience wrestling as I never have before. I can see the dust shoot up from the mat when a wrestler is slammed to the boards. And those boards—I can hear them buckle as the wrestlers move around the ring. In Barclays Center, I saw how far twenty-five men would go for some mediocre pizza; in Philly, I see how far one small-town wrestler with nothing to prove and a lot of pride would go for a crowd of fifty. I saw people indifferently do the wave in Brooklyn; in Williamstown I see a crowd recoil and shriek, "Not the fork noodle!" as a man is pummeled with an object whose composition frankly speaks for itself. I watch a man named Louie endure punishing, agonizing blows from Four Loko cans, from wooden boards, from a bat covered in thumbtacks, and though I have never met this man in my life and know nothing of his backstory, I have never wanted someone to win an altercation more than I do him.

I know for a fact that when "Big Red" Ryan Redfield wrestles Austin Luke, the match is being designed on the fly by the wrestlers, and I know this because Luke's prearranged opponent failed to show up and Red stepped in to put on a delightful show. A three-way women's match ends in an innovative and unexpected tangle; a local hero fights a wrestler with a baseball mask gimmick. During intermission, they do not allude to the forthcoming arrival of a movie star; instead, they sing happy birthday to an audience member as the ring is set up for "an ultra-violent death match."

I finally understand why wrestlers use folding chairs, because I am sitting in one and it's nearby and available, a vestigial affectation that never made sense in a WWE that puts on matches in the largest and most expensive arenas in the country. I also understand why wrestlers crash into tables, because I can see the humble merch hauled in by the wrestlers themselves on folding tables that are one out-of-control match away from annihilation.

The final contest is a grisly, brutal affair that I won't detail, but there are ladders and tables and barbed wire and shopping carts and a sadistic prop that a local fan bought. As it reaches its peak, there is a cry from behind my seat as a garage door opens, the fans quickly evacuating their seats as organizers unveil a large cache of barbed wire upon which the contenders will settle their differences. It is, in every way, the diametric opposite of WWE's *Survivor Series*.

Although the territories that provided options and choices for wrestlers to move freely between them are gone, there has been a rise in the number of independent promotions—a couple big, the vast majority quite small. These have at least begun to provide some job security for performers cut from the WWE roster. The bottom fell out of the business in the 1990s, but slowly, opportunities are emerging in less-lucrative, regional, or independent promotions for wrestlers on the way down or on the rise.

THE RISE OF THE INDIES | WWE killed or consumed the rival territories

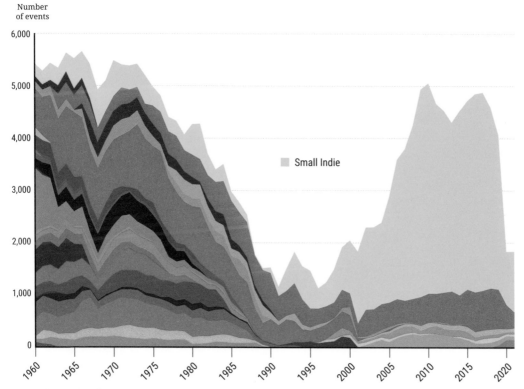

Author's analysis of Wrestlingdata.com

For fans who prefer the more improvisational, unscripted style of Laurence DeGaris's time in the squared circle—the kind of fare that might scare off corporate sponsors—there are plenty of promotions willing to offer what they're looking for, but for now it might entail watching the action in a Williamstown, New Jersey warehouse.

Choose Your Own Adventure

When stories work, when pop culture resonates with us and can hook us, and when we go along for the ride, it comes with positive effects on our brains and our lives as a whole. Someone might talk about a book that changed their life, but when something truly grabs a person, regardless of how intellectual or down-to-earth or frivolous it's perceived to be, it has tremendous potential for changing that person's life.

Fiction reading, often regarded as a mere leisure activity, has remarkable impacts on readers. "As you get older, it prevents cognitive decline," said Sandra Martin-Chang, a professor at Concordia University, in Montreal. "It's associated with making more money," she added. Her studies have found that reading fiction has distinctly positive effects on reading comprehension, far exceeding that of nonfiction.

And the kind of books that your English teachers likely considered garbage? They're great for you. The young adult fiction that *The Scarlet Letter* crowd seems to detest? It's linked directly to great general reading and test scores. And though well proved now, Martin-Chang's data showed that one of the most effective things a parent can do to encourage kids to read on their own later in life is to read to them when they're young.

There's increasing evidence that reading is like exercise, in that the more you do it, the better it is for you—and that every little bit helps, even if it's not the most intellectually strenuous or engaging material. It's about consuming pages, and the more kids consume, the better off they are.

"I think this idea that it [reading] has to be highbrow," said Stephanie Kovacs, a researcher who worked on the study, "I think it's actually doing a disservice. What we want to see is reading over the lifetime, and what we see is a massive falling-off in the upper grades of high school."

When a work of fiction grabs you, it may be for all kinds of reasons. Maybe you see yourself in the hero or her journey. Maybe the villain is so striking, so compelling, so dangerous that your innate moral code simply cannot put the work down until you can confirm that the danger is defeated once and for all. It may play with your mind, whether it's teasing your brain stem with visions of monsters or flattering your brain with clever action. What's so funny is that for all we know about how people can empathize with characters and engross themselves in plots, the overwhelming evidence says that even if we don't completely understand why something works, we can take comfort in knowing that just consuming engrossing stories we love is good for us.

Art Making

Setting aside professional communities, systemic mentoring, or how creativity happens in your brain, why should you even indulge your creative side?

Art therapy has been researched as a mechanism for people wrestling with complex personal issues and events—trauma, grief, a diagnosis—to help process their emotions. It emerged after the world wars, when attempts to treat what would later come to be understood as post-traumatic stress disorder through traditional means were coming up short.

The data on the efficacy of art therapy is still in its early phases, but even for people who haven't endured a blow, an increasing body of scientific evidence shows that doing low-stakes, free-form creative things, to try to lock in on flow, can have positive psychological and health benefits.

"A lot of what I'm trying to understand is what is the worth and value of art in our lives," said Girja Kaimal, a professor in creative arts therapies at Drexel University. "I'm convinced it's more than just 'feel good,' which is important, but . . . something really essential to us."

Across known human history we find people producing art, some of the earliest examples in caves from Europe to South America. In fact, we have yet to discover civilizations that *don't* produce some form of art. It's an irresistible urge on a species-wide level, one that predates cities and agriculture, education and the written word. Kaimal is convinced there's something fundamental about our brains that requires it.

Art can aid in memory formation and help us communicate. When people look at things they enjoy, their brains offer reward signals. When people feel anxiety or stress, art can reduce both. Kaimal's research has led her to explore what happens to people's cortisol levels—a biomarker of stress—when they engage in art making. Does making art reduce cortisol?

"We found that sure enough, it does, and this was with relatively healthy adults," she said. "Then we took the study further, and we had caregivers and patients participate in art making for one session, a forty-five-minute experience. We found that people's mood improved, and people's stress levels went down, and for caregivers their burnout levels went down. There's something about giving people space and time to create that helps their bodies visibly relax and calm down in a high-stress environment."

In other research that involved monitoring people's brains while they made art, she found

that people engage their whole brain when doodling or creating low-stakes art—a simple way to tap into the benefits of flow.

"It's not like watching a movie," said Kaimal. "When you're doing something with your hands and you're actually making it, you have to bring all your senses into the moment—your mind can wander, but your body is still in the moment and attending to this task."

Making things, creating things—even cruddy things—is good for you. Something as simple as doodling can produce maximum activation of the prefrontal cortex, beating out coloring and freehand illustration. After study participants had had three months of art training, researchers were able to detect more white matter in the prefrontal cortex, with the production of art leading to greater gains than active evaluation or just passive engagement. Even viewing art gets things moving, engaging the reward circuitry in your brain. For the sake of your own health—and definitely not to drastically lower the resale value of this book—the reader is strongly encouraged to just grab a pencil and doodle in the margins.

Truly, though, the fact that making art and telling stories has power isn't shocking in the slightest. Time and time again, we find piles of evidence that the stories we tell each other have reverberations that ripple outward, that tales and works and movies affect the people who consume them on a physical, psychological, social, and geopolitical level. Something as simple as entertainment can affect the world and the people in it. So, it should come as little shock that the act of willing those stories into existence has ramifications for the creator and the environment in which they operate. That those effects tend to be positive illustrates just how innate and fundamentally important entertainment really is, and how the stories we tell each other reflect the core of what we are as a society and our very accomplishment and ambition as a species.

Sources

Chapter 1

Boksem, Maarten A. S., and Ale Smidts. 2015. "Brain Responses to Movie Trailers Predict Individual Preferences for Movies and Their Population-Wide Commercial Success." *Journal of Marketing Research* 52 (4): 482–92. doi.org /10.1509/jmr.13.0572.

Christoforou, Christoforos, Timothy C. Papadopoulos, Fofi Constantinidou, and Maria Theodorou. 2017. "Your Brain on the Movies: A Computational Approach for Predicting Box-Office Performance from Viewer's Brain Responses to Movie Trailers." *Frontiers in Neuroinformatics* 11. frontiersin.org/articles/10.3389/ fninf.2017.00072.

Finkelstein, Gabriel. 2003. "M. Du Bois-Reymond Goes to Paris." *The British Journal for the History of Science* 36 (3): 261–300.

"Galvanic Skin Response (GSR): The Complete Pocket Guide." 2020. *Imotions* (blog). February 25, 2020. publish.imotions.com/blog /galvanic-skin-response/.

"Galvanic Skin Response (GSR): The Complete Pocket Guide - IMotions." 2020. February 25, 2020. imotions.com/blog/learning /research-fundamentals/galvanic -skin-response/.

Kaltwasser, Laura, Nicolas Rost, Martina Ardizzi, Marta Calbi, Luca Settembrino, Joerg Fingerhut, Michael Pauen, and Vittorio Gallese. 2019. "Sharing the Filmic Experience - The Physiology of Socio-Emotional Processes in the Cinema." *PLOS ONE* 14 (10): e0223259. doi.org/10.1371/journal .pone.0223259.

Matsukawa, Kanji, Kana Endo, Kei Ishii, Momoka Ito, and Nan Liang. 2018. "Facial Skin Blood Flow Responses during Exposures to Emotionally Charged Movies." *The Journal of Physiological Sciences* 68 (2): 175–90. doi.org/10.1007 /s12576-017-0522-3.

Nemeth, Banne, Luuk J. J. Scheres, Willem M Lijfering, and Frits R. Rosendaal. 2015. "Bloodcurdling Movies and Measures of Coagulation: Fear Factor Crossover Trial." *BMJ*, December, h6367. doi.org/10.1136/bmj.h6367.

Neumann, Eva, and Richard Blanton. 1970. "The Early History of Electrodermal Research." *Psychophysiology* 6 (4): 453–75. doi.org/10.1111/j.1469-8986.1970 .tb01755.x.

Williams, Jonathan, Christof Stönner, Jörg Wicker, Nicolas Krauter, Bettina Derstroff, Efstratios Bourtsoukidis, Thomas Klüpfel, and Stefan Kramer. 2016. "Cinema Audiences Reproducibly Vary the Chemical Composition of Air during Films, by Broadcasting Scene Specific Emissions on Breath." *Scientific Reports* 6 (1): 25464. doi.org/10.1038/srep25464.

Wöllner, Clemens, David Hammerschmidt, and Henning Albrecht. 2018. "Slow Motion in Films and Video Clips: Music Influences Perceived Duration and Emotion, Autonomic Physiological Activation and Pupillary Responses." *PLOS ONE* 13 (6): e0199161. doi.org /10.1371/journal.pone.0199161.

Chapter 2

"ASA 143rd Meeting Lay Language Papers -When Sound Effects Are Better Than The Real Thing." n.d. Accessed January 26, 2023. acoustics.org/pressroom/http docs/143rd/Heller.html.

Barnett, Samuel B., and Moran Cerf. 2017. "A Ticket for Your Thoughts: Method for Predicting Movie Trailer Recall and Future Ticket Sales Using Neural Similarity among Moviegoers." *Journal of Consumer Research*, January, ucw083. doi.org/10.1093/jcr /ucw083.

Barnhart, Anthony S., Francisco M. Costela, Susana Martinez-Conde, Stephen L. Macknik, and Stephen D. Goldinger. 2019. "Microsaccades Reflect the Dynamics of Misdirected Attention in Magic." *Journal of Eye Movement Research* 12 (6). doi.org/10.16910/jemr.12.6.7.

Bezdek, M. A., R. J. Gerrig, W. G. Wenzel, J. Shin, K. Pirog Revill, and E. H. Schumacher. 2015. "Neural Evidence That Suspense Narrows Attentional Focus." *Neuroscience* 303 (September): 338–45. doi.org/10.1016/j.neuro science.2015.06.055.

Boksem, Maarten A. S., and Ale Smidts. 2015. "Brain Responses to Movie Trailers Predict Individual Preferences for Movies and Their Population-Wide Commercial Success." *Journal of Marketing Research* 52 (4): 482–92.

Burleson-Lesser, Kate, Flaviano Morone, Paul DeGuzman, Lucas C. Parra, and Hernán A. Makse. 2017. "Collective Behaviour in Video Viewing: A Thermodynamic Analysis of Gaze Position." *PLOS ONE* 12 (1): e0168995. doi.org /10.1371/journal.pone.0168995.

Christoforou, Christoforos, Spyros Christou-Champi, Fofi Constantinidou, and Maria Theodorou. 2015. "From the Eyes and the Heart: A Novel Eye-Gaze Metric That Predicts Video Preferences of a Large Audience." *Frontiers in Psychology* 6. frontiersin.org/articles/10.3389 /fpsyg.2015.00579.

Cohen, Anna-Lisa, Elliot Shavalian, and Moshe Rube. 2015. "The Power of the Picture: How Narrative Film Captures Attention and Disrupts Goal Pursuit." *PLOS ONE* 10 (12): e0144493. doi.org/10.1371/journal .pone.0144493.

Goldstein, Robert B., Russell L. Woods, and Eli Peli. 2007. "Where People Look When Watching Movies: Do All Viewers Look at the Same Place?" *Computers in Biology and Medicine*, Vision and Movement in Man and Machines, 37 (7): 957–64. doi.org/10.1016/j .compbiomed.2006.08.018.

Hasson, Uri, Yuval Nir, Ifat Levy, Galit Fuhrmann, and Rafael Malach. 2004. "Intersubject Synchronization of Cortical Activity During Natural Vision." *Science* 303 (5664): 1634–40. doi.org/10.1126/science.1089506.

Kirkorian, Heather L., Daniel R. Anderson, and Rachel Keen. 2012. "Age Differences in Online Processing of Video: An Eye Movement Study." *Child Development* 83 (2): 497–507. doi.org /10.1111/j.1467-8624.2011.01719.x.

Lamarre, Thomas. 2018. "This Stuff Called Blink." In *The Anime

Ecology: A Genealogy of Television, Animation, and Game Media, 77–94. University of Minnesota Press. doi.org/10.5749/j.ctt21c4stv.6.

———. 2018. *The Anime Ecology: A Genealogy of Television, Animation, and Game Media.* University of Minnesota Press. doi.org/10.5749/j.ctt21c4stv.

Macknik, Stephen L., S. Martinez-Conde, and Sandra Blakeslee. 2010. *Sleights of Mind: What the Neuroscience of Magic Reveals about Our Everyday Deceptions.* 1st ed. New York: Henry Holt and Co.

Paulich, Katie N., J. Megan Ross, Jeffrey M. Lessem, and John K. Hewitt. 2021a. "Screen Time and Early Adolescent Mental Health, Academic, and Social Outcomes in 9- and 10- Year Old Children: Utilizing the Adolescent Brain Cognitive Development SM (ABCD) Study." *PloS One* 16 (9): e0256591. doi.org/10.1371/journal.pone.0256591.

———. 2021b. "Screen Time and Early Adolescent Mental Health, Academic, and Social Outcomes in 9- and 10- Year Old Children: Utilizing the Adolescent Brain Cognitive Development SM (ABCD) Study." *PLOS ONE* 16 (9): e0256591. doi.org/10.1371/journal.pone.0256591.

Rider, Andrew T., Antoine Coutrot, Elizabeth Pellicano, Steven C. Dakin, and Isabelle Mareschal. 2018. "Semantic Content Outweighs Low-Level Saliency in Determining Children's and Adults' Fixation of Movies." *Journal of Experimental Child Psychology* 166 (February): 293–309. doi.org/10.1016/j.jecp.2017.09.002.

Scott, Hannah, Jonathan P. Batten, and Gustav Kuhn. 2019. "Why Are You Looking at Me? It's Because I'm Talking, but Mostly Because I'm Staring or Not Doing Much." *Attention, Perception, & Psychophysics* 81 (1): 109–18. doi.org/10.3758/s13414-018-1588-6.

Wang, Helena X., Jeremy Freeman, Elisha P. Merriam, Uri Hasson, and David J. Heeger. 2012. "Temporal Eye Movement Strategies during Naturalistic Viewing." *Journal of Vision* 12 (1): 16. doi.org/10.1167/12.1.16.

Chapter 3

Balmford, Andrew, Lizzie Clegg, Tim Coulson, and Jennie Taylor. 2002. "Why Conservationists Should Heed Pokémon." *Science* 295 (5564): 2367–2367.

Bryant, John. 1989. "Situation Comedy of the Sixties: The Evolution of a Popular Genre." *Studies in American Humor* 7: 118–39.

Burns, Sarah. 2012. "'Better for Haunts': Victorian Houses and the Modern Imagination." *American Art* 26 (3): 2–25. doi.org/10.1086/669220.

Butler, Erik. 2010. *Metamorphoses of the Vampire in Literature and Film: Cultural Transformations in Europe, 1732-1933.* Vol. 54. Boydell & Brewer. jstor.org/stable/10.7722/j.ctt81zrh.

Carroll, Noel. 1981. "Nightmare and the Horror Film: The Symbolic Biology of Fantastic Beings." *Film Quarterly* 34 (3): 16–25. doi.org/10.2307/1212034.

Colman, Ian, Mila Kingsbury, Murray Weeks, Anushka Ataullahjan, Marc-André Bélair, Jennifer Dykxhoorn, Katie Hynes, et al. 2014. "CARTOONS KILL: Casualties in Animated Recreational Theater in an Objective Observational New Study of Kids' Introduction to Loss of Life." *BMJ* 349 (December): g7184. doi.org/10.1136/bmj.g7184.

Craig, J. Robert. 2005. "The Origin Story in Werewolf Cinema of the 1930s and '40s." *Studies in Popular Culture* 27 (3): 75–86.

Day, William Patrick. 2002. *Vampire Legends in Contemporary American Culture: What Becomes a Legend Most.* 1st ed. University Press of Kentucky. jstor.org/stable/j.ctt130jsnh.

Fancourt, Daisy, and Andrew Steptoe. 2019. "The Art of Life and Death: 14 Year Follow-up Analyses of Associations between Arts Engagement and Mortality in the English Longitudinal Study of Ageing." *BMJ* 367 (December): l6377. doi.org/10.1136/bmj.l6377.

Fox, Glenn, Mona Sobhani, and Lisa Aziz-zadeh. 2013. "Witnessing Hateful People in Pain Modulates Brain Activity in Regions Associated with Physical Pain and Reward." *Frontiers in Psychology* 4. frontiersin.org/articles/10.3389/fpsyg.2013.00772.

Hudson, Matthew, Kerttu Seppälä, Vesa Putkinen, Lihua Sun, Enrico Glerean, Tomi Karjalainen, Henry K. Karlsson, Jussi Hirvonen, and Lauri Nummenmaa. 2020. "Dissociable Neural Systems for Unconditioned Acute and Sustained Fear." *NeuroImage* 216 (August): 116522. doi.org/10.1016/j.neuroimage.2020.116522.

Kozak, Stephanie, and Holly Recchia. 2019. "Reading and the Development of Social Understanding: Implications for the Literacy Classroom." *The Reading Teacher* 72 (5): 569–77. doi.org/10.1002/trtr.1760.

Lafleur, Jarret Marshall. n.d. "The Perfect Heist: Recipes from Around the World." osti.gov/servlets/purl/1115483.

Martin-Chang, Sandra, Stephanie Kozak, Kyle C. Levesque, Navona Calarco, and Raymond A. Mar. 2021a. "What's Your Pleasure? Exploring the Predictors of Leisure Reading for Fiction and Nonfiction." *Reading and Writing* 34 (6): 1387–1414. doi.org/10.1007/s11145-020-10112-7.

———. 2021b. "What's Your Pleasure? Exploring the Predictors of Leisure Reading for Fiction and Nonfiction." *Reading and Writing* 34 (6): 1387–1414. doi.org/10.1007/s11145-020-10112-7.

Martin-Chang, Sandra, Stephanie Kozak, and Maya Rossi. 2020. "Time to Read Young Adult Fiction: Print Exposure and Linguistic Correlates in Adolescents." *Reading and Writing* 33 (3): 741–60. doi.org/10.1007/s11145-019-09987-y.

Miller, P. Andrew. 2003. "Mutants, Metaphor, and Marginalism: What X-Actly Do the X-Men Stand For?" *Journal of the Fantastic in the Arts* 13 (3 (51)): 282–90.

Noir Urbanisms: Dystopic Images of the Modern City. 2010. Princeton University Press. jstor.org/stable/j.ctt7sw4m.

Posick, Chad. 2017. "Bank Robbery in Popular Culture." Oxford Research Encyclopedia of Criminology and Criminal Justice. January 25, 2017. doi.org/10.1093/acrefore/9780190264079.013.19.

Scrivner, Coltan, John A. Johnson, Jens Kjeldgaard-Christiansen, and Mathias Clasen. 2021. "Pandemic Practice: Horror Fans and Morbidly Curious Individuals Are More Psychologically Resilient during the COVID-19 Pandemic." *Personality and Individual Differences* 168 (January): 110397. doi.org/10.1016/j.paid.2020.110397.

Suan, Stevie. 2021. *Anime's Identity: Performativity and Form beyond Japan.* Minneapolis London: University of Minnesota Press.

Tait, R. Colin. 2011. "Competing Modes of Capital in Ocean's Eleven." In *The Philosophy of Steven Soderbergh*, 231–46. jstor.org/stable/j.ctt2jct7c.17.

The Philosophy of Steven Soderbergh. 2011. University Press of Kentucky. jstor.org/stable/j.ctt2jct7c.

Tremblay, Brittany, Monyka L. Rodrigues, and Sandra Martin-Chang. 2020. "From Storybooks to Novels: A Retrospective Approach Linking Print Exposure in Childhood to Adolescence." *Frontiers in Psychology* 11. frontiersin.org/articles/10.3389/fpsyg.2020.571033.

Tsutsui, William M. 2010. "Chapter 5 Oh No, There Goes Tokyo." In *Noir Urbanisms: Dystopic Images of the Modern City*, 104–26. jstor.org/stable/j.ctt7sw4m.8.

White, Rachel E., Emily O. Prager, Catherine Schaefer, Ethan Kross, Angela L. Duckworth, and Stephanie M. Carlson. 2017. "The 'Batman Effect': Improving Perseverance in Young Children." *Child Development* 88 (5): 1563–71. doi.org/10.1111/cdev.12695.

Chapter 4

"Archery Catching Fire Faster Than Ever Thanks to Pop Culture Boost." n.d. Team USA. Accessed January 26, 2023. teamusa.org/443/News/2013/November/19/Archery-Catching-Fire-Faster-Than-Ever-Thanks-To-Pop-Culture-Boost.

"Asteroids: Perils and Opportunities." n.d. Accessed January 26, 2023. carlkop.home.xs4all.nl/asterimp.html.

Bates, James. 1997. "Face-Off : 'Mighty Ducks' Writer Sues Disney Over Merchandise Take." *Los Angeles Times*. April 11, 1997. latimes.com/archives/la-xpm-1997-04-11-fi-47542-story.html.

"Beach Volleyballer Sarah Pavan Finds New Fans through Love of Anime Series 'Haikyuu' | CBC Sports." n.d. Accessed January 26, 2023. cbc.ca/sports/olympics/summer/volleyball/beach/pavan-anine-series-beach-volleyball-olympics-1.6125571.

Benton, Michael J. 2008. "Fossil Quality and Naming Dinosaurs." *Biology Letters* 4 (6): 729–32. doi.org/10.1098/rsbl.2008.0402.

Brusatte, Stephen. 2018. *The Rise and Fall of the Dinosaurs: A New History of a Lost World.* First edition. New York, NY: William Morrow.

"Clark R. Chapman: Congressional Testimony, May 21, 1998." n.d. Accessed January 26, 2023. boulder.swri.edu/clark/hr.html.

"Collapse and Conservation of Shark Populations in the Northwest Atlantic | Science." n.d. Accessed January 26, 2023. science.org/doi/10.1126/science.1079777.

Consoli, Sarah, Elizabeth A. Fraysse, Natalya Slipchenko, Yi Wang, Jahon Amirebrahimi, Zhiran Qin, Neil Yazma, and Travis J. Lybbert. 2022. "A 'Sideways' Supply Response in California Winegrapes." *Journal of Wine Economics* 17 (1): 42–63. doi.org/10.1017/jwe.2021.26.

Curtis, Tobey H., Camilla T. McCandless, John K. Carlson, Gregory B. Skomal, Nancy E. Kohler, Lisa J. Natanson, George H. Burgess, John J. Hoey, and Harold L. Pratt Jr. 2014. "Seasonal Distribution and Historic Trends in Abundance of White Sharks, Carcharodon Carcharias, in the Western North Atlantic Ocean." *PLOS ONE* 9 (6): e99240. doi.org/10.1371/journal.pone.0099240.

Dahl, Gordon, and Stefano DellaVigna. 2009. "Does Movie Violence Increase Violent Crime?*." *The Quarterly Journal of Economics* 124 (2): 677–734. doi.org/10.1162/qjec.2009.124.2.677.

"Design Fiction: A Short Essay on Design, Science, Fact and Fiction." n.d. Near Future Laboratory Shop. Accessed January 26, 2023. nearfuturelaboratory.myshopify.com/products/design-fiction-a-short-essay-on-design-science-fact-and-fiction.

"Diversity Study | The Palaeontological Association." n.d. Accessed January 26, 2023. palass.org/association/diversity-study.

Dodson, P. 1990. "Counting Dinosaurs: How Many Kinds Were There?" *Proceedings of the National Academy of Sciences* 87 (19): 7608–12. doi.org/10.1073/pnas.87.19.7608.

Dunn, Elizabeth G. 2021. "Murder Shows Are Inspiring Vacations, From 'The Killing' to 'Shetland' (Yes, Really.)." *Wall Street Journal*, September 14, 2021. wsj.com/articles/murder-shows-are-inspiring-vacations-from-the-killing-to-shetland-yes-really-11631649600.

Editors, The. n.d. "Death to Humans! Visions of the Apocalypse in Movies and Literature." *Scientific American*. Accessed January 26, 2023. scientificamerican.com/article/death-to-humans/.

Evje, Mark. 1986. "'Top Gun' Boosting Service Sign-ups" *Los Angeles Times*. July 5, 1986. latimes.com/archives/la-xpm-1986-07-05-ca-20403-story.html.

"Ex-CIA Officer Laments Q's Absence from Modern James Bond." 2008. Gizmodo. November 10, 2008. gizmodo.com/ex-cia-officer-laments-qs-absence-from-modern-james-bon-5082085.

Fancourt, Daisy, and Andrew Steptoe. 2019. "The Art of Life and Death: 14 Year Follow-up Analyses of Associations between Arts Engagement and Mortality in the English Longitudinal Study of Ageing." *BMJ* 367 (December): l6377. https://doi.org/10.1136/bmj.l6377.

"File://C:\Palass Files\Web Backup\palass.Org Backup 23 Feb 2006." n.d.

Francis, Beryl. 2012. "Before and After 'Jaws': Changing Representations of Shark Attacks." NPR.

Gallup, Inc. 2007. "Crime." Gallup.Com. May 18, 2007. news.gallup.com/poll/1603/Crime.aspx.

Gentzkow, Matthew, and Jesse M. Shapiro. 2008. "Preschool Television Viewing and Adolescent Test Scores: Historical Evidence from the Coleman Study *." *Quarterly Journal of Economics* 123 (1): 279–323. doi.org/10.1162/qjec.2008.123.1.279.

Ghirlanda, Stefano, Alberto Acerbi, and Harold Herzog. 2014. "Dog Movie Stars and Dog Breed Popularity: A Case Study in Media Influence on Choice." *PLOS ONE* 9 (9): e106565. doi.org/10.1371/journal.pone.0106565.

Hart, Philip Solomon, and Anthony A. Leiserowitz. 2009. "Finding the Teachable Moment: An Analysis of Information-Seeking Behavior on Global Warming Related Websites during the Release of The Day After Tomorrow." *Environmental Communication* 3 (3): 355–66. doi.org/10.1080/17524030903265823.

Hartke, Kristen. 2017. "'The Sideways Effect': How A Wine-Obsessed Film Reshaped the Industry." NPR. July 5, 2017. npr.org/sections/thesalt/2017/07/05/535038513/the-sideways-effect-how-a-wine-obsessed-film-reshaped-the-industry.

Heatherton, Todd F., and James D. Sargent. 2009. "Does Watching Smoking in Movies Promote Teenage Smoking?" *Current Directions in Psychological Science* 18 (2): 63–67.

Hinnosaar, Marit, Toomas Hinnosaar, Michael Kummer, and Olga Slivko. n.d. "Wikipedia Matters." *Journal of Economics & Management Strategy* n/a (n/a). Accessed January 26, 2023. doi.org/10.1111/jems.12421.

Hood, Grace. 2013. "More Girls Target Archery, Inspired By 'The Hunger Games.'" NPR. November 27, 2013. npr.org/2013/11/27/247379498/more-girls-target-archery-inspired-by-the-hunger-games.

"How 'Haikyuu!!' Made a Surprise Appearance at the Tokyo Olympics." 2021. *Newsweek*. July 27, 2021. newsweek.com/haikyuu-theme-song-olympics-tokyo-2020-volleyball-japan-1613348.

"How 'Mighty Ducks' the Movie Became Mighty Ducks the NHL Team." 2015. *Esquire*. November 25, 2015. esquire.com/sports/a39992/mighty-ducks-movie-nhl-franchise/.

"How The Day After Tomorrow Put Climate Change on the Map." 2019. *The State of SIE Report* (blog). January 28, 2019. thestateofsie.com/the-day-after-tomorrow-climate-change-anthony-leiserowitz-global-issues-audience-behaviour/.

Hudson, Simon, and J. R. Brent Ritchie. 2006. "Promoting Destinations via Film Tourism: An Empirical Identification of Supporting Marketing Initiatives." *Journal of Travel Research* 44 (4): 387–96. doi.org/10.1177/0047287506286720.

"'Hunger Games' Popularity Sends Interest in Archery Soaring." 2013. November 21, 2013. sports.yahoo.com/news/olympics--hunger-games--popularity-sends-interest-in-archery-soaring-232415744.html.

"Impact Hazard Case Study, 2 July 1999." n.d. Accessed January 26, 2023. boulder.swri.edu/clark/ncar799.html.

"Impact Hazard: History." n.d. Accessed January 26, 2023. boulder.swri.edu/clark/ncarhist.html.

Jenkins, Tricia. 2012. *The CIA in Hollywood: How the Agency Shapes Film and Television.* 1st ed. Austin: University of Texas Press.

Jenkins, Tricia and Alford, Matthew. 2012. "Intelligence Activity in Hollywood: Remembering the 'Agency' in CIA." *Scope: An Online Journal of Film and Television Studies*, no. 23 (June). nottingham.ac.uk/scope/documents/2012/june-2012/jenkins.pdf.

Jenkins, Tricia, and Tom Secker. 2021. *Superheroes, Movies, and the State: How the U.S. Government Shapes Cinematic Universes.* Lawrence: University Press of Kansas.

"KFOR Storm Chasers Relive the El Reno Tornado." 2018. *KFOR. Com Oklahoma City* (blog). June 1, 2018. kfor.com/news/kfor-storm-chasers-relive-the-el-reno-tornado/.

Kirby, David A. 2011. *Lab Coats in Hollywood: Science, Scientists, and Cinema.* Cambridge, Mass: MIT Press.

La Ferrara, Eliana, Alberto Chong, and Suzanne Duryea. 2012. "Soap Operas and Fertility: Evidence from Brazil." *American Economic Journal: Applied Economics* 4 (4): 1–31. doi.org/10.1257/app.4.4.1.

Leiserowitz, Anthony. 2004. "Surveying the Impact of 'The Day After Tomorrow.'" *Environment* 46 (January): 23–44.

Leopold, Ariane Lange, Jason. 2017. "How the FBI Shaped It's Image Through Movies." BuzzFeed News, October 9, 2017. buzzfeednews.com/article/arianelange/fbi-in-hollywood.

McCrisken, Trevor, and Christopher Moran. 2018. "James Bond, Ian Fleming and Intelligence: Breaking down the Boundary between the 'Real' and the 'Imagined.'" *Intelligence and National Security* 33 (6): 804–21. doi.org/10.1080/02684527.2018.1468648.

Mellor, Felicity. 2007. "Colliding Worlds: Asteroid Research and the Legitimization of War in Space." *Social Studies of Science* 37 (4): 499–531.

Meyrowitz, Joshua. 1986. *No Sense of Place: The Impact of Electronic Media on Social Behavior.* New York, NY: Oxford University Press.

Mull, Amanda. 2021. "How Netflix Made Americans Care About the Most European of Sports." The Atlantic. September 7, 2021. theatlantic.com/magazine/archive/2021/10/formula-1-drive-to-survive/619814/.

Mutz, Diana C. 2016. "Harry Potter and the Deathly Donald." *PS: Political Science & Politics* 49 (4): 722–29. doi.org/10.1017/S1049096516001633.

New York Times. 1993. "The Dinosaur Society Wants a Bite," June 21, 1993. nytimes.com/1993/06/21/business-the-dinosaur-society-wants-a-bite.html.

News, Bloomberg. 2021. "A Cameo in a James Bond Film Can Increase a Car's Value by 1,000% - BNN Bloomberg." BNN. October 6, 2021. bnnbloomberg.ca/a-cameo-in-a-james-bond-film-can-increase-a-car-s-value-by-1-000-1.1662570.

"News Bulletin Number 168." 1996. Society of Vertebrate Paleontology.

O'Hara, Ross E., Frederick X. Gibbons, Meg Gerrard, Zhigang Li, and James D. Sargent. 2012. "Greater Exposure to Sexual Content in Popular Movies Predicts Earlier Sexual Debut and Increased Sexual Risk Taking." *Psychological Science* 23 (9): 984–93. doi.org/10.1177/0956797611435529.

SOURCES

"Palaeontology Newsletter 29." 1996. palass.org/sites/default/files/media/publications/newsletters/number_29/number29.pdf.

"Paleontology in the 21st Century: Paleoinformatics." n.d. Accessed January 26, 2023. paleonet.org/paleo21/rr/academia.html.

Peach, Sara. 2011. "'The Simpsons' Take on Climate Change » Yale Climate Connections." Yale Climate Connections. February 5, 2011. yaleclimateconnections.org/2011/02/the-simpsons-take-on-climate-change/.

Perkowitz, Sidney. 2010. *Hollywood Science: Movies, Science, and the End of the World.* Paperback ed. New York Chichester: Columbia University Press.

Pro, Archery. n.d. "'Hunger Games' Fuels Archery Renaissance." Accessed January 26, 2023. prnewswire.com/news-releases/hunger-games-fuels-archery-renaissance-236188481.html.

"Publication: Galaxy Science Fiction, May 1952." n.d. Accessed January 26, 2023. isfdb.org/cgi-bin/pl.cgi?58588.

Radio, C. B. C. 2020. "How Hollywood Became the Unofficial Propaganda Arm of the U.S. Military - CBC Radio." CBC. May 11, 2020. cbc.ca/radio/ideas/how-hollywood-became-the-unofficial-propaganda-arm-of-the-u-s-military-1.5560575.

Reporter, By a *Wall Street Journal* Staff. 1998. "'Mighty Ducks' Screenwriter Files Suit Against Walt Disney." *Wall Street Journal,* December 16, 1998. wsj.com/articles/SB913790768453880500.

Rubin, Courtney. 2012. "The Odds Are Ever in Their Favor." *New York Times,* November 28, 2012. nytimes.com/2012/11/29/fashion/hunger-games-heroine-helps-make-archery-hip.html.

Russell, Cristine. n.d. "Jaws: Classic Film, Crummy Science." Scientific American. Accessed January 26, 2023. scientificamerican.com/article/jaws-classic-film-crummy-science/.

Sandomir, Richard. 1993. "HOCKEY; Skate Like a Duck, Quack Like a Duck, Market Like Disney." *New York Times,* August 30, 1993. nytimes.com/1993/08/30/sports/hockey-skate-like-a-duck-quack-like-a-duck-market-like-disney.html.

Schou, Nicholas. 2016. "How the CIA Hoodwinked Hollywood." *The Atlantic.* July 14, 2016. theatlantic.com/entertainment/archive/2016/07/operation-tinseltown-how-the-cia-manipulates-hollywood/491138/.

Shprintz, Janet. 1998. "Writer Bites Ducks." *Variety* (blog). December 16, 1998. variety.com/1998/biz/news/writer-bites-ducks-1117489479/.

———. 1999. "Ducks' Suit Moves Forward." *Variety* (blog). April 6, 1999. variety.com/1999/film/news/ducks-suit-moves-forward-1117492956/.

Sirota, David. 2011. "25 Years Later, How 'Top Gun' Made America Love War." *Washington Post,* August 26, 2011. washingtonpost.com/opinions/25-years-later-remembering-how-top-gun-changed-americas-feelings-about-war/2011/08/15/gIQAU6qJgJ_story.html.

Skatrud-Mickelson, Monica, Anna M. Adachi-Mejia, Todd A. MacKenzie, and Lisa A. Sutherland. 2012. "Giving the Wrong Impression: Food and Beverage Brand Impressions Delivered to Youth through Popular Movies." *Journal of Public Health* 34 (2): 245–52. doi.org/10.1093/pubmed/fdr089.

"Special Report: Are We Reaching Gender Parity among Palaeontology Authors? - The Palaeontological Association." n.d. Accessed January 26, 2023. palass.org/publications/newsletter/spotlight-diversity/special-report-are-we-reaching-gender-parity-among-palaeontology-authors.

"Spy Culture | The State and Popular Culture." n.d. Accessed January 26, 2023. spyculture.com/.

Stokstad, Erik. 1998. "Popular Interest Fuels a Dinosaur Research Boom." *Science* 282 (5392): 1246–47.

Svoboda, Michael. 2014. "A Review of Climate Fiction (Cli-Fi) Cinema . . . Past and Present - Yale Climate Connections." Yale Climate Connections. October 22, 2014. yaleclimateconnections.org/2014/10/a-review-of-climate-fiction-cli-fi-cinema-past-and-present/.

———. 2018. "In 'First Reformed': A Shepherd in Wolf's Clothing? Yale Climate Connections." Yale Climate Connections. June 27, 2018. yaleclimateconnections.org/2018/06/in-first-reformed-a-shepherd-in-wolfs-clothing/.

"Table A-3. Percent of the Population Engaging in Selected Activities by Time of Day : U.S. Bureau of Labor Statistics." n.d. Accessed January 26, 2023. bls.gov/tus/tables/a3-1317.htm.

Telotte, J. P. 2007. "Crossing Borders and Opening Boxes: Disney and Hybrid Animation." *Quarterly Review of Film and Video* 24 (2): 107–16. doi.org/10.1080/10509200500486155.

Tennant, Jonathan P., Alfio Alessandro Chiarenza, and Matthew Baron. 2018. "How Has Our Knowledge of Dinosaur Diversity through Geologic Time Changed through Research History?" *PeerJ* 6 (February): e4417. doi.org/10.7717/peerj.4417.

"The CIA Has Always Understood the Power of Graphic Design." 2021. Eye on Design. January 18, 2021. eyeondesign.aiga.org/the-cia-has-always-understood-the-power-of-graphic-design/.

"The Film 'The Day After Tomorrow' - Comments by Climatologist Stefan Rahmstorf." n.d. Accessed January 26, 2023. pik-potsdam.de/~stefan/tdat_review.html.

"The May 31-June 1, 2013 Tornado and Flash Flooding Event." n.d. Accessed January 26, 2023. weather.gov/oun/events-20130531.

"The Military in the Movies - Transcript of a Programme from America's Defence Monitor." n.d. Accessed January 26, 2023. universityofleeds.github.io/philtaylorpapers/vp01e16d.html.

"The Scully Effect: I Want to Believe in STEM." n.d. *Geena Davis Institute* (blog). Accessed January 26, 2023. seejane.org/research-informs-empowers/the-scully-effect-i-want-to-believe-in-stem/.

"Title: For Your Information (Galaxy, May 1952)." n.d. Accessed January 26, 2023. isfdb.org/cgi-bin/title.cgi?724077.

Twitter, Instagram, Email, and Facebook. 2005. "Disney Will Sell Ducks to Couple." *Los Angeles Times.* February 26, 2005. latimes.com/archives/la-xpm-2005-feb-26-sp-ducks26-story.html.

"Updated 'Complete' List of DOD Films | Spy Culture." 2016.

November 23, 2016. spyculture.com/updated-complete-list-of-dod-films/.

Wang, Steve C., and Peter Dodson. 2006. "Estimating the Diversity of Dinosaurs." *Proceedings of the National Academy of Sciences* 103 (37): 13601–5. doi.org/10.1073/pnas.0606028103.

"What 'Twister' Didn't Tell You About Storm Chasers." 2015. *Popular Mechanics*. May 18, 2015. popularmechanics.com/science/environment/interviews/a15613/emily-sutton-storm-chaser/.

Willmetts, Simon. 2013a. "Quiet Americans: The CIA and Early Cold War Hollywood Cinema." *Journal of American Studies* 47 (1): 127–47.

———. 2013b. "Quiet Americans: The CIA and Early Cold War Hollywood Cinema." *Journal of American Studies* 47 (1): 127–47.

Wills, Matthew. 2021. "When the CIA Was Everywhere—Except on Screen." JSTOR Daily. April 15, 2021. daily.jstor.org/when-the-cia-was-everywhere-except-on-screen/.

Zegart, Amy. 2022. "How Fake Spies Ruin Real Intelligence." *The Atlantic*. January 9, 2022. theatlantic.com/international/archive/2022/01/how-fake-spies-ruin-real-intelligence/621187/.

Chapter 5

Ahmadi, Reza H. 1997. "Managing Capacity and Flow at Theme Parks." *Operations Research* 45 (1): 1–13.

Artistrophe. 2021. "Xenogenesis - The Epic Genesis of James Cameron - Artistrophe." *Artistrophe - Artist & Storyteller* (blog). August 1, 2021. artistrophe.com/xenogenesis-the-epic-genesis-of-james-cameron/.

Bakker, Gerben. 2008. *Entertainment Industrialised: The Emergence of the International Film Industry, 1890–1940.* Cambridge Studies in Economic History. Cambridge, UK ; New York: Cambridge University Press.

Brown, Keith, and Roberto Cavazos. 2005. "Why Is This Show So Dumb? Advertising Revenue and Program Content of Network Television." *Review of Industrial Organization* 27 (1): 17–34.

Businessweek. 1975. "Personal Business Supplement: How to Invest in Movies, The New Tax Shelter: Finance the Filming, Open on Broadway and Sneak into Films," August 25, 1975. NYPL.

Carey, Catherine. 2008. "Modeling Collecting Behavior: The Role of Set Completion." *Journal of Economic Psychology* 29 (3): 336–47. doi.org/10.1016/j.joep.2007.08.002.

Carson, Charles. 2004. "'Whole New Worlds': Music and the Disney Theme Park Experience." *Ethnomusicology Forum* 13 (2): 228–35.

Cieply, Michael. 2009. "A Movie's Budget Pops From the Screen." *New York Times*, November 9, 2009. nytimes.com/2009/11/09/business/media/09avatar.html.

"CONFERENCE COMPARISON ON H.R. 10612 : TAX REFORM ACT OF 1976 JCS-26-76." n.d. JCT. Accessed January 26, 2023. jct.gov/publications/1976/jcs-26-76/.

"DECISIONS ON THE TAX REFORM BILL OF 1975 CORRESPONDING TO SECTIONS OF DRAFT BILL JCS-48-75." n.d. JCT. Accessed January 26, 2023. jct.gov/publications/1975/jcs-48-75/.

"Domestic Sources Box Office Records." n.d. The Numbers. Accessed January 26, 2023. the-numbers.com/box-office-records/domestic/all-movies/sources/.

Dunlap, David W. 1993. "What's Up on 5th Avenue? A Studio Store." *New York Times*, February 10, 1993. nytimes.com/1993/02/10/nyregion/what-s-up-on-5th-avenue-a-studio-store.html.

Eckert, Charles. 1978. "The Carole Lombard in Macy's Window." *Quarterly Review of Film Studies* 3 (1): 1–21. doi.org/10.1080/10509207809391376.

Fleming Jr., Mike. 2020. "Tom Pollock's Legacy: Lawyered Hollywood's Greatest Deal, The One That Gave George Lucas 'Star Wars' Sequel Rights." *Deadline* (blog). August 3, 2020. deadline.com/2020/08/tom-pollock-legacy-architect-hollywood-greatest-deal-george-lucas-star-wars-sequel-rights-1203001950/.

"For Best Performing Shelter . . . " *New York Times.* n.d. Accessed January 26, 2023. nytimes.com/1976/03/28/archives/for-best-performing-shelter-film-investments-earn-tax-breaks-and.html.

"General Explanation Of The Tax Reform Act of 1976, (H. R. 10612, 94th Congress, Public Law 94-455). JCS-33-76." n.d. JCT. Accessed January 26, 2023. jct.gov/publications/1976/jcs-33-76/.

"Harry Potter Wands at the Wizarding World of Harry Potter." 2019. December 16, 2019. cosplayandcoffee.com/harry-potter-wands-wizarding-world-of-harry-potter/.

"How Many Films Are Released Each Year?" n.d. Accessed January 26, 2023. stephenfollows.com/how-many-films-are-released-each-year/.

Hunt, Melissa G., Rachel Marx, Courtney Lipson, and Jordyn Young. 2018. "No More FOMO: Limiting Social Media Decreases Loneliness and Depression." *Journal of Social and Clinical Psychology* 37 (10): 751–68. doi.org/10.1521/jscp.2018.37.10.751.

Imes, Rob. 2021. "History in the Making: The Aging Demographic of Comic Book Readers." *History in the Making* (blog). May 17, 2021. robimes.blogspot.com/2021/05/the-aging-demographic-of-comic-book.html.

Kanter, Burton W., and Calvin Eisenberg. 1975. "What Alice Sees through the Looking Glass When Movieland Seeks Creative Techniques for Financing Films." *Taxes - The Tax Magazine* 53: 94.

Karrh, James A. 1998. "Brand Placement: A Review." *Journal of Current Issues & Research in Advertising* 20 (2): 31–49. doi.org/10.1080/10641734.1998.10505081.

Lee, Lawrence. 1976. "Tax Shelters under the Tax Reform Act of 1976." *Villanova Law Review* 22 (2): 223.

"Los Angeles Public Hearing: Volume 2, Television/Videotape Preservation Study, Preservation Research, National Film Preservation Board, Programs, Library of Congress." n.d. Web page. Library of Congress, Washington, DC 20540 USA. Accessed January 26, 2023. loc.gov/programs/national-film-preservation-board/preservation-research/television-videotape-preservation-study/los-angeles-public-hearing/.

Maddison, David. 2005. "Are There Too Many Revivals on Broadway? A Stochastic Dominance Approach." *Journal of Cultural Economics* 29 (4): 325–34.

Mueller, Shirley M. 2019. *Inside the Head of a Collector: Neuropsychological Forces at Play.* Seattle: Lucia|Marquand.

Muramatsu, Keiji, Yoshihisa Fujino, Tatsuhiko Kubo, Makoto Otani, and Shinya Matsuda. 2019. "Relationship between Treatment and Period of Absence among Employees on Sick Leave Due to Mental Disease." *Industrial Health* 57 (1): 79–83. doi.org/10.2486/indhealth.2018-0055.

Pursell, Carroll. 2013. "Fun Factories: Inventing American Amusement Parks." *Icon* 19: 75–99.

Reuters. 2012. "How Lions Gate Won 'Hunger Games,'" March 22, 2012. reuters.com/article/us-lionsgate-hungergames-idUSBRE82L12A20120322.

"Roaring Success." 2012. *Newsweek.* April 2, 2012. newsweek.com/lions-gate-has-hit-hunger-games-can-it-turn-profit-63989.

"Selling Bugs Bunny." 2012. In *Animation: Art and Industry*, 215–36. Indiana University Press. jstor.org/stable/j.ctt16gz6nm.

Staff, W. W. D. 1996. "WARNER BROS. STORE GROWS UP." *WWD* (blog). October 22, 1996. wwd.com/fashion-news/fashion-features/article-1121121/.

"Streaming Pushes Peak TV to New Heights - Variety." n.d. Accessed January 26, 2023. variety.com/vip/streaming-pushes-peak-tv-to-new-heights-1235135116/.

"TAX REVISION ISSUES, 1976 (H.R. 10612) JCS-8-76." n.d. JCT. Accessed January 26, 2023. jct.gov/publications/1976/jcs-8-76/.

"TAX SHELTER INVESTMENTS : ANALYSIS OF 37 INDIVIDUAL INCOME TAX RETURNS, 24 PARTNERSHIP AND 3 SMALL BUSINESS CORPORATION RETURNS : PREPARED FOR THE USE OF THE COMMITTEE ON WAYS AND MEANS JCS-21-75." n.d. JCT. Accessed January 26, 2023. jct.gov/publications/1975/jcs-21-75/.

"TAX SHELTERS, MOVIE FILMS : PREPARED FOR THE USE OF THE COMMITTEE ON WAYS AND MEANS JCS-26-75." n.d. JCT. Accessed January 26, 2023. jct.gov/publications/1975/jcs-26-75/.

Thompson, Kristin. 2007. *The Frodo Franchise: The Lord of the Rings and Modern Hollywood.*

"Trademark Status & Document Retrieval." n.d. Accessed January 26, 2023. tsdr.uspto.gov/#caseNumber=86313884&caseType=SERIAL_NO&searchType=statusSearch.

Wildschut, Tim, Constantine Sedikides, Jamie Arndt, and Clay Routledge. 2006. "Nostalgia: Content, Triggers, Functions." *Journal of Personality and Social Psychology* 91: 975–93. doi.org/10.1037/0022-3514.91.5.975.

Woletz, Robert G. 1992. "POP MUSIC; Technology Gives the Charts a Fresh Spin." *New York Times*, January 26, 1992. nytimes.com/1992/01/26/arts/pop-music-technology-gives-the-charts-a-fresh-spin.html.

Young, Helen. 2016. "Digital Gaming and Tolkien, 1976-2015." *Journal of Tolkien Research* 3 (3). scholar.valpo.edu/journaloftolkienresearch/vol3/iss3/5.

Chapter 6

Allison, Anne. 2006. *Millennial Monsters: Japanese Toys and the Global Imagination.* 1st ed. University of California Press. jstor.org/stable/10.1525/j.ctt1ppk4p.

Alpert, Steve. 2020. *Sharing a House with the Never-Ending Man: 15 Years at Studio Ghibli.* Berkeley, California: Stone Bridge Press.

Atske, Sara. 2021. "What People Around the World Like—and Dislike—About American Society and Politics." *Pew Research Center's Global Attitudes Project* (blog). November 1, 2021. pewresearch.org/global/2021/11/01/what-people-around-the-world-like-and-dislike-about-american-society-and-politics/.

Bakker, Gerben. 2014. "Soft Power: The Media Industries in Britain since 1870." In *The Cambridge Economic History of Modern Britain: Volume II. 1870 to the Present*, edited by Roderick Floud, Jane Humphries, and Paul Johnson, 416–47. Cambridge, UK: Cambridge University Press.

Breeden, Aurelien. 2021. "France Gave Teenagers $350 for Culture. They're Buying Comic Books." *New York Times*, July 28, 2021. nytimes.com/2021/07/28/arts/france-culture-pass.html.

Chung, Ka Young. 2019. "Media as Soft Power: The Role of the South Korean Media in North Korea." *The Journal of International Communication* 25 (1): 137–57. doi.org/10.1080/13216597.2018.1533878.

"Cinemas Install NEC 3D Digital Projectors for Avatar Launch - Blog." n.d. Accessed January 26, 2023. projectorpoint.co.uk/news/cinemas-install-nec-3d-digital-projectors-for-avatar-launch.

Finler, Joel W. 2003. *The Hollywood Story.* 3. ed. London: Wallflower Press.

"From Netflix Shows to Nintendo: The Resurgence of Japanese Cool." n.d. Nikkei Asia. Accessed January 26, 2023. asia.nikkei.com/Spotlight/The-Big-Story/From-Netflix-shows-to-Nintendo-the-resurgence-of-Japanese-cool.

Giardina, Carolyn. 2010. "How 'Avatar' Changed the Rules of Deliverables." *Hollywood Reporter* (blog). March 25, 2010. hollywoodreporter.com/news/general-news/how-avatar-changed-rules-deliverables-22027/.

Graumans, Wouter, William J. R. Stone, and Teun Bousema. 2021. "No Time to Die: An In-Depth Analysis of James Bond's Exposure to Infectious Agents." *Travel Medicine and Infectious Disease* 44 (November): 102175. doi.org/10.1016/j.tmaid.2021.102175.

"Hallyu at a Crossroads: The Clash of Korea's Soft Power Success and China's Hard Power Threat in Light of Terminal High Altitude Area Defense (THAAD) System Deployment." n.d. Accessed January 26, 2023. kci.go.kr/kciportal/landing/article.kci?arti_id=ART002231023.

Hernandez, Joe. 2022. "COVID-19 Experts, Athletes and Daniel Craig Make the U.K.'s 'Honours List.'" NPR. January 1, 2022. npr.org/2022/01/01/1069677828/uk-new-years-honours-list-daniel-craig.

"How Halloween Became a Thing in Japan." 2021. Kotaku. October 28, 2021. kotaku.com/how-halloween-became-a-thing-in-japan-5954768.

Hu, Tze-Yue G. 2010. *Frames of Anime: Culture and Image-Building*. Hong Kong University Press. jstor.org /stable/j.ctt1xw9xb.

Jenkins, Tricia and Alford, Matthew. 2012. "Intelligence Activity in Hollywood: Remembering the 'Agency' in CIA." *Scope: An Online Journal of Film and Television Studies*, no. 23 (June). nottingham .ac.uk/scope/documents/2012 /june-2012/jenkins.pdf.

Jones, Dorothy B. 1957. "Hollywood's International Relations." *The Quarterly of Film Radio and Television* 11 (4): 362–74. doi.org/10.2307/1209996.

"K-Pop Tirade Reveals Kim Jong Un's Desperate Need for a Hit." n.d. Nikkei Asia. Accessed January 26, 2023. asia.nikkei.com/Opinion/K -pop-tirade-reveals-Kim-Jong-Un -s-desperate-need-for-a-hit.

"K-Pop to 'Squid Game' Lift Korean Soft Power and the Economy." n.d. Accessed January 26, 2023. bloomberg.com/news/articles /2021-10-07/k-pop-to-squid-game -lift-korean-soft-power-and-the -economy.

Lowe, Kinsey. 2012. "Cinema's Digital Takeover: The Decline and Fall of Film as We Have Known It." *Deadline* (blog). February 4, 2012. deadline.com/2012/02/cinemas -digital-takeover-the-decline-and -fall-of-film-as-we-have-known-it -208772/.

Mirrlees, Tanner. 2016. *Hearts and Mines: The US Empire's Culture Industry*. Vancouver: UBC Press.

Otmazgin, Nissim Kadosh. 2014. *Regionalizing Culture: The Political Economy of Japanese Popular Culture in Asia*. University of Hawai'i Press. jstor.org/stable/j .ctt6wqw63.

Penny, Laurie. 2020. "Tea, Biscuits, and Empire: The Long Con of Britishness." Longreads. June 18, 2020. longreads.com/2020/06/18 /the-long-con-of-britishness/.

Pesek, William. 2014. *Japanization: What the World Can Learn from Japan's Lost Decades*. Singapore: Bloomberg Press.

Ro, Christine. n.d. "BTS and EXO: The Soft Power Roots of K-Pop." Accessed January 26, 2023. bbc. com/culture/article/20200309-the -soft-power-roots-of-k-pop.

Roedder, Alexandra. 2014. "The Localization of Kiki's Delivery Service." *Mechademia* 9: 254–67. doi.org/10.5749/mech.9.2014.0254.

Sandbrook, Dominic. 2015. *The Great British Dream Factory: The Strange History of Our National Imagination*. London: Allen Lane.

Sang-Hun, Choe. 2021. "Kim Jong-Un Calls K-Pop a 'Vicious Cancer' in the New Culture War." *New York Times*, June 11, 2021. nytimes.com /2021/06/11/world/asia/kim-jong -un-k-pop.html.

Shin, Byungju, and Gon Namkung. 2008. "Films and Cultural Hegemony: American Hegemony 'Outside' and 'Inside' the '007' Movie Series." *Asian Perspective* 32 (2): 115–43.

"'Squid Game' Shows Hard Economics of South Korea's Soft Power." n.d. Nikkei Asia. Accessed January 26, 2023. asia.nikkei.com/Opinion /Squid-Game-shows-hard-economics-of-South-Korea-s-soft -power.

Suan, Stevie. 2021. *Anime's Identity: Performativity and Form beyond Japan*. Minneapolis London: University of Minnesota Press.

Sun, Rebecca. 2020. "From 'Parasite' to BTS: Meet the Most Important Mogul in South Korean Entertainment." *Hollywood Reporter* (blog). February 7, 2020. hollywoodreporter.com /movies/movie-features/meet -important-mogul-south-korean -entertainment-1275756/.

"The Economic History of the International Film Industry." n.d. Accessed January 26, 2023. eh.net /encyclopedia/the-economic -history-of-the-international-film -industry/.

"The Global Demand for Adult Animated Series." n.d. Parrot Analytics. Accessed January 26, 2023. parrotanalytics.com/insights /the-global-demand-for-adult -animated-series/.

"The Korean Wave: From PSY to BTS -The Impact of K-Pop on the South Korean Economy." 2021. January 22, 2021. asiascot.com /op-eds/the-korean-wave-from -psy-to-bts-the-impact-of-k-pop -on-the-south-korean-economy.

Thorne, Will. 2020. "From 'Masked Singer' to 'Good Doctor,' Korean

Formats Take Hold on U.S. Screens." *Variety* (blog). February 27, 2020. variety.com/2020/tv /news/us-tv-audiences-embrace -korean-content-1203516904/.

Tingley, Anna. 2021. "The 'Squid Game' Costume Effect: White Slip-On Vans Spike 7,800% Since the Series Premiere." *Variety* (blog). October 6, 2021. variety. com/shop/squid-game-halloween -costume-white-slip-on-vans -1235082287.

"TV Sicheong Haengtae Josa" n.d. Accessed January 26, 2023. portal.issn.org/resource/ISSN /2005-498X.

Verma, Rahul. n.d. "The Ramayan: Why Indians Are Turning to Nostalgic TV." Accessed January 26, 2023. bbc.com/culture/article /20200504-the-ramayan-why -indians-are-turning-to-nostalgic-tv.

Winkie, Luke. 2021. "Pokémon Will Outlive Us All." Vox. December 13, 2021. vox.com/the-highlight /22825263/pokemon-nintendo-cartoon-card-game-longevity.

Yossman, K. J. 2021. "From Roald Dahl to Studio Space, Netflix's Reverse British Invasion Is a Mixed Blessing." *Variety* (blog). September 27, 2021. variety. com/2021/streaming/news/ netflix-uk-roald-dahl-longcross-studios-1235073242.

Young, Derek S. 2014. "Bond. James Bond. A Statistical Look at Cinema's Most Famous Spy." *CHANCE* 27 (2): 21–27. doi.org/10.1 080/09332480.2014.914741.

Zhang, Mary. 2020. "Haikyuu!! Isn't Over Yet: The Little Giant's Cultural Legacy." CBR. July 25, 2020. cbr.com /haikyuu-little-giant-cultural -legacy.

기자장슬기. 2021. "[단독] '南영상물, 대량 유입·유포 시 사형'…대남 적개심 노골화 | DailyNK." January 15, 2021. dailynk. com/%eb%8b%a8%eb%8f%85 -%e5%8d%97%ec%98%81%ec %83%81%eb%ac%bc-%eb%8c %80%eb%9f%89-%ec%9c%a0 %ec%9e%85%c2%b7%ec%9c %a0%ed%8f%ac-%ec%8b%9c- %ec%82%ac%ed%98%95-%eb %8c%80%eb%82%a8-%ec%a0 %81%ea%b0%9c/.

Chapter 7

"40 CFR Part 191—Environmental Radiation Protection Standards for Management and Disposal of Spent Nuclear Fuel, High-Level and Transuranic Radioactive Wastes." n.d. Accessed January 26, 2023. ecfr.gov/current/title-40 /chapter-I/subchapter-F/part-191.

Anderson, Ian, Santiago Gil, Clay Gibson, Scott Wolf, Will Shapiro, Oguz Semerci, and David M. Greenberg. 2021. "'Just the Way You Are': Linking Music Listening on Spotify and Personality." *Social Psychological and Personality Science* 12 (4): 561–72. doi.org/10.1177 /1948550620923228.

Aubert, Maxime, Rustan Lebe, Adhi Agus Oktaviana, Muhammad Tang, Basran Burhan, Hamrullah, Andi Jusdi, et al. 2019. "Earliest Hunting Scene in Prehistoric Art." *Nature* 576 (7787): 442–45. doi.org/ 10.1038/s41586-019-1806-y.

Callaway, Ewen. 2019. "Is This Cave Painting Humanity's Oldest Story?" *Nature*, December 11, 2019. doi.org /10.1038/d41586-019-03826-4.

Chevalier, Judith A., and Dina Mayzlin. 2006. "The Effect of Word of Mouth on Sales: Online Book Reviews." *Journal of Marketing Research* 43 (3): 345–54.

Choueiti, Marc, Dr Stacy L Smith, and Dr Katherine Pieper. n.d. "Critic's Choice?: Gender and Race/Ethnicity of Film Reviewers Across 100 Top Films of 2017." assets.uscannenberg.org/docs /cricits-choice-2018.pdf.

Demetriou, Andrew, Andreas Jansson, Aparna Kumar, and Rachel M. Bittner. 2018. "Vocals in Music Matter: The Relevance of Vocals in the Minds of Listeners." 19th International Society for Music Information Retrieval Conference, Paris, France.

Dr. Stacy L Smith. n.d. "Critic's Choice 2: Gender and Race/Ethnicity of Film Reviewers Across 300 Top Films from 2015–2017." assets.uscannenberg.org/docs /critics-choice-2.pdf.

Egermann, Hauke, Mary Elizabeth Sutherland, Oliver Grewe, Frederik Nagel, Reinhard Kopiez, and Eckart Altenmüller. 2011. "Does Music Listening in a Social Context Alter Experience? A Physiological and Psychological Perspective on Emotion." *Musicae Scientiae* 15 (3): 307–23. doi.org /10.1177/1029864911399497.

Epps-Darling, Avriel, Romain Takeo Bouyer, and Henriette Cramer. 2020. "Artist Gender Representation in Music Streaming." 21st International Society for Music Information Retrieval Conference, Montréal, Canada.

Galak, Jeff, Justin Kruger, and George Loewenstein. 2011. "Is Variety the Spice of Life? It All Depends on the Rate of Consumption." *Judgment and Decision Making* 6 (3): 230–38. doi.org/10.1017 /S1930297500001431.

Gardner, Chris. 2018. "Sundance, Toronto to Allocate 20 Percent of Credentials to Underrepresented Critics, Says Brie Larson." *Hollywood Reporter* (blog). June 13, 2018. hollywoodreporter.com/news /general-news/sundance-toronto -allocate-20-percent-credentials -underrepresented-critics-says -brie-larson-1120068/.

Ginsburgh, V., and Sheila Weyers. 2014. "Nominees, Winners, and Losers." *Journal of Cultural Economics* 38 (4): 291–313.

Hansen, Christian, Rishabh Mehrotra, Casper Hansen, Brian Brost, Lucas Maystre, and Mounia Lalmas. 2021. "Shifting Consumption towards Diverse Content on Music Streaming Platforms." In *Proceedings of the 14th ACM International Conference on Web Search and Data Mining*, 238–46. WSDM '21. New York, NY: Association for Computing Machinery. doi.org/10.1145 /3437963.3441775.

"How Music Helped during the Pandemic." 2021. dw.com. Accessed January 26, 2023. dw.com/en/how-music-helped -during-the-pandemic/a-58668728.

Ialenti, Vincent. 2020. *Deep Time Reckoning: How Future Thinking Can Help Earth Now*. One Planet. Cambridge, Massachusetts: The MIT Press.

Juslin, Patrik N., and Daniel Västfjäll. 2008. "Emotional Responses to Music: The Need to Consider Underlying Mechanisms." *Behavioral and Brain Sciences* 31 (5): 559–75. doi.org/10.1017 /S0140525X08005293.

Koo, Minjung, and Ayelet Fishbach. 2010. "A Silver Lining of Standing in Line: Queuing Increases Value of Products." *Journal of Marketing Research* 47 (4): 713–24.

Kovács, Balázs, and Amanda J. Sharkey. 2014. "The Paradox of Publicity: How Awards Can Negatively Affect the Evaluation of Quality." *Administrative Science Quarterly* 59 (1): 1–33. doi.org/10 .1177/0001839214523602.

Lappas, Theodoros, Gaurav Sabnis, and Georgios Valkanas. 2016. "The Impact of Fake Reviews on Online Visibility: A Vulnerability Assessment of the Hotel Industry." *Information Systems Research* 27 (4): 940–61.

Lyubomirsky, Sonja, Kennon M. Sheldon, and David Schkade. 2005. "Pursuing Happiness: The Architecture of Sustainable Change." *Review of General Psychology* 9 (2): 111–31. doi.org/10.1037/1089-2680.9.2.111.

Nazari, Zahra, Christophe Charbuillet, Johan Pages, Martin Laurent, Denis Charrier, Briana Vecchione, and Ben Carterette. 2020. "Recommending Podcasts for Cold-Start Users Based on Music Listening and Taste." In *Proceedings of the 43rd International ACM SIGIR Conference on Research and Development in Information Retrieval*, 1041–50. SIGIR '20. New York, NY: Association for Computing Machinery. doi.org/10.1145/3397271.3401101.

Nelson, Leif D., and Tom Meyvis. 2008. "Interrupted Consumption: Disrupting Adaptation to Hedonic Experiences." *Journal of Marketing Research* 45 (6): 654–64.

Nelson, Leif D., Tom Meyvis, and Jeff Galak. 2009. "Enhancing the Television-Viewing Experience through Commercial Interruptions." *Journal of Consumer Research* 36 (2): 160–72. doi.org/10.1086 /597030.

Pasqualetti, Martin J., ed. 1990. *Nuclear Decommissioning and Society: Public Links to a New Technology*. The Natural Environment—Problems and

Management Series. London and New York: Routledge.

———. 1997. "Landscape Permanence and Nuclear Warnings." *Geographical Review* 87 (1): 73–91. doi.org/10.2307/215659.

———. 2000. "Morality, Space, and the Power of Wind-Energy Landscapes." *Geographical Review* 90 (3): 381–94. doi.org/10.2307/3250859.

Peretti, Peter O., and Kathy Swenson. 1974. "Effects of Music on Anxiety as Determined by Physiological Skin Responses." *Journal of Research in Music Education* 22 (4): 278–83. doi.org/10.2307/3344765.

"Pinocchio in Other Languages." n.d. Accessed January 26, 2023. newitalianbooks.it/pinocchio-in-other-languages/.

Sabin, Sam. 2018. "Most Young Adults Have an Appetite for Binge-Watching Shows." *Morning Consult* (blog). November 6, 2018. morningconsult.com/2018/11/06/most-young-adults-have-an-appetite-for-binge-watching-shows/.

Sackett, Aaron M., Tom Meyvis, Leif D. Nelson, Benjamin A. Converse, and Anna L. Sackett. 2010. "You're Having Fun When Time Flies: The Hedonic Consequences of Subjective Time Progression." *Psychological Science* 21 (1): 111–17.

Setoodeh, Brent Lang, Ramin, Brent Lang, and Ramin Setoodeh. 2019. "How Sundance Is Trying to Diversify Its 'Mostly White Male Critics.'" *Variety* (blog). January 24, 2019. variety.com/2019/film/markets-festivals/sundance-robert-redford-critics-diversity-1203117095/.

Sullivan, W. T., S. Brown, and C. Wetherill. 1978. "Eavesdropping: The Radio Signature of the Earth." *Science* 199 (4327): 377–88.

McGee, Henry, and Sarah McAra. 2017. "The Black List." Harvard Business School Case 317-027, November 2016 (revised May 2017). Accessed January 26, 2023. hbs.edu/faculty/Pages/item.aspx?num=51874.

Trauth, K. M., S. C. Hora, and R. V. Guzowski. 1993. "Expert Judgment on Markers to Deter Inadvertent Human Intrusion into the Waste Isolation Pilot

Plant." SAND—92-1382, 10117359. doi.org/10.2172/10117359.

Way, Samuel F., Santiago Gil, Ian Anderson, and Aaron Clauset. 2019. "Environmental Changes and the Dynamics of Musical Identity." arXiv. doi.org/10.48550/arXiv.1904.04948.

Zamani, Hamed, Markus Schedl, Paul Lamere, and Ching-Wei Chen. 2019. "An Analysis of Approaches Taken in the ACM RecSys Challenge 2018 for Automatic Music Playlist Continuation." *ACM Transactions on Intelligent Systems and Technology* 10 (5): 57:1–21. doi.org/10.1145/3344257.

Chapter 8

Abbing, Annemarie, Anne Ponstein, Susan van Hooren, Leo de Sonneville, Hanna Swaab, and Erik Baars. 2018. "The Effectiveness of Art Therapy for Anxiety in Adults: A Systematic Review of Randomised and Non-Randomised Controlled Trials." *PLOS ONE* 13 (12): e0208716. doi.org/10.1371/journal.pone.0208716.

Abbing, Annemarie, Leo de Sonneville, Erik Baars, Daniëlle Bourne, and Hanna Swaab. 2019. "Anxiety Reduction through Art Therapy in Women. Exploring Stress Regulation and Executive Functioning as Underlying Neurocognitive Mechanisms." *PLOS ONE* 14 (12): e0225200. doi.org/10.1371/journal.pone.0225200.

Alexander, Julia. 2021. "From Fanfiction to Netflix Hits." Verge. January 14, 2021. theverge.com/2021/1/14/22215052/wattpad-authors-fanfiction-netflix-hulu-streaming-movies-romcom-teen-drama.

Aragon, Cecilia Rodriguez, Katie Davis, and Casey Fiesler. 2019. *Writers in the Secret Garden: Fanfiction, Youth, and New Forms of Mentoring.* Cambridge, Massachusetts: The MIT Press.

Beaty, Roger E. 2015. "The Neuroscience of Musical Improvisation." *Neuroscience & Biobehavioral Reviews* 51 (April): 108–17. doi.org/10.1016/j.neubiorev.2015.01.004.

Berkowitz, Aaron L., and Daniel Ansari. 2010. "Expertise-Related Deactivation of the Right Temporoparietal Junction during Musical Improvisation." *NeuroImage* 49 (1): 712–19. doi.org/10.1016/j.neuroimage.2009.08.042.

Brown, Eleanor D., Mallory L. Garnett, Kate E. Anderson, and Jean-Philippe Laurenceau. 2017. "Can the Arts Get Under the Skin? Arts and Cortisol for Economically Disadvantaged Children." *Child Development* 88 (4): 1368–81. doi.org/10.1111/cdev.12652.

Campbell, Julie, Cecilia Aragon, Katie Davis, Sarah Evans, Abigail Evans, and David Randall. 2016. "Thousands of Positive Reviews: Distributed Mentoring in Online Fan Communities." In *Proceedings of the 19th ACM Conference on Computer-Supported Cooperative Work & Social Computing*, 691–704. CSCW '16. New York, NY: Association for Computing Machinery. doi.org/10.1145/2818048.2819934.

Conner, Tamlin S., Colin G. DeYoung, and Paul J. Silvia. 2018. "Everyday Creative Activity as a Path to Flourishing." *The Journal of Positive Psychology* 13 (2): 181–89. doi.org/10.1080/17439760.2016.1257049.

De Garis, Laurence. 2005. "The 'Logic' of Professional Wrestling." *Steel Chair to the Head*. Durham, NC: Duke University Press. doi.org/10.1215/9780822386827-009.

Eisenberger, Robert, Jason R. Jones, Florence Stinglhamber, Linda Shanock, and Amanda T. Randall. 2005. "Flow Experiences at Work: For High Need Achievers Alone?" *Journal of Organizational Behavior* 26 (7): 755–75.

Evans, Sarah, Katie Davis, Abigail Evans, Julie Ann Campbell, David P. Randall, Kodlee Yin, and Cecilia Aragon. 2017. "More Than Peer Production: Fanfiction Communities as Sites of Distributed Mentoring." In *Proceedings of the 2017 ACM Conference on Computer Supported Cooperative Work and Social Computing*, 259–72. CSCW '17. New York, NY: Association for Computing Machinery. doi.org/10.1145/2998181.2998342.

"Every Time I See More of the 'Ao3 Is Evil' Crap Circulating I Think, 'Well, Tumblr Is Evil Too and I Don't See You Stop Using It'" Fanlore. n.d. Accessed January 26, 2023. fanlore.org/wiki/Every_time_I _see_more_of_the_%E2%80%98 ao3_is_evil%E2%80%99_crap _circulating_I_think,_%E2%80 %98well,_tumblr_is_evil_too_ and_I_don%E2%80%99t_see_you _stop_using_it%E2%80%99.

Garis, Laurence de. 1999. "Experiments in Pro Wrestling: Toward a Performative and Sensuous Sport Ethnography." *Sociology of Sport Journal* 16 (1): 65–74. doi.org/10.1123/ssj.16.1.65.

Hanstock, Bill. 2020. *We Promised You a Great Main Event: An Unauthorized WWE History*. First edition. New York, NY: Harper.

Hornbaker, Tim. 2018. *Death of the Territories: Expansion, Betrayal and the War That Changed pro Wrestling Forever*. Toronto, Ontario, Canada: ECW Press.

Jeff Pressing. 2001. "7 Improvisation: Methods and Models." In *Generative Processes in Music, The Psychology of Performance, Improvisation, and Composition*. Oxford University Press. doi.org/10.1093/acprof:oso /9780198508465.001.0001.

Kaimal, Girija, Hasan Ayaz, Joanna Herres, Rebekka Dieterich-Hartwell, Bindal Makwana, Donna H. Kaiser, and Jennifer A. Nasser. 2017. "Functional Near-Infrared Spectroscopy Assessment of Reward Perception Based on Visual Self-Expression: Coloring, Doodling, and Free Drawing." *The Arts in Psychotherapy* 55 (September): 85–92. doi.org/10 .1016/j.aip.2017.05.004.

Kaimal, Girija, Kendra Ray, and Juan Muniz. 2016. "Reduction of Cortisol Levels and Participants' Responses Following Art Making." *Art Therapy* 33 (2): 74–80. doi.org /10.1080/07421656.2016.1166832.

Kalir, Jeremiah. 2019. "Proceedings of the 2018 Connected Learning Summit." Carnegie Mellon University. doi.org/10.1184/R1 /7793804.v1.

Katahira, Kenji, Yoichi Yamazaki, Chiaki Yamaoka, Hiroaki Ozaki, Sayaka Nakagawa, and Noriko Nagata. 2018. "EEG Correlates of the Flow State: A Combination of Increased Frontal Theta and Moderate Frontocentral Alpha Rhythm in the Mental Arithmetic Task." *Frontiers in Psychology* 9. frontiersin.org/articles/10.3389 /fpsyg.2018.00300.

Landau, Andrew T., and Charles J. Limb. 2017. "The Neuroscience of Improvisation." *Music Educators Journal* 103 (3): 27–33.

Melas, Chloe. 2021. "Dwayne Johnson Reflects on His Record-Breaking Year, Becoming the Tequila King and Whether He'll Run for the White House." CNN. December 29, 2021. cnn.com/2021/12/29 /entertainment/dwayne-the-rock -johnson-interview/index.html.

Men, Mat. 2021. "The Rock Originally Planned for WWE Survivor Series Appearance." Wrestling Observer. November 22, 2021. f4wonline .com/news/wwe/rock-originally -planned-wwe-survivor-series -appearance-360396.

Perretti, Fabrizio, and Giacomo Negro. 2007. "Mixing Genres and Matching People: A Study in Innovation and Team Composition in Hollywood." *Journal of Organizational Behavior* 28 (5): 563–86.

Sammond, Nicholas, ed. 2005. *Steel Chair to the Head: The Pleasure and Pain of Professional Wrestling*. Durham, NC: Duke University Press.

Sandmire, David Alan, Sarah Roberts Gorham, Nancy Elizabeth Rankin, and David Robert Grimm. 2012. "The Influence of Art Making on Anxiety: A Pilot Study." *Art Therapy* 29 (2): 68–73. doi.org/10. 1080/07421656.2012.683748.

Silk, Michael L., and David L. Andrews, eds. 2012. *Sport and Neoliberalism: Politics, Consumption, and Culture*. Philadelphia: Temple University Press.

Sport and Neoliberalism: Politics, Consumption, and Culture. 2012. Temple University Press. jstor.org /stable/j.ctt14bt86n.

Stuckey, Heather L., and Jeremy Nobel. 2010. "The Connection Between Art, Healing, and Public Health: A Review of Current Literature." *American Journal of Public Health* 100 (2): 254–63. doi.org/10.2105/AJPH.2008.156497.

"Theory" selfdeterminationtheory.org. n.d. Accessed January 26, 2023. selfdeterminationtheory.org /theory/.

Williams, Ben. 2003. "Encomium for Jeff Pressing." *Music Perception: An Interdisciplinary Journal* 20 (3): 315–21. doi.org/10.1525/mp.2003 .20.3.315.

Yang, Qingqi, Qunhui Shao, Qiang Xu, Hui Shi, and Lin Li. 2021. "Art Therapy Alleviates the Levels of Depression and Blood Glucose in Diabetic Patients: A Systematic Review and Meta-Analysis." *Frontiers in Psychology* 12. frontiersin.org/articles/10.3389 /fpsyg.2021.639626.

Index

ACKNOWLEDGMENTS

I want to thank Jack Gernert, my agent, whose advice and expertise and encouragement during the development process of this book was a rock. I'd also like to thank Seth Fishman for his counsel early on.

◆

I also want to thank Heather Jones, data visualist extraordinaire and my closest collaborator throughout this project, and John Meils at Workman, who wholeheartedly believed in this book when I really needed someone to, and whose edits made it into what it is. A huge thanks to Janet Vicario, whose design made the material sing, and Kim Daly, who kept everything in order. And to the publicity and marketing team, including Rebecca Carlisle, Meghan O'Shaughnessy, and Abigail Sokolsky.

◆

Thank you to the friends who helped me shape the ideas that went into this book, including my earliest and constant confidant, Olivia Walch. Thank you to my friend Maureen McNabb, who was the first editor to ever shape it into what it became. Thanks to Felicity Smith for her early thoughts, to Colin Davis, and especially Rachael Dottle, whose early work on visualizing the data was an inspiration.

◆

Thanks as well to my many friends who watched movies while wearing galvanic skin response devices, especially during one of the worst times in our collective lives. In no particular order, thank you to Winston Wolf, Lindsey Rupp, Robert Hoffmann, Beck Edson, Megan Willet-Wei, Will Wei, Joel Eastman, Julia Wolf, Matt Fernandez, Karen Toney, Brittany Koffer-Kelly, John Koffer-Kelly, Mario Alexandre, Geenie Rose Enriquez, Felicity Smith, Olivia Walch, Jon Katora, and Amana Katora. Thank you specifically to the brave souls who watched *The Handmaiden* (2016) while under arousal surveillance (while the data was absolutely unusable, it was extremely funny for me).

Thank you to Katherine Chiglinsky, Luke Kawa, Noah Belanich, Kim Bhasin, Winston Wolf, and Kevin Wolf for volunteering to have their vision tracked while watching *Star Wars*. Thank you to Pupil Labs for their excellent software and for making open-source plans available to construct an eye tracking device.

◆

Thank you to current and former colleagues who assisted me during the reporting of this book, including Harry Enten for his help obtaining historical polling data, Neil Paine for his expertise in sports, Ben Casselman for advice on using the American Time Use Survey, Bobby Kogan and Joe Thorndike for their insights on US tax policy, Jacob Shamsian for help obtaining court documents, and Hanna Kim for translation assistance. Thank you to Cassius Adair for helping me navigate the research. A big thank you to Kim Bhasin for his expertise and companionship during the wrestling portions of this book.

◆

Thank you to the long-time sources who have been instrumental in helping me not just in this book but in the path leading up to it, including Dr. Stacy Smith and the whole team at the Annenberg Inclusion Initiative as well as Bruce Nash, the genius behind box office resource The Numbers, who has always been so generous with his data. Thank you to the dedicated volunteers who build and maintain Fandom's system of Wikis, the people who update and maintain IMDb, the librarians who assisted me in archival research, and to the fans who maintain amazing projects whose data was used in this book. Thank you to Charin Polpanumas, who designed the core code used to simulate Pokémon battles and generously allowed me to adapt it for my needs.

◆

Thank you to the many, many people who spoke to me for this book, the researchers

ACKNOWLEDGMENTS

who took time away from their amazing work to chat with me, the people who shared their stories and the scientists who took me in and showed me what they were doing at a time when the world felt very fragile. I am particularly grateful to Gordon Bakker, Stephen Macknick, Susanna Martinez-Conde, David Kirby, and Dominic Sandbrook for their books.

◆

Thank you especially to Peter Starrett, Tom Secker, Jon Lomberg, Linda Simensky, Alex Newton, and David Hancock, who provided firsthand documents and reporting that were instrumental in reporting the book. A special thank you to the folks from the Warner Bros. Studio Store as well as the Waste Isolation Pilot Plant who took time to tell me stories about the fascinating history they were part of.

◆

As I wrote a whole chapter about, none of this would be possible if not for the journalists and friends who have surrounded me, encouraged me, coached me, and motivated me. I am so grateful for the opportunities I have had but mostly because I got to spend them writing alongside the people I did. Thanks to the artists whose work motivated me during the reporting process. Thank you to my friends for their valiant efforts in keeping me sane, unsuccessful they ultimately may have been. Thanks to the people who spent years indulging me, colleagues, bartenders, artists, and more, and the readers of Numlock who have always supported me. Thank you to the statistics mentors I had at William & Mary, Tanujit Dey, and Ross Iaci. Thanks to Joe Weisenthal and Julie Zeveloff West for hiring me into this business, to Nate Silver for giving me the opportunity of a lifetime, and to all the wonderful people at FiveThirtyEight and Insider who have motivated me. Thank you to all the editors who have coached me into the writer I am, especially Micah Cohen, Blythe Tyrell, Meghan Ashford-Grooms, Maureen McNabb, and Dave Levinthal, and all the colleagues who surrounded me and put me in the kind of creative community where a book like this is possible.

◆

Thank you to my family for indulging me and for letting me do reckless things like entering journalism. Thank you to my grandmother for showing me *Titanic* when nobody else would.

◆

Finally, and most of all, thank you Michael.

PHOTO CREDITS

For readers who want to download the data sets behind the data visuals in this book, plus view additional sources, please visit: www.whatyou.watch/data.

Alamy: 1492 PICTURES/HEYDAY FILMS/WARNER BROS/Album p. 83 (Harry Potter); AJ Pics pp. ix, 16, 32, 41, 82 (*Dances with Wolves*), 137 (*The Terminator*); Album pp. 30, 136 (*Ocean's Eleven*, right), 203; Allstar Picture Library Limited pp. 8, 13, 22, 34 (Star Wars), 44 (Dracula, left), 69, 82 (*Dallas*), 137 (*The Godfather*), 149 (Elton John), 149 (Emma Thompson), 199 (Dwayne Johnson), 183 (*Alice in Wonderland*, center); Archives du 7e Art/Toei Company p. 163; Istvan Bajzat/DPA p. 85; Radu Bercan p. 162; Ira Berger pp. 195, 199 (Bruno Sammartino); BFA/Alamy Stock Photo p. 1; Cinematic Collection pp. 11, 34 (*Big*), 39, 70, 98, 136 (*The Silence Of The Lambs*), 138 (The Avengers); colin black p. 192; Columbia Pictures p. 83 (*Sense and Sensibility*); dpa picture alliance p. 199 (Hulk Hogan); dpa picture alliance archive p. 199 (John Cena); FlixPix p. 111; Focus Features/The Hollywood Archive p. 190; Glasshouse Images p. 9; MARKA p. 61; MARVEL STUDIOS/Album p. 138 (*Avengers: Age of Ultron*) ; Maximum Film pp. 34 (Shrek), 77, 136 (*Ocean's 11*, left), 138 (*2 Fast 2 Furious*); Moviestore Collection Ltd pp. 34 (*Moana*), 37, 169; George Napolitano p. 199 (Ric Flair); NetPics p. 174; NEW LINE PRODUCTIONS/Album p. 83 (*The Lord of the Rings: The Two Towers*); North Wind Picture Archives p. 183 (*Alice's Adventures in Wonderland*, top); Paramount Pictures p. 94; Kim Petersen p. 84; Photo 12 pp. 20, 46; Pictorial Press Ltd pp. 17, 55, 67(*The Mary Tyler Moore Show*); PictureLux/The Hollywood Archive pp. 18, 29, 67 (*30 Rock*), 130, 145, 149 (Judy Dench); RGR Collection pp. 137 (*X-Men: The Last Stand*), 183 (*Alice in Wonderland*, bottom); Steve Robson/The National Trust Photolibrary p. 84; Ronald Grant Archive pp. 44 (Dracula, center), 103; ScreenProd/Photononstop p. 10; Sipa USA p. 124; Dom Slike p. 141; Bruce Springsteen p. 17; TCD/Prod.DB pp. 44 (Twilight), 137 (Men in Black), 138 (Halloween II); The Artchives p. 19; Twentieth Century Fox/Entertainment Pictures p. 87 (Freddie Mercury, right); Universal Pictures/Entertainment Pictures p. 138 (*Fast & Furious 9*); WARNER BROS. PICTURES/Album p. 34 (*The Matrix Reloaded*); Wilson Webb/Sony Pictures/ The Hollywood Archive p. 82 (*Little Women*); WENN Rights Ltd pp. 149 (Sidney Poitier), 149 (Ian McKellen); ZUMA Press p. 197. **Everett Collection, Inc.:** © 20th Century Fox Film Corp p. 28; © Buena Vista Pictures p. 171 (*Pirates of the Caribbean: At World's End*); © Paramount p. 94; © Universal p. 106. **Getty Images:** Juan Bautista Ruiz p. 186; Lloyd Bishop/NBCU Photo Bank/ NBC Universal via Getty Images p. 176; Ian Hitchcock p. 94; Don Kelsen/Los Angeles Times p. 117; Ollie Millington p. 131; Pete Still/Redfern p. 87 (Freddie Mercury, left); Transcendental Graphics p. 144; Universal p. 73; Kevin Winter p. 164. **Lionsgate Publicity:** Murray Close p. 72. **Sandria National Labortories** p. 171. **Wikimedia Commons:** Mercer p. 178; NASA/JPL p. 170; Zunkir p. 172.

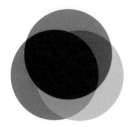